Tennessee Bird Watching

A Year-Round Guide

Copyright © 2004, Bill Thompson, III

All Rights Reserved. No part of this book may be reproduced or transmitted in any form, or by any means, electronic or mechanical, including photocopying, recording, or by any information storage and retrieval system, without permission in writing from the publisher.

Published by Cool Springs Press, a Division of Thomas Nelson, Inc., P. O. Box 141000, Nashville, Tennessee, 37214.

Thompson, Bill, III.
    Tennessee bird watching : a year-round guide / Bill Thompson, III, and the staff of Bird watcher's digest.
       p. cm.
    Includes bibliographical references and index.
    ISBN 1-59186-096-2 (pbk.)
    1. Bird watching--Tennessee. 2. Birds--Tennessee. I. Bird watcher's digest. II. Title.
QL684.T2T48 2004
598'.072'34768--dc22
                                2004014177

First Printing 2004
Printed in the United States of America
10 9 8 7 6 5 4 3 2 1

Managing Editor: Billie Brownell
Interior Designer: Bill Kersey, Kersey Graphics
Production Artist: S.E. Anderson
Map and Icon Illustrator: Heather Lynch
Sighting Notes Illustrator: Julie Zickefoose

Visit the Thomas Nelson website at www.ThomasNelson.com, and the Cool Springs Press website at www.coolspringspress.net

Photography Credits

Arthur Morris/Birds as Art: Front cover featured photo (American goldfinch); front cover top photo (American kestrel); front cover bottom photo (American robin); Intro photo page 6 (northern mockingbird); Pages 8; 10; 11; 12; 14; 15 (both photos); 16; 19; 20; 21 (bottom photo); 23 (blue grosbeak); 23 (common loon); 25 (least tern and sandhill crane); 26 (snow goose)
Tom Vezo: Pages 13; 17; 18; 21 (top photo); 23 (Bonaparte's gull); 24 (broad-winged hawk)
Brian Henry: Back cover bottom photo (eastern bluebird); Page 9
Brian Small: Page 26 (Swainson's warbler)
Maslowski Photography: Front cover middle photo (ruby-throated hummingbird)
Robert McCaw: Pages 22 (American woodcock)
Charles Melton: Back cover top photo (scarlet tanager)
Barth Schorre: Page 7
John Trott: Page 22 (black-throated blue warbler)

Tennessee Bird Watching

A Year-Round Guide

Bill Thompson, III
and the staff of
Bird Watcher's Digest

Cool Springs Press
A Division of Thomas Nelson Publishers
Since 1798

www.thomasnelson.com

Dedication and Acknowledgements

Dedication

To my parents, Bill and Elsa Thompson, who were bird watching *way* before it was cool and who had the courage and optimism to launch *Bird Watcher's Digest* in the living room of our home back in 1978. Thank you, Mom and Dad, for opening the door to my lifelong passion for birds and bird watching.

To Julie, Phoebe, and Liam (my own little family) who make each day sweeter than the last.

And to my siblings, Andy and Laura, for always being there.

Acknowledgements

There is no such thing as "too many cooks spoiling the broth" when creating a book. From the outset I leaned on and drew upon the talents of publishing professionals and birding experts in creating this book. At *Bird Watcher's Digest*: Deborah Griffith (special editorial blue ribbon), Heather Lynch (maps and cover design kudos), Andy Thompson, Ann Kerenyi, Linda Brejwo, Nate Wooley, Elsa "Catbird" Thompson, Helen Neuberger, Susan Hill, and David Scheimann deserve my never-ending thanks for their help with this project and for covering for me at *BWD* so I could stay home and write.

Andy Thompson, Charles Kirkwood, and Russell Galen made early and important contributions to the launching of this book.

My deep gratitude to the folks at Cool Springs Press—especially Billie Brownell, Hank McBride, David Dunham, and Roger Waynick—for their enthusiasm, guidance, and support. Thanks also to the many people who helped in the development of this book "behind the scenes"—to Tama Fortner for her copyediting expertise, to Bill Kersey for his art direction, and to S.E. Anderson for pulling it all together.

Helping with the content creation were Norma Siebenheller, Howard Youth, and Julie Zickefoose—three peerless bird authors. Without them I'd still be laboring over a smoking-hot laptop.

Jim Hiett was my Tennessee birding expert for this book, and I am grateful for his work writing the "Welcome to Bird Watching in Tennessee" chapter. Jim is, by profession, an educator who serves as an academic administrator and teacher of psychology at Volunteer State Community College. He confesses that he has found no answers in his 35 years of study to the problem of addiction to birds and birding. Jim would like to thank his wife Sharon, who knows her birds and her words; and he also sends a special thank you to Pamela and Steve Lasley.

Creating a book requires a lot of "cooks" and I am grateful for everyone's contributions. Any errors, omissions, or factual errors contained herein are utterly inadvertent and remain the responsibility of the author (me).

Finally, thank *you* for reading this book. I hope our paths cross someday in a beautiful natural place where there are lots and lots of birds. What could be better?

—*Bill Thompson, III*

Table of Contents

Welcome to Bird Watching in Tennessee — 7
Ecoregions of Tennessee 12
Tennessee Bird Watching by Season 14
Tennessee's Ten Must-See Birds 22

American Woodcock 22
Black-throated Blue Warbler 22
Blue Grosbeak 23
Bonaparte's Gull 23
Broad-winged Hawk 24
Common Loon 24
Least Tern 25
Sandhill Crane 25
Snow Goose 26
Swainson's Warbler 26

Tennessee's Ten Best Bird-Watching Spots 27
Resources for Tennessee Bird Watchers 32

Getting Started in Bird Watching — 33

Feeding and Housing — 37

How to Use *Tennessee Bird Watching* — 44

100 Most Commonly Encountered Birds in Tennessee — 45

Resources — 146
Solutions for Common Feeding Problems 146
Food/Feeder Chart 147
Nest Box Chart 148
A Glossary of Common Bird Terms 150
Frequently Asked Questions 152
How to Build a Simple Birdhouse 157
Bird-Friendly Plants for Your Yard 162
National Organizations for Bird Watchers 166
  (National Organizations, Field Guides, Audio Guides, and Periodicals)

Index — 169

Meet Bill Thompson, III — 176

Welcome to Bird Watching
in Tennessee . . . Jim Hiett

The great state of Tennessee is a fantastic place to watch birds, whatever your level of interest or skill—and it's not just the abundant bird life, but also the people that make it so. The citizen-scientist movement has been alive and well in the state for many decades, and your own interest in birds will only add to it.

Bird watching has a long and storied history in Tennessee, beginning with the journal entries made about birds by some of the area's earliest explorers in the 1600s. The famous American ornithologist Alexander Wilson (1766 to 1813) spent several weeks studying birds in the state in the spring of 1810. He (among others) observed the Nashville and Tennessee warblers, which he first described from specimens collected in Middle Tennessee. John James Audubon (1785 to 1851), who spent several years in neighboring Kentucky, made a number of trips on the Mississippi River in the early 1800s and traveled overland across Tennessee at least once. The records of those trips are sparse, but they do mention the ivory-billed woodpecker and the Carolina parakeet, both now considered to be extinct. Systematic ornithology began after the Civil War with visits and reports by William Brewster (1851 to 1919) and a number of others. The first comprehensive list of state birds was published in 1895.

In 1915, the first state bird club in the Southeast—the Tennessee Ornithological Society (TOS)—was founded in Nashville, and the study of the state's birds by Tennesseans has grown exponentially since that time. From the beginning, the objectives of this independent, nonprofit, educational, and scientific organization have been to promote the scientific study and conservation of birds and to publish the results of its investigations. The TOS publishes a quarterly journal, *The Migrant*, which includes seasonal and other sight records, along with articles to facilitate the tracking of changes in the state's bird populations. The organization is open to all with an interest in birds and includes professional scientists, educators, and non-professionals from all walks of life. There are currently 11 local chapters from Memphis to Bristol and some 800 members. There is a statewide member's newsletter, *The Tennessee Warbler*, and the local chapters also publish periodic newsletters. Communication is facilitated through monthly meetings and an Internet discussion list. Local field trips, counts, and forays are frequent, and visitors are always invited. State meetings are

Tennessee warbler

Bald eagle

held in different locations across Tennessee in spring and winter.

What Makes Birding in Tennessee Special?

Tennessee is a big, beautiful, ecologically diverse state. Topographically, it is interesting, rising almost 6,500 feet in elevation from the west to the east over a distance of 500 miles. Its 42,144 square miles are 50 percent forested and include more than 900 square miles of inland water. There are three major rivers and an abundance of open agricultural land with sufficient wild areas, so that one can still—as the oldest natives might say—"get way back up in the woods." It has good roads, including the confluence of several interstate highways, so key bird-watching areas throughout the state can be easily and quickly accessed.

The state is home to approximately 5 million people who are noted for being friendly, helpful, and nature-oriented. Though not precisely its original meaning, every year many Tennesseans "volunteer" their yards and patios, even their dens and living rooms, to scores of birders who come to view an unusual bird visiting their feeder. Driving directions are usually easy to come by if one will ask, and permission is often granted to watch birds on private property. In general, people who live in the rural areas of the state enjoy the natural world and appreciate others who take a special interest in it.

The climate contributes positively to the birding experience in Tennessee. Most days of the year afford comfortable weather for birding in the field. In general, the winters are mild, the summers are hot, and the rainfall is abundant. Compared with the more northerly states, there is no spring thaw to speak of. Even the harshest winter only holds its grip on the water and land for a few days at a time. Snowfall is light in Middle and West Tennessee, but is often heavy in the mountains of East Tennessee.

The weather begins to moderate in February. By early March the temperature occasionally climbs to 60 degrees Fahrenheit and even into the 70s by the end of the month. Primarily because of the elevation, it is always a bit cooler, on average, in the eastern part of the state, and the warming may be a few days later than in the west and middle. The eastern mountains are the latest to warm. Precipitation is variable (some years drier than others), and the east is wetter, but on average the rainfall is around 50 inches per year. It can be very wet in the higher mountains, though, with the peaks averaging over 80 inches per year. The late summer and early fall is downright hot in the lower elevations of the state, averaging well above 80 degrees Fahrenheit, and the humidity is high—but this only lasts for a few weeks. Fall is pleasantly cool, crisp, and beautiful as it progresses.

All the birds that can be regularly found in Tennessee can also be found in other states, particularly nearby inland states. However, some can be found more readily in Tennessee because they breed or winter here in significantly greater numbers. Some species are easier to find because they regularly hang out in specific habitats and locations. The current list of species verified as having been seen at least once in the state totals close to 400, but this number changes annually. With more of us watching birds, the number of birds found in Tennessee is certain to grow.

A note on terminology: If you are new to the state, you need to know that it is divided—even by state law—into three so-called grand divisions: West Tennessee, Middle Tennessee, and East Tennessee. These divisions have deep, historical roots and have not been without controversy at times. Residents use the shorthand readily, although to newcomers or visitors, the use of "middle" rather than "central" may seem awkward.

Key Species and Phenomena

As birds go, Tennessee is known for its woodland breeders, particularly its high-altitude nesters (such as the black-throated blue warbler), its large number of wintering waterfowl, and the American bald eagles on its lakes and rivers. The gathering of gulls and loons on some of these waters, on their regular timetable, is impressive. Situated on the major migration route of many birds, the state is also known for its spectacular shorebird migration along the Mississippi River, the passing of thousands of sandhill cranes (primarily through the eastern parts of the state), and a statewide passerine migration that can introduce the novice birder to many unfamiliar species.

Bird watching in Tennessee can yield rewards at any time of the year, but there is a day during the spring each and every year when your interest in birds and your patience and careful observation can be greatly rewarded. No one can ever predict exactly which day it will be, although many bird watchers try. But if you are out in your yard or in the woods anywhere in the state every day from about the middle of April through the middle of May, and if you pay close attention, you will know it. The summer visitors have arrived, and the number and variety of migrants who are passing through are at their peak.

The birds in the trees—many different species—may seem to come in waves, moving first in one direction and then the other, feeding on invisible insects and other morsels. Many, if not most, are singing and the confusing mixture of songs may even seem dissonant to the listener. There may be so many species of wood warbler at one time that it could be described as a "warbler attack." And it's not long before the condition known as "warbler neck" sets in, and you have to tuck your chin, stretch, and take a break. "Warbler neck" is caused by continuously looking upward at treetops in order to spot warblers.

Knowing this, some birders may set out in teams (of no more than four) to set a record for the total number of species seen in a single 24-hour period in a form of competition called a "Big Day." As many as 174 species thus far have been seen on a single Tennessee Big Day. It is telling that the highest counts have been on May 7, 8, 9, and 10 in various years. (On one record-breaking April day in Texas, a total of 258 species were seen!) You may never participate in a Big Day other than in your own backyard, but as you stand amidst the wonder of it, you can see the possibility and understand the allure.

Maybe the most important thing about the Big Day records, which are available from the American Birding Association (www.americanbirding.org), is what they can teach us about the seasonal distribution of birds in our area. Careful study of the details and the counts—knowing that the competitors had developed

Eastern bluebird

a strategy and were trying to see every possible species—can be instructive. So can the Audubon Christmas Bird Count results (www.audubon.org/bird/cbc), which include all the species and individual birds counted in some twenty-five different 15-mile diameter circles across the state on one day each year from December 14 through January 5. These data cover more than 100 years of bird watching and counting.

The distribution of species through the seasons is important to note. Sixty or so species winter in Tennessee and then repair to more northerly climes for the warmer months to breed. By mid-May, most of the 80 or so species that regularly migrate through the state, but do not stay, are no longer here. Of the 50 or so species that leave for the cold months and then return to their summer homes here, about 30 are among the top 100 birds that are common to the state and are depicted in this book. More than 160 species have been found breeding in the state, though the number of significant, regular breeders is around 120.

A bonus for Tennessee birders watching for passing sandhill cranes is the occasional sight of the rare whooping crane. The Whooping Crane Eastern Partnership (WCEP), a project to restore the endangered whooping crane to the eastern United States, is located in Wisconsin and uses ultralight aircraft to assist captive-bred and raised birds to make their first migratory journeys to the upper Florida Gulf Coast. These flights are tracked each year on the Internet, and with planning and a little luck one can get a glimpse of these special birds from a vantage point somewhere in East Tennessee. The routes and timetables vary with the weather and other factors, and every effort is made to protect the birds from harm, including unnecessary human contact. A few of the nearly 20 wild whoopers have been seen using the Hiwassee Refuge north of Chattanooga.

Tips for Successful Birding

Good preparation and planning are keys to successful birding. Use the resources at your disposal, including this book, as you prepare to observe birds more closely at home or in the field. Consult field guides and other published materials. Look at your own field cards or journals, if you keep them. And check out your questions on the Internet, using a public library connection if necessary.

A specific caution: Homeland Security Issues and attendant restrictions have become a concern to bird watchers. At a time when there are more binocular- and scope-using birders than ever in our history, the level of suspicion of those who wield the tools of our hobby is the highest ever. Today, increasingly—especially near dams and reservoirs, water treatment plants, airports, and military installations—there is heightened security. Never enter a posted or blockaded area. If possible, identify yourself in advance, even if looking into such an area from outside. Even "public space" has a different meaning in this era than in the past. When birding, strive to maintain a comfort zone that works for everyone concerned, including you. Ask permission. Explain yourself. Never violate private property, even by looking through your binoculars.

Another caution: Hunting, including the hunting of game birds, is a popular sport in Tennessee. Besides the obvious wild turkey, dove, quail, ducks, and geese, there are a dozen other species—sought by bird watchers and hunters alike—that have a hunting season,

Wood duck

including Wilson's snipe, rails, and American woodcock. For safety's sake, always check the hunting season dates (www.state.tn.us/twra) when headed for the open fields, woods, or water to watch birds.

Learn and practice the etiquette and the ethics of birding; you will stay in the good graces of your fellow travelers and the others you encounter along the birding trail. You will be rewarded, stay out of harm's way, and ensure that the birds are taken care of as well. (See the American Birding Association's Code of Ethics at www.americanbirding.org/abaethics.htm.)

Spreading Your Wings: Birding Beyond This Book

According to a survey by the U.S. Fish and Wildlife Service, 46 million people in the United States are bird watchers. That's nearly 20 percent of the adult population. Tennessee has its fair share, and you are among them. Bird watching has always been popular in the state and is becoming increasingly so. Even watching a feeder hung on an upper balcony of an apartment building in the city brings us closer to the wonders of nature.

Interest in the field study of birds has been called a diversion, a pastime, a hobby, a passion—even an affliction! There may be a natural progression from first noticing birds and then paying closer attention to them, to the all-consuming passion it becomes for some few. Behavioral scientists have attempted to flesh out the psychology of it, and it is an interesting question. We know that one can enhance his or her skill and enjoyment by making choices that lead to more experience—vicarious and direct—with birds. Reading this book is one choice. Later, we will explore some things you can do that will lead to a greater understanding of the birds around you.

A funny thing happens to many bird watchers. The more time one spends studying and observing birds, the less bias one seems to have for the beautiful, the colorful, and the striking. Cardinals and bluebirds, goldfinches and wood ducks still catch the eye. But the more plain or confusing—

Wild turkey

and possibly more common—blackbirds, grackles, female ducks, winter gulls, and shorebirds, along with the "little brown jobs" and the many species of sparrow begin to draw one's interest. The increasing sense of challenge to make positive identifications is part of it. Getting to know these birds better certainly can sharpen your skills overall.

Another funny thing that happens is that as one becomes more expert, adding more species to the list and sightings to the journal, he or she may begin to focus on just one aspect of bird watching, or maybe on just one particular bird. Bird watching may lead to becoming a bird bander, and then to just banding and studying hummingbirds.

So we don't know and can't really predict where this interest in birds will lead us, but wherever it does, Tennessee is a great place to see it play out. For many people, nothing comes closer to the definition of "life-long learning" than the study of birds. And as you spread your wings, don't neglect your own "backyard"—whatever form that might take. Remember to create habitats and to provide food and provide nesting possibilities if you can. Encourage the birds to come to you, for their sake and for your pleasure, knowledge, and satisfaction.

Ecoregions of Tennessee

Tennessee is diverse in physiography, vegetation, and habitat types. For bird monitoring and reporting purposes, the state is divided into four regions (see the map on page 27). Within these regions, there are other divisions representing distinct features important to understanding bird life.

Western Coastal Plain

This region begins at the Mississippi Alluvial Plain and is bordered on the east by the north-flowing Tennessee River. In the west, the land is gently rolling and mainly agricultural, while the rougher and higher parts are closer to the eastern boundary. The forests are mainly oak, hickory, and pine with swamp forests in the far west. The winter birds are ducks, geese, and sparrows. Red-tailed hawks rule in the warmer months.

Mississippi Alluvial Plain

Within the Western Coastal Plain is included the Mississippi Alluvial Plain—a narrow strip of low-lying, swampy bottomland along the Mississippi River in the westernmost part of the state. Natural vegetation is primarily bald cypress, oak, and tupelo. Higher ground supports beech, elm, sweetgum, and shagbark hickory. Spring here sees the earliest neotropical migration with many birds stopping along the river to nest. Migrating shorebird numbers are impressive in spring and fall.

Highland Rim and Basins

Western and Eastern Highland Rim

The Highland Rim and Basin region includes the Western and Eastern Highland Rims and the Central Basin: The Western and Eastern Highland Rims lie between the Tennessee River and the Cumberland Plateau. The rim is an upland plain of low-to-moderate fertility that surrounds the Nashville or Central Basin. The Eastern Highland Rim is higher, averaging 1,000 feet above sea level. The forests of the rim are primarily oak and hickory with prairie on portions of the Western Rim. The important birds of the area are breeding woodland species and passerines in migration. Pileated and other woodpeckers and owls are omnipresent.

Central Basin

The Central Basin, an oval-shaped lower region (550 feet in elevation) extending some 80 miles

Red-tailed hawk

Pileated woodpecker

north to south and 50 miles east to west, is surrounded by the Western and Eastern Highland Rims. Some parts of the basin have deep soils with good agriculture, but other portions have thin soils fit only for grazing. The distinctive forest feature of the area is the red cedar glade. Scattered oak, hickory, hackberry, winged elm, and redbud occur as well. In the basin, prolific summer birds are indigo buntings, American goldfinches, American robins, and eastern bluebirds. Swallows, chimney swifts, and common nighthawks are everywhere as well. Winter sparrows cover the grasslands and forest edges.

Eastern Ridge and Valley

The Eastern Ridge and Valley proper stretches a width of some 60 miles from the eastern escarpment of the Cumberland Plateau to the Tennessee portion of the Blue Ridge Mountains known as the Unaka Range. The Eastern Ridge and Valley, which contains the Great Valley of the Tennessee River, is a succession of cultivated valleys (running generally southwest to northeast) that are separated by forested ridges. The elevations range from 2,000 to 2,500 feet. Appalachian oak forest predominates, but other tree types, including shortleaf and Virginia pine, also occur. On the rivers and lakes, ducks, geese, and sandhill cranes abound in colder months. The northern rough-winged, tree, cliff, and even bank swallow breed here, as do loggerhead shrike and eastern bluebird. The mixed farmland and upland woods makes for a variety of good birds in any season.

Cumberland Plateau

The Eastern Ridge and Valley region includes the Cumberland Plateau, which is some 50 miles wide and runs northeast to southwest between the Eastern Highland Rim and the Eastern Ridge and Valley. The average elevation of the plateau is 2,000 feet, but some of the mountains on the upturned eastern edge climb to more than 3,600 feet. The once-flat plateau has been deeply carved by streams into deep, steep valleys. Much of the area is rugged terrain and virtually inaccessible. The forest is oak, hickory, and pine with some mixed beech, tulip poplar, sugar maple, oak, and hemlock to the north. Black-throated green and several other warblers breed here. Alder and great crested flycatcher do also. Broad-winged hawks hold sway in the woods. In winter, white-breasted nuthatches and yellow-bellied sapsuckers are here.

Eastern Mountain

The Eastern Mountain region is the chain of mountains known as the Blue Ridge Mountains, forming the southern part of the Appalachians. The Tennessee range, the Unakas, runs southwest to northeast and includes a large portion of the Great Smoky Mountains National Park. The highest point in the state, Clingman's Dome, is in the park. The area is sparsely populated and heavily forested. The forests of the lower elevations are deciduous hardwoods of the Appalachian oak type. At the higher elevations, spruce and Frasier fir dominate. Some of the higher peaks have no trees and are called *balds*.

Ruffed grouse can be seen throughout the mountains. Many high-altitude breeding birds—such as the veery, winter wren, rose-breasted grosbeak, and Canada, black-throated blue, and other warblers—can be found. The mountains are cool, pleasant, and good for birds and birders alike.

Tennessee Bird Watching by Season

Spring

When March "comes in like a lion," as it often does in Tennessee, what some bird watchers think of as the most interesting, if not the most exciting, season of the year begins. Spring. Glorious spring!

A Carolina wren *teakettling* at the bedroom window before first light is more effective than an alarm clock and several decibels louder. The mantra-like background chorus of American robins builds in number and volume as the month goes on. A woodpecker has found the most sonorous spot on a pole, the side of a building, or even a piece of metal and is adding rhythm to the swelling cacophony. Chickadees are rushing to and from the feeders and adding their incessant, high-pitched *dee, dee, dee* to the mix. The *cheer, cheer* of the northern cardinal and the *peter, peter, peter* of the tufted titmouse fill in the middle. On the ground beneath the feeders, the mourning doves are grazing, and in the trees they sit serenely as they *coo* what could be the base line to this symphony that many have called "the dawn chorus." The invitations are out. The offer is made to make new life and to get on with it as quickly as possible.

By the first week of March, the first of the migrating purple martins have arrived. For many, this is *the* signal that spring is here and that life will be renewed. Most often, the first report is from West Tennessee. If you have a martin house, or if there are some nearby, you will soon hear the sweet, urgent chortle of the colony as it builds in size as the adults and then later the sub-adults come. One caution: Be careful in your identification of single, early birds on the wing. European starlings in just the right form are sometimes misidentified as martins.

By the first day of spring, the daffodils are in profusion, the forsythia and the ornamental shrubs and trees are in full bloom, and many of the wildflowers are already past. The redbuds bloom as April begins, covering the woods and city landscapes in vivid purple; by the end of April, the native dogwoods do the same with their pure white and shades of pink.

Flocks of starlings, grackles, cowbirds, and red-winged blackbirds seem to be everywhere—at feeders, on lawns, and in the woods and fields. In the fields, sometimes more than a dozen species can be spotted on the ground from one vantage point. Along with blackbirds, the lemon-yellow-breasted eastern meadowlark (and the western, occasionally, near the river in West Tennessee) may be seen feeding in small flocks. The northern flicker, with its distinctive black bib, may be there, too—often in pairs. Robins stand stock-still and cock their heads toward the ground. And killdeer—often in large numbers—scurry and stop, scurry and stop, and then scream and fly a short distance when alarmed. One day an expanse of lawn or a close-

Purple martin

Gray catbird

cropped field may be teeming with birds, but the next day it may be completely empty. Some birds are on the move north, some have found another food source, and some are beginning to settle into the routine of breeding and nesting.

American goldfinches may cover the feeders and are in every stage of changing to their brilliant summer colors. The eastern bluebirds have long-since settled into their territories. The piercing cry of the red-shouldered hawk echoes through the woods. The state bird, the northern mockingbird, has begun to sing its varied repertoire, frequently at night, and the other mimics—the brown thrasher and the gray catbird—chime in.

In April and May, the big show is the hundreds of thousands of neotropical migrants coming through, on some rare days seeming to drip from the trees. Some stay, but most—even the namesake Tennessee warbler—pass on through to their summer haunts. Though the wood thrush stays and begins to bless the woods with its lilting *ee-o-lay*, the Swainson's and the gray-cheeked thrushes move on.

By the first of May, almost all the wintering waterfowl have flown away, but along the rivers and smaller streams the green herons have begun to arrive with the other herons and egrets that occur in lesser numbers. The great blue heron and a few black-crowned night-herons have lingered through the winter, and their numbers begin to increase as the weather moderates. Great blues can sometime be seen in the fields, as well, carefully stalking dry land prey.

By late April or early May, you may hear the last plaintive songs of the white-throated sparrows as they end their winter in the South. In a few weeks, they will begin to arrive on their breeding grounds over most of Canada, along with some of the other sparrows and the dark-eyed juncos who have visited the state over the cold months but don't stay for the summer.

Great blue heron

Summer

For birders, the summer birding season is primarily the months of June and July. These months are normally not the hottest or the driest in Tennessee, but they may sometimes be—particularly July. As usual, the weather affects the birds and the bird watchers, so visits to the field may slow down as the temperature rises. And the foliage seems to obscure many of the sought-after birds. Relying on our hearing becomes more necessary, but in general the birds have less to say. Summer is the nesting season. Birds have grown more silent as their offspring have come along and that provides more safety and security for the hatchlings. But resist the temptation to stay inside in air-conditioned comfort; there is still a lot shaking out there to hear and see.

The color of spring continues into the summer with many of the birds still in their breeding plumage. Look for the bright blue of our most abundant neotropical migrant—the indigo bunting—in brushy areas and along the margins of woodlands. The indigo rarely occurs in urban areas, so beginning birders may not yet have seen it. The first view is a knockout, as are all the others after that. In the woods, look for the red of the male summer tanager, the red and black contrast of the male scarlet tanager, and the chestnut and black of the male orchard oriole. The greenish and yellow females will be nearby. When you hear the *wheeep* of the great crested flycatcher from the treetops look patiently for it. And in thickets, listen and watch for that big old warbler, the yellow-breasted chat. Its whistled song and explosive *whoots* and *kooks* may be accompanied early in the summer by a humorous, leaping display that has caused the bird to be nicknamed the "buffoon of the briar patch."

Summer is southern magnolia time in Tennessee. This native tree with its huge, fragrant, creamy-white blossoms and shiny green leaves enlivens the landscape, and its fruit feeds a score of avian species, including the mockingbird, catbird, northern flicker, and eastern kingbird. In June, the blackberries are just past full bloom and are beginning to show small, pale fruit. Blue grosbeaks prefer the dense vines for nest sites, and indigo buntings like them, too. By mid-June, the rhododendrons blanketing the eastern mountains are in full bloom. The red flowers of the native honeysuckles (growing in old fields and thickets) and the orange-, yellow-, or scarlet-flowered trumpet vines draw ruby-throated hummingbirds by the score.

In June and into July, the Carolina wrens have multiplied and their sometimes piercing songs seem to come rapid-fire from every direction, beginning before dawn and continuing until well after dark. The young are now out and about and—along with the adults—are trying out the more than 30 songs and sounds in their repertoire. They may have nested anywhere around human habitation, including a spot inside a barn, shed, garage, or even inside the house. Local newspapers frequently run interest articles praising the gracious hosts of gregarious

Northern flicker

Eastern wood-pewee

wrens that have nested inside the domicile in a location apparently suited to them, but often quite inconvenient for the accommodating human residents.

Though much less common in most areas of the state than the Carolina wren, house wrens may have actually used the house put up just for them to successfully hatch a brood. The rapid, bubbling song of the house wren is much less varied than that of its larger cousin; once learned, it is easily recognized around the neighborhood or the farm—even from a distance—and can also be detected in the background in movies, television shows, and commercials.

American robins still seem to be chanting incessantly, and the variety in their song seems to increase as the young come along. Juvenile robins—as well as the young of the other common thrush, the Eastern bluebird—sometimes surprise and confuse the novice bird watcher if seen without the parent nearby. For a few weeks after they have fledged, they look quite different from the adult. Both have speckled breasts and may appear as large or even larger than the adult, but the rust color on the robin and the bluish wing feathers of the bluebird are giveaways in their identification.

In late summer, chimney swifts in squadrons twitter overhead from dawn to dusk, and common nighthawks join them late in the day, *peenting* as they bat their long wings lazily overhead. The secretive yellow-billed cuckoo—sometimes called the rain crow—may be frequently heard but seldom seen. The *pee-a-wee* of the eastern wood-peewee and the namesake call of another common flycatcher, the eastern phoebe, can be heard in many areas as the birds move through the treetops, sweeping out from upper branches to eat flying insects.

At the lake or by a pond, look for the great blue heron stalking its luckless prey along the shore and the spotted sandpiper teetering along the water's edge nearby. The green heron, whose legs have now turned from the red-orange of breeding back to greenish-yellow, may be resting on the low branches of a tree or bush near the water or stealthily crouching along the bank. A common yellowthroat may call aggressively from nearby, its repeated *witchity* hard to miss. As the shorebirds begin to leave, it is a sure sign that summer will soon end.

Autumn

By the "dog days of August," even though it feels like summer in Tennessee, birders are thinking fall. Fall for birders includes the months of August through November, and there is no better time to be bird watching. The nesting season is drawing to a close, and some birds are already starting to head south. While the summer for birds has been about staying close to home, fall is about movement and moving. The juveniles are finding their wings and many of the older birds, even the year-round residents, are in post-breeding dispersal.

By the first of August, the shorebird migration is in full swing, although it will not be complete until almost November. By early September, many of the purple martins have already flown, but the barn and bank swallows will stay on for another month. Tree swallows are coming through and those that have summered here join them as they head for the coast. The chimney swifts may hang on through October before they leave for South America.

The fall wildflowers are in profusion, and by September the leaves of the deciduous trees are beginning to change color. Many of the neotropical migrants that are leaving—and those passing through from the North—have changed color. Some, mainly the wood warblers, have molted to the drab colors so confusing to us at some stages of bird watching; but with patience and study even these birds can be learned. The vireos and warblers are mostly all gone by mid-October.

Some say that a number of fall warblers are confusing, some say they are not, or at least they shouldn't be. Either way, warbler watching during fall migration can certainly be interesting. Warbler identification at this time of year is made more difficult by the fact that the birds sing little, if at all, and the immatures do not yet look like the adults. The key to avoiding confusion and frustration may be to only attempt small successes in identification at any one outing and to prepare by reviewing your field guides and other sources in advance. Some guides sort the warbler species with obvious wing bars from those with no wing bars. In Tennessee, this group includes the migrating immature chestnut-sided, black-throated green, Blackburnian, magnolia, and palm warblers, along with both the immature and adult bay-breasted warbler. The species that are either migrating or have summered here include the northern parula, yellow, pine, and prairie immatures, and the adult pine warbler. You might want to focus your attention on these birds first to sharpen your skills.

"Wire birding"—spotting and identifying birds perching on wires, mainly those along the roadsides—is a pastime for many Tennessee bird watchers because so many of us spend so much time on the road. Once a passion for birds develops, it is almost unavoidable for those who

White-eyed vireo

spend time on the road, but one should remember that the rules for safe driving should always be observed. It is best to let passengers do the close watching. When driving, pull safely off the road and stop to observe an especially interesting bird. Some birders who keep lists even keep separate lists of the species they have seen on wires, and these lists can include some unexpected entries of birds small and large. You might believe great blue heron, but would you believe a wood duck doing a balancing act?

Fall is a great season for finding birds on the high wires and low fences along the highways and byways of the state. Look for the jaunty belted kingfisher and the female in her patriotic red-white-and-blue pattern, hunting from wires over or near water, sometimes in puddles too small to discern. Look for swallows arrayed along wires as they stage to migrate. Some field guides depict swallow species side by side on a wire to aid the learner. The young birds in the mix can always provide an interesting identification challenge because they don't look quite like the adults. And, near where they have nested (often on the flat, graveled roofs of large buildings), you might spot one of the goatsuckers—the common nighthawk—perching on a wire even in broad daylight. Typically the bird will squat long-ways with the wire as if it were a tree limb and never seem to lose its balance.

Another regularly seen wire bird, the American kestrel, is our state's smallest and most common falcon. The kestrel is a permanent resident and breeds from one end of Tennessee to the other. By fall, the wires along a particular route may seem to be there just for them because there are so many. Like the kingfisher, the kestrel often leaves the wire to hover in one spot with rapid wingbeats, searching for prey. This is a good time to note the difference between the male, with its distinct blue-gray wings, and the female, whose wings are more the color of the back and tail.

Broad-winged hawks are leaving the woods for their long journey to the tropics, but the northern harriers, sharp-shinned hawks, and Cooper's hawks are returning for the winter. Red-tailed and red-shouldered hawks are year-round resi-

American kestrel

dents, but they now seem to be soaring more beside the other raptors. Rising kettles of black and turkey vultures signal their movement to the south, although some overwinter here. (*Kettle* is the name given to the tornadolike formation created by migrating hawks when they locate a thermal, or mass of rising warm air. Thermals facilitate easy, energy-conserving flight by providing lift. The hawks will climb the thermal and, as they reach the top, the swirling mass of birds will peel off one at a time, gliding southward on angled, fixed wings.)

Canada geese fly over in tight "V" formations, calling to each other to keep up. Snow geese arrive in numbers in October. On the lakes, as huge flocks of double-crested cormorants are seen staging for the trip south, some 20 species of wintering duck are just arriving. Wild turkeys are found in large grazing flocks almost anywhere these days in most parts of the state.

By November our yard birds—the blue jays and northern cardinals—provide some remaining color as the season nears its end. The raucous blue jays seem louder in the crisp air as the trees become more and more bare. The *caw* of the American crow seems less urgent, more resigned. Winter is coming.

Winter

Old Man Winter comes to Tennessee with a vengeance some years, bringing much colder temperatures and more precipitation than on average, but many winters are mild throughout. December through February is the winter for birds. When winters are more severe, unusual birds may be driven from the North and show up here. Be on the lookout at your feeders and for area reports of birds we don't normally see. Pine siskins, purple finches, evening grosbeaks, and even snow buntings can occur. Your regular feeder birds—the Carolina chickadee, tufted titmouse, house finch, and downy and red-bellied woodpecker—will welcome them. Dark-eyed juncos and white-throated sparrows frequent the ground below or a tray feeder supplied with seed.

The results of the Audubon Christmas Bird Counts can give you a good idea of "what's shaking" in your area and across the state, bird-wise, as the season begins; check these out at www.audubon.org/bird/cbc. Only some preliminary results of the current year may be reported, but the previous year's data and the entire history are there for you to use.

The big shows in Tennessee in winter are the ducks and geese on the lakes and rivers. The variety and numbers are sometimes impressive. Look for ring-necked duck, lesser scaup, bufflehead, and hooded and red-breasted merganser. You'll find pied-billed grebe and American coot in the same places. The large herring gull may also be seen on water nearby in several plumages, and the ring-billed may be seen anywhere, including shopping mall parking lots.

American bald eagles visit the state in good numbers, and a few stay here to breed. A great way to see eagles is to go on a bird club field trip or agency-guided tour to Reelfoot Lake in West Tennessee or Dale Hollow Lake in north-central Middle Tennessee in January or February.

With its relatively moderate winters, Tennessee attracts many birds from the North that make a short migration to the South while they wait out the extreme weather. The hermit thrush, eastern bluebird, northern flicker, eastern towhee, and song sparrow are among these. A bird we see in January, a bluebird for example, may be a short-range migrant and not the bird we saw last summer. Our bird may be even farther south.

One of our most beautiful ground-feeding birds is the eastern towhee. Although they are typically fairly wary, in winter they can often be spotted by listening for their loud scratching and rustling through dry leaves in woods and brushy areas. The bird's pattern of dark above and lighter below with white tail corners is striking. The black hooded male and the brown

Herring gull

Hooded merganser

hooded female seen together in contrast are always a treat. When feeding on the ground in our occasional snow cover, they are even more impressive. Some do regularly come to tray feeders.

While trying to spot a rustling towhee, a birder might be surprised to find the much less common fox sparrow, with its reddish back and heavy streaks on the underside. Winter is the prime time for this bird and many of the other sparrows to be found in the state. Primarily because they are generally thought to be drab and known to be difficult to identify, the sparrows are among the last group of birds most watchers attempt to learn. But for some, no better day can be had than to move through brushy fields and along the margins scouting up the "little brown jobs." The Savannah, swamp, white-throated, white-crowned, and—rarely—the Le Conte's and American tree sparrows can be found and sorted out. They join the year-round species, the field and song sparrows, which may be seen on a day in the field or even at the feeder.

Winter is probably the best time to add to your understanding of what attracts birds to your window, yard, or garden. Try adding different types of feeders and new and different foods. Experiment with the locations of feeders and note the results. A resident bird—a mockingbird or woodpecker—you have never seen at your feeders might become a regular. Find time to simply sit and watch your feeders for most of a day and see what surprises you might have been missing. An evening grosbeak or pine siskin may just show up.

Many fruit-eating birds have made Tennessee their winter home because our shrubs and fruiting trees survive through winter and carry their fruit through to spring—that is until the robins, grackles, and cedar waxwings find them. Sometimes flocks, even in late winter, will sweep back through trees that one would have thought were already picked clean, finding whatever morsels they can. White-breasted nuthatches and kinglets pick through what still hangs in the fruit orchards with success.

It seems that more and more reports of wintering hummingbirds are coming in each year from across the state. With our mild winters, it is possible to leave the nectar feeders out for most of the cold months, especially if they are hung in a protected area, such as under the eave of a building. It is important to keep the liquid from freezing if a bird is feeding; a light bulb can be an effective overnight heater. The rufous hummingbird is now reported statewide each winter and many of the other western species, such as the Anna's and the Allen's hummingbirds, have appeared as well. If a late or wintering hummer visits your yard, let the local bird club know.

As the season draws to a close and the weather warms, eastern screech and great horned owls have already begun to nest. Their calls may be heard, even in the city, on cold February nights. Spring is not far away.

Eastern towhee

Tennessee's Ten Must-See Birds

American Woodcock
Scolopax minor

The American woodcock is a short-legged, short-tailed, dumpy-looking bird with no apparent neck and a long, sharp bill. Its bulging, dark eyes with dark eyeline are set high on the head, adding to its odd look. Both males and females are orangish underneath with camouflage-patterned, gray and reddish brown back and wings and broad bars on the crown. The woodcock is a shorebird whose short wings let it live easily in the wet woods, swamps, and shrubby fields it prefers. It is known and sought out for its courtship displays.

One of the best ways to see the bird, anywhere in the state, is to join a "woodcock walk" to one of its singing grounds sponsored by local parks or bird clubs. The best time is from late January through March, as long as it is above freezing, and at dawn, dusk, or on a moonlit night. From about 15 minutes after sunset, for about a half hour, the male woodcock will explode skyward, its wings twittering in song, and then settle back into the open grassy field from which it flew. During the show, he will repeatedly give his *peent* call to keep the attention of the female below.

Black-throated Blue Warbler
Dendroica caerulescens

A neotropical migrant, this warbler nests in the Northeast and in eastern Canada, as well as in the higher altitudes of the Appalachians, including the high mountains of East Tennessee. The male is striking in dark blue-black above, black on the face and sides, and snow-white underneath, with a white "handkerchief" wing patch. The adult female is olive-drab above, buffy underneath, with a light eyebrow line and dark cheek. She also has a small, white wing spot in the same location as on the male. The bird is usually seen foraging low in the understory of deciduous trees. Its song is a lazy, wheezy series of *zhwee* notes with the last note rising.

These beautiful wood warblers begin nesting shortly after they arrive in the mountains in April, but they may extend breeding through the summer into August. They can be found above 3,000 feet in elevation all along the North Carolina border. A good time to search is in July or August, when it is steamy down below, but refreshingly cool in the high mountains. The birds can be found at many spots in the Smokies and at Roan Mountain farther north.

Along with the dark-eyed junco, it is thought to be the most abundant bird in these mountains, so a search should be rewarding. Look for the birds foraging low in the canopy and brushy understory, not in the treetops.

Blue Grosbeak
Guiraca caerulea

The blue grosbeak goes through several plumage changes as it matures, and though it is larger, it is sometimes confused with the indigo bunting, a bird that goes through similar changes. Adult male blue grosbeaks are deep blue with two rusty-red wing bars. Adult females are pale gray-brown with buff-brown wing bars and noticeable blue on the rump. The bills of both are large and silver-gray. The song is an unbroken series of rich, mumbled warbles, similar to the house finch and may be confused with the song of the orchard oriole. Get to know the song since blue grosbeaks are often hard to see. Until the 1940s, none were recorded in the state. Now they are widespread, common, and breeding.

A good place to look for the blue grosbeak is Land Between the Lakes (www.lbl.org), a recreation area managed by the Tennessee Valley Authority (TVA) that lies at the northwestern corner of Middle Tennessee and stretches some 40 miles into Kentucky. This 300-square-mile natural area lies between the impounded Tennessee and Cumberland Rivers (Kentucky Lake and Lake Barkley) and offers many areas of good habitat for the bird. Go in mid-May to late-June, and listen and look for them early and late in the day in the brushy clearings, fencerows, and blackberry thickets where they prefer to nest.

Bonaparte's Gull
Larus philadelphia

One of our three regular winter gulls—along with the ring-billed and the herring gull—this small bird has been called dainty, petite, and ternlike, all of which are apt descriptors. The winter adult is gray above and white below with black wing tips; it lacks the black hood of the summer bird. It has a dark smudgy ear spot, its bill is slender and black, and its legs are orange-red. This is a two-year gull (meaning it takes two years for it to reach adult plumage), and the first-winter bird has pinkish legs and dark brown on the leading edge of the wing. The "Bonie," as it is called, is seen less frequently than the others, but when seen may be in large flocks.

A good time to see the Bonaparte's gull is in December or January as they gather on our human-made lakes throughout the state. A good place to see them is at Pickwick Landing Dam and State Park, near Savannah in Hardin County (park office: 731-689-3129 or www.state.tn.us/environment/parks), and at nearby areas along the river frequented by gulls. A number of rare or uncommon gulls have been seen in this area, including the state's only ivory gull seen here in February of 1996.

Broad-winged Hawk
Buteo platypterus

This small, stocky hawk is not as large as the average crow. It is quite common in the summer in the woods of the state. The adult male and female are both brown on the back with reddish bars on the chest. The immature is more streaked on the sides and chest. In flight the tail is banded black and white, with the terminal band the broadest. The wings are white underneath, trimmed in black, and the wing tips are black. During spring and summer, listen for the broad-winged hawk's high whistling two-note call of Teee-teee!

Within their territory, they are often quite tame. When found feeding along a wooded country lane, along some other roadside, or in the deep woods, they can be approached closely and may tolerate your presence for a long period.

If you have not yet seen the broad-winged somewhere in the woods or along the country lanes by summer's end, look for it in mid- to late-September at the peak of its southern migration through the state. It can be best seen from a ridge or a fire tower toward the eastern part of the state. Try the Soddy Mountain Hawk Watch north of Chattanooga or Sharp's Ridge in Knoxville.

Common Loon
Gavia immer

The common loon (shown in the photo in its breeding plumage) is a large, long-bodied, fish-eating diver. Among the loons, the common loon is second only to the yellow-billed in size. On the water it appears to be, and is, much larger than most of the ducks with which it may be seen. In winter plumage, the back of the head and neck is dark, but there is a whitish indentation midneck. The back is lighter than the neck and head, and the undersides are whitish. The bill is stout, straight, and gray with a slightly darker tip in winter juveniles and adults. Its haunting, yodeling calls are not often heard in winter.

Migration of the common loon through the state is in November and March, and many winter here. Sometimes hundreds, even thousands, form in rafts on the larger bodies of water. From November on, a great place to see this bird and other loons is the Pace Point Area of the Tennessee National Wildlife Refuge, near the town of Big Sandy (www.tennesseerefuge.fws.gov). Just recently, for the first time ever reported anywhere in the state, all four loons—common, Pacific, red-throated, and the very rare yellow-billed—were seen at this site in one scope view!

Single common loons, or small groups, may be found on smaller lakes or large ponds, some even in heavily populated areas. It is sometimes possible to observe the same bird in such a location for weeks or even months through the cold season. Some birds do stay in the state over the summer.

Least Tern
Sterna antillarum

The interior least tern (Sterna antillarum athalassos) is a locally common summer resident that nests on sand and gravel bars in the Mississippi River along the state's western border. It has been on the U.S. Fish and Wildlife Service Endangered Species list since 1985, but the Tennessee area population is reportedly relatively secure, assuming no increase in the recreational use of its nesting grounds.

The least tern is the smallest American tern, 8 to 9 inches long, with a wingspan of 20 inches. The breeding adult is gray above with a white underside, a black cap and nape with a white forehead. Its sharp-pointed bill is orange-yellow in the early season with a black tip; later, it is greenish. The legs are bright orange or yellow. The flight is rapid, sometimes bouncy, often punctuated with squeaks or squeals. The bird feeds mainly on small fish caught in shallows, often knifing straight down into the water with wings folded.

Look for the least tern beginning in mid-May along the Mississippi river from Memphis to Tiptonville. In most years, they nest at 20 or more locations on this stretch of "The Big Muddy." Check the Internet for where they are being seen. Fall migration, from July through early September, provides looks at these terns and others from locations upriver. Some migrants are seen in other parts of the state.

Sandhill Crane
Grus canadensis

The sandhill crane is one of the tallest, if not largest, birds seen in Tennessee. Along with the more common great blue heron, it may stand over 4 feet tall and its wingspan can be 7 feet. Only the bald eagle's wingspan surpasses it. The sandhills that migrate through Tennessee in fall are from nesting areas around the Great Lakes; they are moving to wintering grounds in Florida. They return north by the same route in the spring. The bird is long-necked, with long blackish legs and feet, and is all-gray with a red crown.

During their stopovers in the state, the cranes roost together at night, standing in flocks, often in shallow water. At dawn, they fly to nearby fields or marshes to feed. Their rattling, bugle-like *garooo-a-a-a* calls can be deafening in unison. They are high-altitude migrants, and their calls can often be heard from far overhead—even before they can be seen descending rapidly in small squadrons to join a flock already gathered on the ground. It is an amazing spectacle when the entire resting flock lifts off all at once in response to a raptor or some other alarm.

For more than a decade, one of the best ways to see sandhill cranes has been to attend the annual festival of the Cherokee Heritage and Sandhill Crane Viewing Days in early February at the Hiwassee Wildlife Refuge in Meigs County north of Chattanooga. More than 5,000 cranes are often present.

Snow Goose
Chen caerulescens

The snow goose is smaller than most Canada geese and most other goose species found in Tennessee, except for the much less common Ross' goose, with which it is sometimes seen. In its white morph, it is white with black primary feathers. Its bill is pink and always has a black grin patch on the side (the Ross' lacks this). Its feet are pink. Its voice is different from the honk of the Canada, more of a whouk, which is often given in unison by a flock.

Until recent years, the bird was not commonly seen in the state, and the darker morph (once considered a separate species and called the "blue goose") was reportedly the plumage type seen most often. Today, large winter flocks are regularly seen in both the western and the eastern parts of the state, and the white juveniles and adults seem to predominate. The month of January is good for seeing snow geese, and there are no better spots than Reelfoot and Hiwassee. Sometimes thousands of snow geese can be seen in one flock.

Snow geese feed by uprooting grass and grain shoots, and this can cause significant damage to commercial operations and can be costly in managed feeding areas. For this reason, there may be more liberal hunting regulations on this species at certain times and in various areas, and there may generally be more "hard feelings" on the part of nonbirders toward this beautiful bird.

Swainson's Warbler
Limnothlypis swainsonii

The Swainson's warbler is a neotropical migrant that breeds regularly in the state, but it is uncommon, very secretive, and elusive. A birder, even looking for it intentionally, may not see the first one for years. It is a small, plain, brown bird, slightly lighter below, but with a strong, whitish eyebrow stripe and dark eyeline. It has a long, pointed, straight bill that it uses to search for insects among the leaves on the ground. Its legs are pink, and the sexes are alike. It is best found by its loud, slurry, five-note song on the nesting grounds. Learn to distinguish it from the similar Louisiana waterthrush's song to know you are on the right bird; the waterthrush song seems to splutter more at the end.

The Swainson's warbler is found in three distinct breeding areas of the state. In West Tennessee, it is found in swamps, thickets, and bottomland canebrakes. In East Tennessee, on the plateau and in the Cumberland Mountains and the higher mountains, it is found in ravines, near water in thickets of great laurel, often near hemlocks, and in other dense undergrowth. A good place to look for it, beginning in late April, is the lovely mountain valley Cove Lake State Park at Careyville, on the eastern edge of the Cumberland Mountains (http://www.state.tn.us/environment/parks). The bird has been reliably found here for several years, and the site is quite accessible. But remember, with the Swainson's there's no guarantee.

Tennessee's Ten Best Bird-Watching Spots

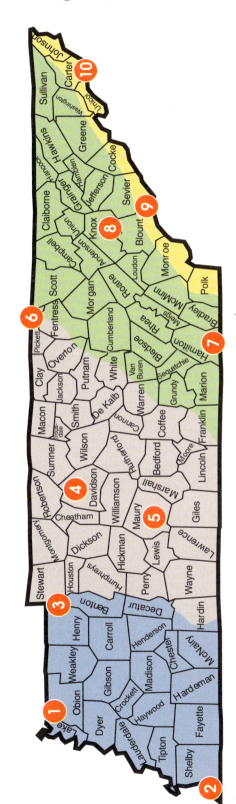

Key Code

1. Reelfoot NWR
2. EARTH Complex
3. Pace Point, Big Sandy Unit
4. Radnor Lake State Natural Area
5. Williamsport Lakes
6. Pickett State Park
7. Standifer Gap Marsh
8. Sharp's Ridge Memorial Park
9. Great Smoky Mountains National Park
10. Roan Mountain State Park

Tennessee Ecoregions

- WESTERN COASTAL PLAIN
- HIGHLAND RIM AND BASIN
- EASTERN RIDGE AND VALLEY
- EASTERN MOUNTAIN

❷

EARTH Complex
At the west end of Mitchell Rd. off US 61
Memphis, TN
(901) 576-6720
www.tnbirds.org
(Check out the Memphis chapter for more information about this bird-watching spot.)

This large, municipal sewage-treatment facility, located to the southwest of Memphis, has become one of the most popular birding spots in the area. Just mention "the pits," and any birder in this part of the state will know you are referring to this site. In spite of the obvious olfactory drawbacks, birders have come to relish "sewey ponds" wherever they have access to them. The birds, particularly the shorebirds, can be fabulous, and the unexpected often show up. No need to call ahead, but do check in at the office.

During the colder months, waterfowl, terns, and gulls are seen here. In summer, black-necked stilts nest here and, when the young hatch, the show is something to see. Fall and spring bring the migrants in flocks. One can spot lesser yellowlegs, spotted sandpiper, and most of the other sandpipers, as well as Wilson's snipe, plovers, and dowitchers. In fall, or from July on, every day brings a new mix of hundreds, sometimes thousands, of birds. Reeves, as the female ruffs are called, have even been seen here. As at any shorebird or open water area, a spotting scope is best.

❾

Great Smoky Mountains National Park
107 Park Headquarters Road
Gatlinburg, TN 37738
(865) 436-1200
http://www.nps.gov/grsm/

It is no wonder that this park is the most-visited in the national system. More than 800 square miles—with altitudes ranging from 857 to 6,643 feet and the greatest diversity of plant and animal life one can find in an area this size in a temperate climate—the Smokies are indeed a treasure. More than 200 bird species stop here, and 110 species breed here. The many life zones attract breeding species typically found farther north. The black-capped chickadee, dark-eyed junco, red-breasted nuthatch, and the black-throated blue, Blackburnian, and Canada warblers (among others) nest at high elevations in the park. Red crossbill can sometimes be found, as well.

In warm weather (some roads are closed in winter), a good starting point is at the top. From the Sugarlands Visitor Center on U.S. 441 (where bird lists and information are available), drive the 12.9 miles to Newfound Gap on the Tennessee and North Carolina border, and then on to the Clingman's Dome parking area (6,311 feet). A half-mile paved trail leads to this second highest point in the eastern United States. All along your drive and climb, at pull-offs and trailheads, listen and look for the birds. Hike the trails for closer looks. There is much good birding at the lower elevations, as well, including the visitor center area. The park has been named an International Biosphere Reserve and one of the state's Important Bird Areas.

③

Pace Point, Big Sandy Unit
Tennessee National Wildlife Refuge
3006 Dinkins Lane
Paris, TN 38242
(731) 642-2091
www.tennesseerefuge.fws.gov

The Pace Point area of this 50,000-acre refuge (which stretches, in three units, some 65 miles along the Tennessee River's Kentucky Lake) is becoming famous for its great diversity of waterfowl, gulls, and terns. It seems that every year some new rarity shows up to join the refuge's list of almost 300 species. In winter, great rafts of ducks and loons can be seen off this peninsula that juts north into a body of water over four miles wide. In the surrounding fields, sparrow species abound and short-eared owls are nearby. In fall, black terns come through, feeding in good-sized flocks. Bald eagles nest here. Several nearby areas, including Britton Ford, are good, too. To the south, the Duck River Unit also provides excellent waterfowl birding. The refuge has also been named one of Tennessee's Important Bird Areas (IBAs).

⑥

Pickett State Park
4605 Pickett Park Highway
Jamestown, TN 38556
(931) 879-5821
http://www.state.tn.us/environment/parks

This 17,000-acre park and forest, with pine and deciduous woods, is a great place to experience the bird life and all the other wonders of the upper Cumberland Plateau. The park provides a look at a variety of woodland birds, easy access to unusual geological formations, and a botanical diversity rivaled only by the high mountains to the east. Look for the dozen or so species of summer wood warblers, including ovenbirds and hooded warblers. You'll find the Acadian flycatcher along streamsides and ravines. At night, listen for eastern screech-owls, great horned and barred owls, and whip-poor-wills. The park has good accommodations, including rustic stone cabins. Next door is the 100,000-acre Big South Fork National River and Recreation Area, hosting many of the same species.

④

Radnor Lake State Natural Area
1160 Otter Creek Road
Nashville, TN 37220
(615) 373-3467)
http://www.state.tn.us/environment/parks

"Nashville's Walden Pond," as it has been reverently called by nature lovers, is truly a superlative place for birds. The 85-acre lake is nestled in steep, wooded hills and is surrounded by trails through some 900 acres of the best habitat to be found for migrating wood warblers and breeding woodland birds. Though very much in the city, it is not a recreation-oriented park, but a natural area functioning as a sanctuary. It is a magnet for birds and birders.

In spring, more than 20 warblers species can be seen in a day, including Tennessee, magnolia, American redstart, and hooded and—with skill and luck—Connecticut and mourning warblers as well. Yellow-billed cuckoo, white-eyed vireo, scarlet tanager, blue-gray gnatcatcher, and scores of others nest here. In winter, pied-billed grebe, ring-necked duck, lesser scaup, bufflehead, and gadwall are regulars, along with many other species of waterfowl that visit the lake. Viewing of the water is best from Otter Creek Road and a scope is helpful. Several miles of trail are wheelchair accessible.

①

Reelfoot National Wildlife Refuge
4343 Highway 157
Union City, TN 38261
(731) 538-2481s
http://reelfoot.fws.gov

Earthquakes along the New Madrid fault in the winter of 1811 to 1812 changed the course of the Mississippi River and left the lowland that is today one of the more unusual physical features and all-around best birding spots in Tennessee—Reelfoot Lake. The shallow, swampy, bald cypress-edged, black water teems with fish and in summer is decorated with water lilies, herons, and egrets. This National Wildlife Refuge includes or manages some 25,000 acres of open water, close to 2,000 acres of bottomland forests, and many acres of croplands. The refuge and the nearby wildlife management area, Black Bayou Waterfowl Refuge, and Reelfoot Lake State Park are winter homes to more than a half million ducks and geese and more than 200 American bald eagles. Although the refuge lands are closed to the public from March 15 to November 15, the auto-tour route is open year-round and many other nearby areas are accessible.

Birding is excellent almost anytime of year at Reelfoot. The lake and its surroundings are not only regular stopovers for millions of migrating birds in spring and fall, but are also breeding grounds for a number of neotropical migrant species. Ospreys, wood thrushes, prothonotary warblers, hooded mergansers, wood ducks, and red-shouldered hawks nest here along with many others. The red-headed woodpecker is resident here along with the other five woodpeckers commonly found in the state year-round; the yellow-bellied sapsucker winters here. Reelfoot Lake area has recently been named one of the 500 globally most significant Important Bird Areas (IBAs) in the United States by the American Bird Conservancy.

⑩

Roan Mountain State Park
1015 Highway 143
Roan Mountain, TN 37687
(423) 772-0190
http://www.state.tn.us/environment/parks

This park is some 2,000 acres of fine hardwood forest, situated at the base of 6,285 feet high Roan Mountain. There is a great diversity of plant and animal life in the woods and hollows and along the ridges. Rhododendrons are spectacular in June, and birds are good year-round. In the park, and along the 8-mile drive to Carver's Gap at the top of the mountain on the North Carolina border, look for the magnolia warbler, veery, winter wren, golden-crowned kinglet, and peregrine falcon. Northern saw-whet owls are also found here. Park accommodations are good and include camping and cabins.

##

Sharp's Ridge Memorial Park
329 Sharp's Ridge Memorial Drive
Knoxville, TN 03790
(423) 215-2090

To find Sharp's Ridge, follow these directions: From Interstate 40, exit 389A/U.S. 441 North/Broadway. Travel 1.5 miles and turn left onto Ludlow Avenue. Bear right in 0.4 miles, then left onto the ridge. The road ends after 1.3 miles.

One of the most well-known gathering spots for birds and birders in East Tennessee, this 1,300-foot high outcropping of sandstone in the center of the city is literally above it all. The views are spectacular, and from mid-April to mid-May the birds rival the view. Waves of warbler, thrush, vireo, and tanager species and other northbound migrants assault this promontory and fill the senses of the visiting birder. From the road, looking down the steep slopes into the treetops gives great looks at birds from angles seldom seen. The ridge is a good hawk watch in fall and spring. This site is sometimes closed due to national security alerts. Be sure to call ahead to confirm park access.

Standifer Gap Marsh

6601 Standifer Gap Road
Chattanooga, TN 37421
(423) 899-3933
Property of Living Covenant Christian Center (public access available)

From Interstate 75, exit onto Shallowford Road west. Turn right on Hickory Valley Road, and then left on Standifer Gap Road. Travel approximately 1/2 mile to the church. Turn right on the black-top road by the church; the marsh is on the left.

This freshwater marsh has become a popular site for birders looking for migrant rails and wetland species in season. Virginia rails are sometimes abundant, and king rail, sora, Wilson's snipe, and bitterns are also found. In winter, the Canada goose and many species of duck are here. Boots are recommended for walking the edges.

Another well-known marsh and seasonal mudflat, the city-owned Brainerd Levee is a short distance away to the west at the corner of Shallowford Road and North Moore Road.

Williamsport Lakes

Maury County
On Highway 50, approximately 10 miles northwest of Columbia on Hwy 50
(931) 583-2477
http://www.state.tn.us/twra/fish/pond/famlake/williamsport.html

The six lakes along with the forests and fields of this state wildlife management area cover 1,850 acres. Managed by the Tennessee Wildlife Resources Agency, the site is being reclaimed from its former use as a phosphate mining operation. The results have been the creation of a prime bird and wildlife watching area. Two of the lakes are wetlands, and no fishing is allowed.

In fall and winter, ducks—including blue-winged teal, mallard, and ring-necked—are in good number, and the fields hold many species of sparrow. Song, field, white-throated, and white-crowned sparrows are here, and grasshopper and Henslow's sparrows can also be found. In summer, the nesting yellow-breasted chat, prairie warbler, indigo bunting, and American goldfinch are a feast for the senses. Roads through the complex provide easy access. The Natchez Trace Parkway is only 2 miles away and provides a wonderful birding drive in either direction.

Resources for Tennessee Bird Watchers

Books and Publications

Bierly, M. L. 1980. *Bird Finding in Tennessee.* Nashville, Tennessee: Published by the author. This title is out of print, but used copies can be found. After more than two decades, it is still very useful.

Nicholson, C. P. 1997. *Atlas of the Breeding Birds of Tennessee.* Knoxville, Tennessee: The University of Tennessee Press.

Parmer, H. E., compiler. 1985. *Birds of the Nashville Area.* 4th ed. Nashville: Tennessee Ornithological Society, Nashville Chapter. The 5th edition is soon to be released.

Robinson, J. C. 1990. *An Annotated Checklist of the Birds of Tennessee.* Knoxville, Tennessee: The University of Tennessee Press. This title is currently out of print, but used copies can be found.

Stedman, S. J., and Stedman, B. H. 2002. *Notes on the Birds of the Big South Fork National River and Recreation Area and Obed National Wild and Scenic River.* Cookeville, Tennessee: Tennessee Technological University.

Agencies, Organizations, and People

The National Audubon Society
www.audubon.org
Audubon chapters in the state offer a number of bird- and nature-related activities throughout the year. Contact the local chapters in Chattanooga, Clarksville, Memphis, and Nashville.

State Ornithologist
Tennessee Wildlife Resources Agency
P.O. Box 40747
Nashville, TN 37204
(615) 781-6653
http://www.state.tn.us/twra

Tennessee Ornithological Society
P.O. Box 22682
Memphis, TN 38122
www.tnbirds.org
The society's website includes a comprehensive list of birding resources, checklists, membership information, chapter and events information, and links to a number of useful state bird-related sites.

Tennessee Travel and Tourism Information
312 8th Avenue North, 25th Floor
Nashville, TN 37243
(615) 741-2159
www.tnvacation.com

Getting Started in Bird Watching

Bird watching, or birding, is one of North America's fastest-growing and most popular hobbies. According to a recent survey by the U.S. Fish & Wildlife Service, there are as many as 44 million bird watchers in the United States. Back in 1978, when my family began publishing Bird Watcher's Digest *in our living room, bird watching was still considered a bit odd. The image many people associated with bird watching was Miss Jane Hathaway of* The Beverly Hillbillies. *Fortunately, that stereotype is long gone now, and our culture has come to embrace bird watching as an enriching, exciting pursuit—one that can be done with little expense and enjoyed almost anywhere at any time.*

Why Do We Watch Birds?

Birds have inspired humans for thousands of years. Birds can fly—something we humans have mastered only in the past 100 years. Birds have brilliant plumage, and some even change their colors seasonally. Birds are master musicians, singing beautiful and complex songs. They possess impressive physical abilities—hovering, flying at high speeds, and withstanding extreme weather conditions, as well as the rigors of long migration flights. Birds also have behaviors to which we can relate, such as intense courtship displays, devotion to their mates, and the enormous investment of effort spent in raising their young. Sound familiar? In short, birds are a vivid expression of life, and we admire them because they inspire us. This makes us want to know them better and to bring them closer to us. We accomplish this by attracting them to our backyards and gardens, and by using optics to see them more clearly in an "up close and personal" way.

Early Bird Study

Before the advent of modern optics that help us view birds more closely, humans used a shotgun approach to bird watching. Literally. Famed ornithologist and bird artist John James Audubon was the first European to document many of the North American bird species in the early 1800s. He did so by shooting every unfamiliar bird he encountered. Having a bird in the hand allowed him to study it closely and draw it accurately. This was an excellent method of learning a lot about birds quickly, but it was rather hard on the birds. This method of bird study continued largely unchecked until the

Millions of Americans enjoy bird watching.

early 1900s, when the effects of market hunting on birds became unhappily apparent. In 1934, a young bird enthusiast and artist named Roger Tory Peterson published *A Field Guide to the Birds*, with a system of arrows showing key field marks on the plumage of each species. This enabled a person to identify a bird from a distance, with or without the aid of magnifying optics. Modern bird watching was born, and it was no longer necessary to shoot birds in order to positively identify them. The era of shotgun ornithology was over.

Modern Bird Watching

Bird watching today is about seeing or hearing birds and then using these clues to positively identify them. To reach this identification, we use two important tools of the bird-watching trade: binoculars and a field guide. The binoculars (or perhaps a *spotting scope*, which is a telescope especially designed for nature watching) help you to get a closer, clearer look at the bird. The field guide helps you interpret what you see so that you can identify the bird species.

I like to say that we live in the golden era of bird watching. When I started birding more than 35 years ago, feeders, seed, birdhouses, and other supplies were hard to come by—we had to make our own. Now they are available in almost any store. We can buy a field guide or a book like the one you're holding in any bookstore. We can try out optics at camera stores, outdoor suppliers, and at birding festivals. We can learn about birds in special bird courses, on the Internet, in magazines, or from CD-ROMs, DVDs, and videos. We can join a local or state bird club and meet new bird-watching friends. We can take birding tours to far-off places.

There's never been a better time to become a bird watcher. So let's get started!

Basic Gear

If you're just starting out as a birder, you may need to acquire the basic tools—binoculars and a field guide.

Binoculars

You may be able to borrow optics from a friend or family member, but if your interest takes off, you'll certainly want to have your own binoculars to use anytime you wish. Fortunately, a decent pair of binoculars can be purchased for less than $100, and some really nice binoculars can be found used on the Internet or through a local bird club for just a bit more. The magnification powers that are commonly used for bird watching are 7x, 8x, and 10x. This is always the first number listed in the binoculars' description, as in 8x40. The second number refers to the size of the objective lens (the big end) of the binocular. The bigger the second number, the brighter the view presented to your eye. In general, for bird-watching binoculars the first number should be between 7x and 10x, and the second number should be between 30 and 45.

Try to find binoculars that are easy and comfortable to use. Make sure they focus easily, giving you a clear image, and that they are comfortable to hold (not too large or heavy) and fit your eye spacing. Every set of eyes is different, so don't settle for binoculars that just don't feel right. The perfect pair of binoculars for you should feel like a natural extension of your hands and eyes. Over time you will become adept at using your optics and, with a little practice, you'll be operating them like a pro.

Field Guide

When choosing a field guide, you'll need to decide what type of birding you'll be doing and where you plan to do it. If nearly all of your bird watching will be done at home, you might want to get a basic field guide to the backyard birds of your region, or at least a field guide that limits its scope to your half of the continent. Many field guides are offered in eastern (east of the Rocky Mountains) and western (from the

Select binoculars that feel good in your hands and are easy to use.

A field guide is one of birding's essential tools.

Rockies west) versions. These geographically limited formats include only those birds that are commonly found in that part of the continent, rather than continent-wide guides that include more than 800 North American bird species. Choose a field guide that is appropriate for you, and you'll save a lot of searching time—time that can be better spent looking at birds!

It Starts at Home

Most bird watchers like to start out at home, and this usually means getting to know the birds in your backyard. A great way to enhance the diversity of birds in your yard is to set up a simple feeding station. Even a single feeder with the proper food can bring half a dozen or more unfamiliar bird species into your yard. And it's these encounters with new and interesting birds that make bird watching so enjoyable.

Start your feeding station with a feeder geared to the birds that are already in your backyard or garden. For most of us this will mean a tube or hopper feeder filled with sunflower seeds. Place the feeder in a location that offers you a clear view of bird activity, but also offers the birds some nearby cover in the form of a hedge, shrubs, or brush pile into which the birds can fly when a predator approaches. I always set our feeding stations up opposite our kitchen or living room windows because these are the rooms in which we spend most of our daylight hours, and because these rooms have the best windows for bird watching. We'll discuss bird feeding and attracting in greater detail in the next section.

Once you've got a basic feeder set up outside, you'll need to get yourself set up inside your house. You've probably already selected the best location for viewing your feeder. Next you should select a safe place to store your binoculars and field guide—somewhere that is easily accessible to you when you suddenly spot a new bird in your backyard. At our house we keep binoculars hanging on pegs right next to our kitchen windows. This keeps them handy for use in checking the feeders or for heading out for a walk around our farm.

Keeping Your Bird List

Most bird watchers enjoy keeping a list of their sightings. This can take the form of a written list, notations inside your field guide next to each species' account, or in a special journal meant for just such a purpose. There are even software programs available to help you keep your list on your computer. In birding, the most common list is the *life list*. A life list is a list of all the birds you've seen at least once in your life. Let's say you noticed a bright, black-and-orange bird in your backyard willow tree one morning, then keyed it out in your field guide to be a male Baltimore oriole. This is a species you'd never seen before, and now you can put it on your life list. List keeping can be done at any level of involvement, so keep the list or lists that you enjoy. I like to keep a property list of all the species we've seen at least once on our 80-acre farm. Currently, that list is at 180 species, but I'm always watching for something new to show up. I also update my North American life list a couple of times a year, after I've seen a new bird species.

Bird Watching Afield

Sooner or later you may want to expand your bird-watching horizons beyond your backyard bird feeders. Birding afield—away from your own home—can be a wonderfully exhilarating experience. Many beginning bird watchers are shy about venturing forth, afraid that their inexperience will prove embarrassing, but there's really no reason to feel this way. The best way to begin

35

Ten Tips for Beginning Bird Watchers

1. Get a decent pair of binoculars, ones that are easy for you to use and hold steady.
2. Find a field guide to the birds of your region (many guides are divided into eastern and western editions). Guides that cover all the birds of North America contain many birds species uncommon or entirely absent from your area. You can always upgrade to a continent-wide guide later.
3. Set up a basic feeding station in your yard or garden.
4. Start with your backyard birds. They are the easiest to see, and you can become familiar with them fairly quickly.
5. Practice your identification skills. Starting with a common bird species, note the most obvious visual features of the bird (color, size, shape, and patterns in the plumage). These features are known as field marks and will be helpful clues to the bird's identity.
6. Notice the bird's behavior. Many birds can be identified by their behavior—woodpeckers peck on wood, kingfishers dive for small fish, and swallows are known for their graceful flight.
7. Listen to the bird's sounds. Bird song is a vital component to birding. Learning bird songs and sounds takes a bit of practice, but many birds make it pretty easy for us. For example, chickadees and whip-poor-wills (among others) call out their names. The Resources section of this book contains a listing of tools to help you to learn bird songs.
8. Look at the bird, not at the book. When you see an unfamiliar bird, avoid the temptation to put down your binoculars and begin searching for the bird in your field guide. Instead, watch the bird carefully for as long as it is present—or until you feel certain that you have noted its most important field marks. Then look at your field guide. Birds have wings, and they tend to use them. Your field guide will still be with you long after the bird has gone, so take advantage of every moment to watch an unfamiliar bird while it is present.
9. Take notes. No one can be expected to remember every field mark and description of a bird. But you can help your memory and accelerate your learning by taking notes on the birds you see. These notes can be written in a small pocket notebook, in the margins of your field guide, or even in the back of this book.
10. Venture beyond the backyard and find other bird watchers in your area. The bird watching you'll experience beyond your backyard will be enriching, especially if it leads not only to new birds, but also to new birding friends. Ask a local nature center or wildlife refuge about bird clubs in your region. Your state ornithological organization or natural resources division may also be helpful. Bird watching with other birders can be the most enjoyable of all.

birding away from the backyard is to connect with other local bird watchers via your local bird club. Most parts of North America have local or regional bird clubs, and most of these clubs offer regular field trips. Bird watchers are among the friendliest people on the planet, and every bird club is happy to welcome new prospective members. If you don't know how to find a local bird club, ask your friends and neighbors if they know any bird watchers, check the telephone directory, search the Internet, or ask at your area parks, nature centers, and wild bird stores.

Getting out in the field with more experienced bird watchers is the fastest way to improve your skills. Don't be afraid to ask questions ("How did you know that was an indigo bunting?"). Don't worry if you begin to feel overwhelmed by the volume of new information—all new bird watchers experience this. When it happens, relax and take some time to simply watch. In time you'll be identifying birds and looking forward to new challenges and new birds.

Feeding and Housing

Birds need four basic things to live: food, water for drinking and bathing, a safe place to roost, and a safe place to nest. These vital elements are actually quite easy for you to offer to birds, even if your backyard is small.

Food

Bird feeding is a good place to start your bird-attracting efforts. It's wise to begin with a single feeder, such as a hopper feeder or tube feeder filled with black-oil sunflower seeds. The black-oil sunflower seed is the most common type of sunflower seed available, because it's the seed type that most of our feeder birds can readily eat. Think of it as the hamburger of the bird world. The black-oil sunflower seed has a thin shell (easy for seed-eating birds to crack) and a large, meaty seed kernel inside. As you can see from the seed preference chart on page 147, many backyard bird species eat sunflower seeds.

Other excellent foods for birds include: mixed seed (a blend that normally includes millet, milo, cracked corn, and other seeds), sunflower bits (shells removed), peanuts (best offered unsalted and without the shell), suet or suet cakes, cracked corn, thistle seed (also known as Niger or nyjer seed), safflower seed, nectar (for hummingbirds), mealworms, fruits, and berries. Bird feeding varies from region to region—don't be afraid to experiment with new feeders or food. Birds will vote with their bills and stomachs and will let you know their preferences

Eating the food at feeders is not the only way birds find sustenance. A backyard or garden that includes natural food sources for birds—such as seed-producing flowering plants and fruit-bearing trees and shrubs—will further enhance its attractiveness to birds. In fact, it's often the natural features of a backyard habitat that attract the birds' attention rather than the bird feeders. Read the Bird-Friendly Plants section on page 162 for more specific suggestions.

Feeder Types

It's important to match the foods and feeders to each other, as well as to the birds you wish to attract. Sunflower seed works in a wide variety of feeders, including tube, hopper, platform, and satellite or excluder feeders (that permit small birds to feed, but exclude larger birds), as well as for ground feeding. Mixed seed does not work as well in tube or hopper feeders for a couple of reasons. First of all, the birds that prefer mixed seed tend to be ground feeders, so it's less natural for them to go to an elevated feeder for food. Secondly, elevated feeder designs (such as tubes or hoppers) are built to dole out seed as it is eaten and the smaller size of most mixed seed kernels causes excess spillage. Mixed seed works best when offered on a platform feeder or when scattered on the ground.

Pictured from the top down: Black-oil sunflower seed, peanuts, mixed seed, and cracked corn.

A fruit feeder.

When purchasing your feeders and foods, make sure they will work effectively with each other. Specialty foods such as suet, peanuts, thistle (Niger), mealworms, fruit, and nectar require specific feeders for the best results for you and the birds. The Food and Feeder Chart on page 147 is a great place to start.

Your Feeding Station

Place your feeding station in a spot that is useful and attractive to you and the birds. When we moved into our farmhouse, we looked out all the windows before choosing a spot for our feeding station. You may want to do the same thing. After all, the whole point of bird feeding is to be able to see and enjoy the birds. From the birds' perspective, your feeders should be placed adjacent to cover—a place they can leave from and retreat to safely and quickly if a predator appears. This cover can be a woodland edge, brushy area or brush pile, hedges or shrubs, or even a weedy fencerow. If your yard is mostly lawn, consider creating a small island of cover near your feeding station. This will greatly enhance the feeders' appeal to birds.

Be patient. You've spent the money and effort to put up feeders, but don't expect immediate dividends. Birds are creatures of habit, and it may take a few days or even a few weeks before they recognize your offering as a source of food. Sooner or later, a curious chickadee, finch, or sparrow will key into the food source, and the word will spread along the local bird "grapevine."

Housing for Birds

Almost every bird species builds or uses some type of nest to produce and rear its young. However, only a small fraction of our birds use nest boxes provided by humans. Birds that use next boxes or birdhouses are called *cavity nesters*, because they prefer to nest inside an enclosed space, such as hole excavated in a tree, as many woodpeckers do. Nest boxes simulate a natural cavity, but they have the added advantage (for humans) of our being able to place them in a convenient spot. To the birds' advantage, we can protect the nest box from predators, bad weather, and other problems.

Being a landlord to the birds is a thrilling experience. You are treated to an intimate peek inside the lives of your "tenants" and rewarded with the presence of their offspring, if nesting is successful. To help ensure the nesting success of your birds you need to provide the proper housing in an appropriate setting, and you should monitor the housing during the nesting season.

The Right Housing

Two factors are key to providing the right nest box for your birds: the size of the housing and

Male northern cardinals at a sunflower feeder.

Exterior latex stain helps prolong the life of a birdhouse and protects the birds inside.

the size of the entry hole. Not all cavity nesters are picky about the interior dimensions of the cavity, except when it is excessively big or small. But the size of the entry hole is important because it can effectively limit the entrance of large, aggressive nest competitors, predators, and inclement weather. For example, an entry hole with a diameter of 1 1/2 inches on a bluebird nest box will permit entry by bluebirds and many smaller birds, including chickadees, titmice, nuthatches, wrens, and tree swallows. But this same size keeps European starlings out and prevents them from usurping the box.

Use the Nest Box Chart (page 148) to help you determine the appropriate nest box details for your backyard birds. Whether you build your own birdhouses or buy them at your local wild bird products supplier, see page 40 for a few tips for "landlords" that you will want to consider.

An Appropriate Setting

Place your nest boxes where they will be most likely to be found and used by birds. Bluebirds and swallows prefer nest sites in the middle of large, open, grassy areas. Wrens, chickadees, nuthatches, flycatchers, woodpeckers, and other woodland birds prefer sites that are in or adjacent to woodlands. Robins, phoebes, Carolina wrens, barn swallows, and purple martins prefer to nest near human dwellings, perhaps for the protection from predators that we provide.

Monitoring Your Nest Boxes

By taking a weekly peek inside your nest boxes, you will stay abreast of your tenants' activities, and you'll be able to help them raise their families successfully. During most of the year, your birdhouses will appear to be empty. This does not mean that the boxes are going unused. In fact, many birds use nest boxes during the win-

An example of a pole-mounted predator baffle.

Nest Box Tips for Landlords

- Do build or buy sturdily constructed nest boxes that are built from untreated wood (or another weatherproof material) with walls that are at least 3/4 inch thick. See page 157 for a simple bird house plan.
- Do not stain or paint the interior of the box. Stain or paint on the box exterior will help the box last longer. Light colors reflect sunlight and keep box interiors from getting too hot.
- Perches by the entry hole are unnecessary and may actually encourage competitors and predators.
- The box roof should be slanted and extend out several inches over the entry hole to keep out the weather.
- Nest boxes should have an access door for monitoring. Access doors that swing upward to open on the side or front of the box are easiest to use and safest for birds.
- The box should have holes for ventilation at the top of the vertical walls. Drainage holes in the floor will permit excess moisture to escape.
- Mount boxes on poles away from nearby trees and structures.
- Place a pole-mounted predator baffle beneath the nest box to keep snakes and mammals from gaining access to the nest.

ter months as nighttime roosts. A loose feather, insect parts, berry seeds, or a few droppings are classic evidence of roosting activity.

During breeding season, your regular visits will help you know when nest building begins and when eggs are laid, and will give you an idea about how soon the eggs will hatch and the babies leave the nest. Bird nests are vulnerable to a variety of dangers, including harsh weather and predators such as cats, raccoons, snakes, and even birds, as well as nest-site competitors. These dangers are greatly reduced when nest boxes are monitored because the birds' landlord (you) can take steps to protect the nest.

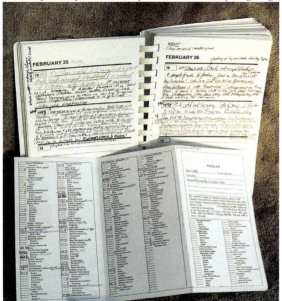

Top: A daily bird notes diary. Bottom: A checklist for sightings.

On my trips to check each of our 10 nest boxes, I keep a small notebook with me to record my observations. Each nest box has its own name and number in my notebook, along with the date of each visit and a note about what I've found. When nesting starts in a box I note the date, what materials are used to construct the nest, and the date that the first egg was laid. Once the clutch is complete and the female begins incubating the eggs, I can estimate the hatching date. This usually takes about 14 days. Another 14 to 21 days later, I know the young birds will be ready to leave the nest.

Peeking Inside

When checking a nest box, approach quietly. During the breeding season, you may scare the female off the nest temporarily when you open the box. Don't worry. If you keep your visit brief, she'll be back to the nest soon. I visit nest boxes

Checking the nest box.

in the late morning on sunny days, when the adult birds are likely to be away finding food. I open the box, quickly count the eggs or young, close the box and move away before pausing to record my notes. It's a myth that opening a nest box or checking the young will cause the adults to abandon the nest. In fact, over time many cavity-nesting birds that use nest boxes grow quite accustomed to regular visits.

One final note on nest monitoring. As fledging time approaches for the young birds—normally about two weeks after the eggs hatch—you should curtail your box visits to avoid causing a premature nest departure.

When Things Go Wrong

You open your nest box, and you find broken or missing eggs and the nest in disarray. What happened? The bad news is: A predator has raided your nest, and, in the natural order of things, the eggs or nestlings have been eaten. The good news: There are steps that you can take to avoid such an event in the future.

It's important to protect your nest boxes so predators cannot easily access them. For many landlords the best option is to mount the housing on galvanized metal poles with pole-mounted predator baffles installed beneath the boxes. An added advantage to pole-mounting (as opposed to mounting on a fencepost or tree) is that the housing can be moved to a new location fairly easily.

Follow the steps outlined on page 148 for nest box placement, mounting, and baffling. You may also wish to consult one of the publications listed in the Resources section for specific strategies for dealing with nest box predators and pests.

Creating Bird Habitat

To make your backyard or garden a haven for birds, all you need to do is think like a bird. Look around your yard. Where is the food, the water? Where are the places to hide from predators or to shelter in bad weather? Is nesting habitat available?

An ideal bird habitat can be created in a tiny, urban garden just as it can be created in a large, rural setting. Birds love varied habitats; so when you are planning your yard, landscape, or gardens, resist the urge to plant matching plants in straight lines. Instead, let your imagination go wild—literally. Give the edges of beds or gardens natural curves. Scatter trees, shrubs, and vines in clumps or islands around the area you are designing. On the edges of your property, try to create natural transitions from the grass of your yard to the tops of your trees with short- and medium-height plants that provide food and shelter for birds.

Edible Habitat

Birds have evolved over millions of years right alongside the native plants with which they share the planet. These same native plants can work for you in your bird-friendly habitat plan. Your local nursery, nature center, or native plant society should be able to recommend plant species that are native to your region. Native plants not only provide food in the form of fruits and nuts, but birds may also eat the plants' buds, leaves, nectar, and sap, as well as the insects that live on the plants. When choosing your native plants, select a wide variety of species, sizes, shapes, and seasonality. Planting only one or two plant species will minimize the number of birds your habitat will attract. Consult the Bird-Friendly Plants chart on page 162 for suggested plant families.

Water

Birds need water all year long for drinking and bathing. The best way to offer water to birds is in a shallow birdbath with about 2 inches of water in it. I've always had good luck attracting birds to water in my yard when the bath was on or near the ground and when the water had some motion to it.

The sight and sound of moving water are highly attractive to birds. You can add motion to any birdbath or water feature with a mister, dripper, or a recirculating pump. Misters and drippers attach to your garden hose and let out a small amount of water that disturbs the surface of the bath; these ripples are eye-catchingly attractive to birds. Recirculating pumps, which require electricity, recycle the water from the main bath through a pump and filter, and then back to the bath. If you live in an area where water freezes in winter, add a small, electric birdbath heater to keep the water open and available to birds.

If you already have a water garden or water feature, consider making part of it accessible to birds. This can be accomplished by placing a flat rock shelf on or near the water's surface, or by allowing recirculating water to trickle over an exposed flat rock. Our backyard water garden is ringed with goldfinches almost every day all year-round. They use a large, flat piece of slate that gets splashed by our small waterfall as a place to grab a quick drink.

A male scarlet tanager bathes in a water feature.

Water is a universal attractant for birds—species that might otherwise never visit your yard, feeders, or birdhouses will visit a clean and alluring birdbath or water feature.

Shelter

When they need to rest, hide from danger, or get out of the weather, birds seek deep cover in the form of thick vegetation, vine tangles, dense evergreens, or brushy areas. These bits of habitat may not be first on a landscaper's list of backyard beautifying accents, but to a bird they are vital havens. Even a brush pile in a corner of your property can offer enough shelter during a storm to help sparrows, cardinals, and other backyard birds survive.

Look at your bird habitat, and observe where the birds go just before a storm or at dusk. These are the places in which they shelter themselves. Consider adding more habitat, and your yard will be even more attractive to birds.

Places to Nest

The majority of North American birds do not use nest boxes. Most build their nests in places that are hidden from view—in trees, bushes, or in secluded spots on or near the ground. Birds—such as phoebes, barn swallows, and Carolina wrens—are bold enough to build nests on porch ledges, in garages, and in barns. House finches and mourning doves are known for building their nests in hanging flower baskets, but these sites won't satisfy most of our birds.

The places where birds choose to nest are similar to the places they choose to roost and shelter—in thick vegetation and deep cover out of view of passing predators. In providing a nesting habitat for birds, the key is diversity. As you read through the species profiles in this book, notice the habitat features that each species prefers. Then factor this information into your habitat plans.

Helping Other Nesting Birds

There are many things you can do to help non-cavity nesters—all those birds that build

Allow lawn edges to grow wild.

open-cup nests and will never use one of our nest boxes. The most important thing is to offer variety in your landscaping or backyard habitat. A backyard that is mostly lawn with a tree or two staked out in the middle will not be nearly as appealing as a yard featuring a variety of plant types, including grasses, perennial plants, shrubs, bushes, trees, and other natural elements. The more your landscape looks like nature, the more attractive it will be for birds.

Places for You

As you plan for your bird-friendly habitat, you'll also want to incorporate elements that you can use and enjoy, such as a water garden, benches, shady relaxation spots, and perhaps a location for your feeding station. Remember, the whole point of attracting birds to your property is so that you can enjoy them while they enjoy your offerings. Plan with your favorite viewing spots in mind, and you'll be rewarded with year-round free (and natural) entertainment.

Tips for Helping Nesting Birds

- Consider letting a portion of your yard grow up into a weedy patch for sparrows, finches, and towhees to enjoy.
- Offer a basket of nesting material, such as 2- to 3-inch pieces of natural fibers (yarn, pet or human hair, stiff dry grasses, and the like).
- Keep pets, especially cats, from roaming freely in your yard during nesting season.
- Try to limit or eliminate the use of lawn and garden chemicals in and around the parts of your property being used by nesting birds.
- Trim hedges, shrubs, and trees in early spring before nesting season, or in late fall, after nesting season. This way you'll avoid disturbing nesting birds, which are often so secretive that you are unaware of the nest until you stumble onto it.

How to Use This Book

Hello! *and welcome to the fun, friendly, and exciting word of bird watching. Birding is America's fastest-growing hobby and requires little more than some basic tools—binoculars and a field guide—and an interest in the fascinating world of birds. The primary purpose of this book is to start you down the path to a greater understanding and enjoyment of this engaging pastime. To that end, we've chosen the content carefully to provide you, the reader, with the ideal blend of information and detail on many of the most commonly encountered birds of your state. If we've done our job right, this will* not *be the last bird book you buy.*

At the heart of this book is a set of profiles of your state's 100 most commonly encountered birds. These are the birds that you're most likely to see and hear regularly. *But remember*—birds have wings and they tend to use them, so you'll certainly see and hear many other species as your bird-watching experience grows. For this reason we suggest that you augment this book with a good field guide to help you identify those unfamiliar species you encounter.

Each species profile features a beautiful photograph of the bird, typically an adult male in breeding plumage since this is the most identifiable version of many birds. Please note that adult females, winter-plumage adults, and young birds can look very different. We describe these plumage differences in the profile, but space constraints prevent us from showing images of all these variations. Once again, a good field guide (see the Resources section on page 166 for suggestions) will be useful in identifying any mystery birds you encounter.

We cover all the interesting and useful natural history information about each of the 100 birds—appearance, sounds, behavior, nesting, feeding, range, and migration—and we even tell you where to go and what to do in order to encounter a particular bird in the "Backyard and Beyond" section.

The profiles in the main body of the book are organized *taxonomically*—this means that related species are grouped by bird family using the same general order that ornithologists use to list and classify birds. See the facing page to find a convenient alphabetic listing. In the 100 species profiles, we've used a series of symbols to provide instant insight into the lives of these birds. Here is a key to what each of these icons represents:

 Will use a birdhouse for nesting or roosting.

 Can be attracted to bird feeders.

 Will visit birdbaths or water features for bathing and drinking.

 Has a song or call and can be identified by its vocalizations or sounds.

 A migrant species, seen primarily during spring or fall migration.

Also, turn to pages 7 through 32 to read more about the natural history and ecology of your state and its bird life. We focus on bird watching by season—the specific birds you're likely to encounter and how to attract them—by feeding and by offering the appropriate bird-friendly habitat. This section also describes the many migrants that pass through in spring and fall. As an extra bonus, we briefly describe the "Ten Must-See Birds" for your state. We also include a summary of the "Ten Best Bird-Watching Spots."

At the end of this book you will find a resources list for bird watching (feeding and planting charts, answers to frequently asked questions, birdhouse plans, bird books, field and audio guides, and more) to help you enjoy this hobby more.

Happy bird watching!

—*Bill Thompson, III*

100 Most Commonly Encountered Birds

Acadian Flycatcher 92
American Coot 68
American Crow 100
American Goldfinch 144
American Kestrel 65
American Redstart 123
American Robin 112
Bald Eagle 63
Barn Swallow 103
Barred Owl 78
Belted Kingfisher 84
Black Vulture 59
Blue-gray Gnatcatcher 110
Blue Jay 99
Blue-winged Teal 53
Brown-headed Cowbird 139
Brown Thrasher 117
Bufflehead 56
Canada Goose 50
Carolina Wren 107
Carolina Chickadee 105
Cedar Waxwing 119
Chimney Swift 82
Chipping Sparrow 134
Common Grackle 141
Common Nighthawk 81
Common Yellowthroat 125
Cooper's Hawk 60
Dark-eyed Junco 137
Double-crested Cormorant 47
Downy Woodpecker 87
Eastern Bluebird 111
Eastern Kingbird 95
Eastern Phoebe 93
Eastern Screech Owl 79
Eastern Towhee 132
Eastern Wood-Pewee 91
Eastern Meadowlark 138
European Starling 118
Field Sparrow 133
Golden-crowned Kinglet 109
Gray Catbird 115
Great Blue Heron 48
Great Horned Owl 77
Great Crested Flycatcher 94
Green Heron 49
Hairy Woodpecker 88
Herring Gull 73
Hooded Merganser 57
Hooded Warbler 126

House Finch 143
House Sparrow 145
House Wren 108
Indigo Bunting 131
Killdeer 69
Lesser Scaup 55
Lesser Yellowlegs 70
Loggerhead Shrike 96
Magnolia Warbler 121
Mallard 52
Mourning Dove 74
Northern Bobwhite 66
Northern Cardinal 130
Northern Flicker 89
Northern Mockingbird 116
Northern Rough-winged Swallow 102
Orchard Oriole 142
Osprey 64
Ovenbird 124
Pied-billed Grebe 46
Pileated Woodpecker 90
Purple Martin 101
Red-bellied Woodpecker 86
Red-eyed Vireo 97
Red-headed Woodpecker 85
Red-shouldered Hawk 61
Red-tailed Hawk 62
Red-winged Blackbird 140
Ring-billed Gull 72
Ring-necked Duck 54
Rock Pigeon 75
Ruby-throated Hummingbird 83
Scarlet Tanager 129
Song Sparrow 136
Spotted Sandpiper 71
Summer Tanager 128
Swainson's Thrush 114
Tennessee Warbler 120
Tufted Titmouse 104
Turkey Vulture 58
Whip-poor-will 80
White-breasted Nuthatch 106
White-eyed Vireo 98
White-throated Sparrow 135
Wild Turkey 67
Wood Duck 51
Wood Thrush 113
Yellow-billed Cuckoo 76
Yellow-breasted Chat 127
Yellow-rumped Warbler 122

Pied-billed Grebe
Podilymbus podiceps

Most North American grebes either breed far to the north or in the West, but the stocky little pied-billed grebe also breeds through much of the South. You can find this frequent diver in varied wetlands, including ponds, lakes, and marshes that have a thick cover of cattails or other vegetation. Pied-billed grebes most often are seen singly or in twos or threes. They don't often vocalize, except during breeding season when they call out a series of penetrating, barking notes.

All About
In general, pied-billed grebes occur in sheltered, lush wetlands. The other grebes that show up during winter migrations in the South are normally seen in bays or on large rivers or other open water. This bird is smallish but has a big head, stocky neck, and a thick bill that differs from the more pointed bills of horned and eared grebes. During breeding season, the bill (which is pale in winter) becomes distinctively adorned with a thick, black band that wraps around an otherwise horn-colored bill. Breeding pied-billed grebes also have black throats, but at other times their soft-brown necks and bodies contrast with whitish throats and puffy whitish undertails. The Southeast's other grebes have much sharper contrasting patterns on their heads and necks, and they are not as compact.

Habitat & Range
Pied-billed grebes nest in well-vegetated lakes, ponds, and pockets of marsh. You may find them in brackish water in winter, but they prefer freshwater habitats. The numbers of pied-billed grebes swell in the South during winter and migration, when many northern nesters abandon their frigid habitats for warmer, more productive wintering areas.

Feeding
Pied-billed grebes are frequently seen diving for food or diving to evade predators or observers. Their wide-lobed feet push them beneath the water's surface in search of small fish, amphibians, and a wide variety of aquatic invertebrates, including crayfish and insects. They also eat some plant matter.

Nesting
Mates call to each other as part of their courtship. Together, they build a nest that is basically a mound of matted vegetation. This mound is fastened to nearby plants and may float or rise from the shallows. The female lays four to six eggs, with the pair sharing the three-week incubation period. Both parents feed the young, which can fly by two months of age.

Backyard & Beyond
Scan marsh edges and ponds to find pied-billed grebes; they are rarely spotted in flight. They have a tendency to appear as if by magic and to disappear just as fast, often leaving a ring of ripples on the water's surface as the only evidence of their presence.

Double-crested Cormorant
Phalacrocorax auritus

Often, the somewhat snakelike black neck and head is all that betrays the presence of a swimming double-crested cormorant. In general, this water bird is most numerous in the Southeast during late fall, winter, and early spring. Double-crested cormorants declined earlier in the twentieth century due to disturbance and hunting at nesting grounds, followed by DDT and other pesticide contamination. Protection, wetland conservation, and the DDT ban have helped these birds recover.

All About
With practice, birders can easily distinguish a distant, flying double-crested cormorant from a pelican, goose, heron, or other large bird by its all-dark form, thick and somewhat wavy neck, longish tail, and slow wingbeats. The cormorant's bright orange throat, bill, and lores stand out on its otherwise black body. Even its heavy webbed feet are blackish. Immatures are dull brown with whitish necks and chests. In this species, it's usually not visible. On the Gulf Coast, from Texas to western Louisiana, watch for the smaller, thinner, longer-tailed neotropic cormorant. During spring, this smaller species has an angled, white fringe behind its smaller, orange throat.

Habitat & Range
Most double-crested cormorant populations are migratory, and these birds turn up at rivers, marshes, swamps, large lakes, bays, and along the coast. Because they travel widely during the day, don't be surprised to see cormorants flying over inland habitats in loose formation. Double-crested cormorants breed in western Alaska, central Canada, and down both coasts of the United States; they winter along the coast and well inland throughout the Southeast.

Feeding
Double-crested cormorants are very adaptable, seeking a wide variety of fish, and also crustaceans, amphibians, and other aquatic animals. Their webbed feet propel them under water after their aquatic prey, and much of their feeding is done not far beneath the surface.

Nesting
Double-crested cormorants nest in colonies in trees, on cliffs, and on islands. Females build much of the platform nest, while males provide the many sticks and other materials. Females usually lay three or four eggs, which both parents incubate for about a month. Young leave the nest 21 to 30 days after hatching, but are not fully on their own until after two months.

Backyard & Beyond
Watch for the "periscope" heads of partially submerged cormorants and try not to confuse them with those of the more dagger-billed anhinga or loons, which have slimmer, straighter bills and at least some light coloration on the head. After long swims, cormorants often sun themselves on dead trees and shoreline, holding out their wings to dry.

Great Blue Heron
Ardea herodias

North America's largest and most widespread heron is found, at one time or another, virtually wherever water and small aquatic creatures are found. Although the best known of our dozen heron species, the great blue heron is not always called by its correct name. Many non-birders call it a crane or a stork, but the heron can be instantly distinguished from these other large, long-legged birds by its folded-back neck in flight and the S-shaped curvature of its neck at rest.

All About
Adult great blue herons have a black stripe running from the eye to the back of the neck; immature birds have a blackish cap. Southern Florida is home to the great white heron, an all-white race of the great blue that can be distinguished from egrets by its large size and long, thick, orange bill and orange legs. The great blue heron's croaking *ccrraaaaaaaank* call is often heard as it takes flight.

Habitat & Range
Found across the United States, southern Canada, and up the Pacific coast to Alaska, the great blue heron ventures where few other herons dare. Many eastern birds migrate to the South or to the tropics—as far south as northwestern South America—in winter. Outside of the Appalachians, great blue herons occur throughout the South all year.

Feeding
Great blue herons seek a variety of prey in a range of wet habitats. Fish are a mainstay, but amphibians, reptiles, birds, small mammals, and invertebrates feature on the menu, as well. Feeding strategy varies as well. They may hunt alongside each other, wading slowly up to their bellies, or may stand alone for long periods, waiting to thrust their bills at unsuspecting prey. Great blue herons sometimes stalk rodents in dry fields or haunt beaches and docks in search of live or discarded sea life.

Nesting
Great blue herons nest in large colonies, often in tall trees away from human disturbance. They will nest in the company of other water birds, often in areas with water beneath nesting trees, probably to thwart predators. Each year, great blue heron pairs form bonds through a series of posing displays, including stretching, preening, crest raising, circling in flight, and twig shaking. Males provide sticks, which females place in the large platform nest. Females usually lay three to five eggs, which incubate for almost a month. Both parents feed the young, which take flight 2 to 2½ months after hatching.

Backyard & Beyond
Despite their large size, great blue herons sometimes turn up at small backyard ponds seeking fish and frogs. They are far more frequent in marshes, swamps, rivers, lakes, and reservoirs.

Green Heron

Butorides virescens

The green heron isn't exactly green, but it's the most greenish of the North American herons. Perhaps a better name would have been "squat heron" or "little heron" or "common pond heron." The bird was known until recently as the "green-backed heron," and this is an apt moniker since the adults have blackish green backs.

All About

The least bittern is our smallest heron, but the green heron is the smallest *easily seen* heron. While a green heron will sometimes stretch its neck out to peer at approaching birders or predators, its head is usually held close to the body, giving the bird a squat look. Identification of adults is straightforward: The back and crown are blackish with a green tinge, the neck and face are dark chestnut, and the belly is gray. Yellow legs flush to bright orange during breeding season. Young birds are brown streaked, and care should be taken not to mistake them for bitterns. Subadults are a mixture of brown and streaky and rusty necked. The piercing *KEEE-OWK* call will draw attention to flushed birds that might otherwise be missed.

Habitat & Range

In spring and summer, look for green herons along wooded streams and ponds, around lakes, at drainage ditches, and in marshes, often near woody cover. In winter, green herons move south from northern nesting areas, spending the winter in Florida and the Gulf States and southward into the tropics. Green herons also nest throughout the West Indies and in Central America south to Panama.

Feeding

Like stock-still balls of rust and greenish feathers, green herons wait patiently by the water's edge for fish, frogs, crayfish, various insects, and other small prey. They also slowly walk through the water and wait for prey to show. They have even been known to drop small baits, such as fish food pellets, bits of bread (from people feeding park ducks), or flower petals into the water to attract curious fish and other potential prey.

Nesting

Green herons nest in pairs or small clusters, but avoid large colonies. They nest in trees or shrubs that may either be near or fairly far from water and feeding areas. Three to seven eggs are laid in a stick platform nest primarily built by the female. Both parents incubate the eggs for about three weeks; both then feed their young, which can fly by three weeks of age.

Backyard & Beyond

Green herons may visit backyard ponds to investigate the goldfish or frogs. They also frequently fly over neighborhoods en route to golf course ponds, streams, lakes, or drainage ditches. Green herons are frequently overlooked until startled into flight.

Canada Goose
Branta canadensis

The Canada goose enjoys an almost iconic status with human observers (though large, nonmigratory flocks can wear out their welcome). Their huge, V-shaped flights mark the passing of seasons, their honking is reminiscent of wilderness itself, and their strong family bonds (they mate for life) endear them to us. Many non-bird watchers mistakenly call this bird the Canadian goose.

All About
The Canada goose's black neck and white cheek strap are unmistakable. In flight, Canadas beat their wings deeply and slowly and show a black-and-white tail. Their familiar call is a deep, two-syllable *ha-ronk* and is given by mated pairs as well as flocking birds. Canadas also give a variety of softer cackling calls to each other, especially when they are on the ground. More than a dozen different subspecies exist in North America, and their sizes vary from 25 to 45 inches in length.

Habitat & Range
The Canada goose is a habitat generalist when it comes to water, settling in lakes, bays, rivers, and city parks and ponds. The species has enjoyed unprecedented success in living with or near humans, and today it nests all across the upper two-thirds of North America. Some re-established populations of Canada goose are year-round, nonmigratory residents, though many birds nesting in northern North America migrate to the southern United States in winter. Spring migration begins early, and many females are incubating by mid-March.

Feeding
Aquatic plants, grasses, grains, and seeds are the Canada's primary foods. To reach submerged food, it will tip its tail in the air and extend its neck below the water's surface. Flocks leave roosting areas in the morning to forage in nearby fields, meadows, and marshes. Urban populations often live on handouts of cracked corn near city park lakes and golf course ponds.

Nesting
Located on a high spot near water, the nest is a small mound made of surrounding sticks and vegetation and lined with down plucked from the female. Half a dozen or more eggs are laid and incubated by the female for nearly a month while the male stands guard and brings her food. Within two days of hatching, young goslings are herded by their parents to the nearest water. Families stay together until the following breeding season, though young birds become self-sufficient in about two months.

Backyard & Beyond
Some housing developments and golf courses find them (and their droppings) a nuisance. To best see Canadas, visit a wildlife refuge where large flocks congregate during winter and during spring and fall migration. Watching hundreds of loudly honking Canadas is quite a spectacle.

Wood Duck
Aix sponsa

The up-slurred WHEEEP of the wood duck is a familiar sound to anyone frequenting areas where woodland and fresh water mix. Patience and a bit of stealth will reward the birder seeking a good look at these cagey, dazzling ducks. Across much of the South, wood ducks abound, finding ample habitat and welcoming nest boxes.

All About
The male wood duck takes its colorful plumage to an extreme. In breeding plumage, it has a green crown and black face offset by white slashes reaching up from its white throat. The bill looks painted, a bright red-orange with black and white touches. Breast and undertail are chestnut, while the sides are adorned with vertical white and blackish slashes followed by a panel of butterscotch yellow. The male's back is metallic green. These colors fade during summer, as the birds molt into *eclipse*, or nonbreeding, plumage, but the bright bill and eye and face pattern remain. Both male and female have backward-facing crests that give them a helmeted look. The female wood duck is easy to identify, not only because of her head shape, but also because of her white, tear-shaped eye rings. Otherwise, females are grayish brown and generously flecked with whitish spots on their sides.

Habitat & Range
The perfect setting for wood ducks combines tranquil fresh water with plenty of trees—bottomland swamps, riverside forests, and tree-lined ponds and lakes. Wood ducks are permanent residents in much of the South, except in the Appalachians, where populations withdraw during the cold months. Northern populations, from southern Canada through the Northeast, retreat to the South in winter.

Feeding
Wood ducks eat a variety of seeds and some fruits from aquatic and forest plants, including acorns. Sometimes, they eat grain. Insects and other small animals supplement their diet; though, for recently fledged birds, these are a mainstay.

Nesting
Wood ducks are cavity nesters, setting up house in holes high in mature or dead trees. They also nest down low in nest boxes. The nest is simply an accumulation of down placed on the cavity floor, where the female incubates her 8 to 15 pale eggs for between $3^{1}/_{2}$ and 5 weeks. Chicks usually tumble out of their nest the day after hatching. Females accompany them for about six weeks, and they can fly at about two months of age.

Backyard & Beyond
If you live near fresh water, you may see wood ducks fly over your property. If your property includes a pond or wetland, you may attract wood ducks with a nesting box, which ideally would be set in the water on a post fitted with a collar-like, predator baffle.

Mallard
Anas platyrhynchos

- Spring/Summer
- Year-Round
- Winter

Of all the North American duck species, there's one that nearly everyone knows—the mallard. Abundant all across the continent, the mallard is known to interbreed commonly with black ducks and other wild duck species, as well as with domesticated ducks. Large numbers of semitame mallards exist on city park ponds, golf courses, and reservoirs, getting by on handouts from humans.

All About
The male mallard's green head and yellow bill are easily recognizable, but female mallards—with their overall dark brown coloration—can be confused with black ducks, mottled ducks, and other female ducks. Look for her orange and black bill and listen for the loud, raucous *quack, quack-quack, quack-quack* call, given only by female mallards. Mallards are fairly large ducks with a 23-inch body length.

Habitat & Range
Like other dabbling ducks, mallards prefer shallow bodies of fresh water at all times of year, including marshes, flooded woodlots, ponds, and swamps. They can be found year-round across most of the United States, but a large number of mallards breed in the Far North and spend the winter in the Southeast.

Feeding
Mallards feed by scooping up seeds and plant material from the water's surface, by tipping up—tails in the air—to reach submerged plants, and by grazing for waste grain in agricultural fields. They eat everything from seeds and vegetation to insects, small fish, crawfish, and frogs.

Nesting
Mallards pair up well before the spring breeding season. The hen mallard chooses the nest site, usually in or near thick vegetation on the ground. She then builds a small bowl out of nearby plant material and lines it with her own down. Between 7 and 12 eggs are laid and incubated by the hen for a month. Like other ducks, mallard ducklings leave the nest within hours after hatching and follow their mother to the nearest water. Though ducklings feed themselves right away, it's nearly two months before they are able to fly. Predators take a heavy toll on nests and young, especially in parks where natural predators are augmented by domestic pets.

Backyard & Beyond
If you want to feed the mallards in your local park, don't bother with stale bread, which holds little nutritional value for birds. Instead, offer some cracked corn. This inexpensive food is available at most stores selling birdseed and is relished by mallards. When you've got a hungry flock of panhandling mallards nearby, take time to look at the birds' fine plumage. Look, too, for wild ducks of other species that may be "hanging out" with the local flock of tame mallards, as well as for the many interesting hybrids that result from the mallard's promiscuous nature.

Blue-winged Teal
Anas discors

- Spring/Summer
- Year-Round
- Winter

A fast-flying, small (14 inches long) duck, the blue-winged teal shows the blue shoulder patch for which it is named only when the wings are extended. Blue-wingeds fly in tight flocks and seem to be wary as they pass repeatedly over a body of water before landing. However, they are not as skittish as other ducks when approached by humans, perhaps because they know they can explode off the water and straight into the air in seconds.

All About
Males have a blue-gray head and a distinctive white face crescent and hip patch, making them easy to identify even from a distance. Females are a warm, gray-brown overall with a slight echo of the males' white face crescent. Identifying them is made somewhat easier by the fact that blue-winged teal pairs form in early winter and stay together through spring migration.

Habitat & Range
Blue-winged teal breed throughout the northeastern, central, and western United States, but bird watchers in the southeastern states are most likely to see them during spring and fall migration and in winter. Most blue-winged teal spend the winter south of the United States, as far as South America. They are considered fair-weather ducks by many bird watchers because they stay far to the south until spring is in full force. Perhaps it is their later spring arrival and their earlier fall departure that has earned them the nicknames "summer teal" and "August teal." Their preferred habitats—at all seasons—are shallow, freshwater marshes and ponds.

Feeding
Teal feed on seeds and plant matter gleaned from the water's surface or by swimming with their heads submerged to find snails, aquatic insects, and crustaceans. Unlike other dabbling ducks, blue-wingeds do not "tip up" to feed on submerged vegetation.

Nesting
Like many other ducks, blue-winged teal nest on the ground in a spot concealed by thick vegetation. The female builds a shallow, basket-shaped nest out of dried grasses lined with her down. A clutch of nine or more eggs is laid and incubated by the hen for slightly more than three weeks. Teal ducklings leave the nest almost immediately and are able to feed themselves right away, but it will be six weeks before they are fully flighted.

Backyard & Beyond
The blue-winged's preference for shallow water means that it can show up almost anywhere—from farm or city ponds to coastal marshes, mudflats, and sewage settling pools. If you see a flock of small ducks flying pell-mell, twisting and turning as one, chances are they are blue-winged teal. You can clinch the identification by looking for the male teal's white face crescent, or for the flash of blue, white, and green in the wings.

Ring-necked Duck
Aythya collaris

The ring-necked duck is a characteristic bird of the South—not because it nests there, but because of its widespread occurrence there in winter. Flocks of ringnecks frequent marshes, swamps, and sheltered and wooded corners of lakes. These birds are often found in areas where the only other regularly sighted ducks are wood ducks and mallards (in interior areas). Ringnecks are also found on open water and areas with a wider diversity of ducks.

All About
Closely related and superficially similar to the greater and lesser scaup, this diving bird has a few embellishments that easily set it apart from the scaup. Like the scaup, the male ringneck is blackish—in most light—on head, chest, and back. However, even at a distance, the adult male ring-necked duck has a vertical white comma that edges its gray sides. Its bill is three-toned: The tip is black, followed by a white band, then much gray, then a white border where bill meets head. Like the scaup, the female ringneck is more somber in coloration and markings, but she has a noticeably dark crown compared with the rest of the head. She sports a white eye ring, and usually has a clearly three-toned bill. As with the red-bellied woodpecker, the ring-necked duck's name was poorly chosen by "dead-bird-in-the-hand" early ornithologists: Only in rare circumstances will you see its namesake rusty collar.

Habitat & Range
Most ring-necked ducks winter in the United States, below the northern tier of states, and south into central Mexico. Others winter in the West Indies, and a few are found as far south as Panama. Unlike scaup, ring-necked ducks frequent small or smallish bodies of water, and they rarely enter salt water. Summer finds them nesting in Canada, Alaska, and a good number of northern U.S. states in freshwater wetlands, usually surrounded by forest.

Feeding
Ring-necked ducks dive for their supper, snipping roots and stems of plants, eating seeds, insects, and mollusks. Like other waterfowl, their recently hatched young eat mostly insects.

Nesting
The female ring-necked duck usually lays between 8 and 10 eggs in a nest of grasses or other plants clipped from nearby. She incubates the eggs for almost a month. After they hatch, she accompanies her chicks until they can fly, shortly before two months of age.

Backyard & Beyond
Early in the morning or in well-protected areas, you may catch close-up looks at ring-necked ducks on small ponds or lakes. Even at a distance, though, the gray, white, and black markings on the male's sides help identify these birds as they dive underwater and pop back up to the surface.

Lesser Scaup
Aythya affinis

We have two scaup species in North America—greater and lesser scaup—both are medium-sized, black-and-white ducks, and they can be difficult to tell apart. The lesser scaup is by far the more commonly encountered of the two, especially on inland bodies of water. Both species are named for their characteristic skawwp! call, but the similarities don't end there. Both scaup species are excellent swimmers and divers, both have drab brownish mates, and both show lots of white in the wing in flight.

All About
Older field guides suggest that greater and lesser scaup can be identified based upon head color, but this is very unreliable in poor light. Separating scaup species in the field is most accurately done based on head shape—lessers have a thinner head with more of a peak on top, while greaters have a rounder head and larger bill. Female scaup are brownish gray overall with a white ring around the base of the bill. Hens can be identified based on the males with which they associate because the two scaup species are rarely seen in mixed flocks. All scaup show a blue-gray bill with a black tip—an important clue to separate the scaup from the superficially similar ring-necked duck, which has a white ring on its bill.

Habitat & Range
Lesser scaup are one of most common wintering ducks on inland bodies of water, with flocks sometimes numbering in the thousands. They are very late migrants in both spring and fall migration, arriving on the breeding grounds as late as mid-May and not leaving until just before the winter freeze-up.

Feeding
Specialists in diving for their food, lesser scaup eat snails, mussels, small clams, fish, and aquatic insects. They also rely on plant matter and seeds for food, especially in fall and winter.

Nesting
Preferring to nest in thick vegetation on dry ground or islands near water, the female lesser scaup does nearly all of the hard work. The nest is a scrape lined with dry grass and lots of the hen's down into which 8 to 10 eggs are laid. Hen scaup incubate their eggs for longer than three weeks before hatching. Hatchlings leave the nest within a day of emerging and are able to feed themselves immediately. Within two weeks they are diving for food, and two months later they are fully flighted.

Backyard & Beyond
Lesser scaup can be found on almost any open (ice-free) body of water in the continental United States in winter, but they are especially abundant along the Gulf and southern Atlantic coasts. Look for flocks of black-and-white ducks actively diving and bobbing to the surface of a pond, lake, or reservoir.

Bufflehead
Bucephala albeola

One of North America's most common diving ducks, the striking bufflehead spends migration and winter on brackish and saltwater bays, reservoirs, rivers, and lakes. This little duck gets its name from its swollen head shape, which—apparently to some observers—resembles that of a buffalo.

All About
The bufflehead is small, but strikingly marked. Even a distant bird seen in the binoculars can often be identified. Both male and female have a large, rounded head, small bill, and striking white markings on the heads. In most light, the male appears to have a black forehead, crown, and lower neck and back; the rest—including all of the cheek and back of neck and underparts—gleams with white. The female is darker, smudged with gray below and dark brown above, but her head is punctuated with a large, horizontal oval of white on each cheek. Considered by many to be our smallest duck, the bufflehead is close in length to the green-winged teal and ruddy duck. All are less than 16 inches long, with the bufflehead measuring in at about 13 1/2 inches. Buffleheads are not as social as some other diving ducks; they are usually seen in small groups.

Habitat & Range
Buffleheads nest in trees close to or within wetlands. Pairs begin to form in late winter, and mates are paired off by the time they reach their breeding grounds in April. Most of them breed in Canada and Alaska, but there are some populations nesting in northwestern states. During migration and winter, buffleheads are seen on waters virtually throughout the United States and south to central Mexico.

Feeding
Buffleheads usually dive in search of food, snatching up crustaceans, mollusks, small fish, and other aquatic fauna. They also eat some aquatic plant seeds. Their summer diet is rich in insects and insect larvae.

Nesting
Cavity nesters, and small ones at that, buffleheads frequently move into old flicker nest holes to lay their eggs and raise their young. They sometimes use nest boxes. The female lays up to a dozen pale eggs on a bed of down placed at the cavity bottom, and she incubates them for about a month. Hatchlings tumble out of the nest shortly after hatching and are followed by their mother. It takes almost two months until the young birds can fly.

Backyard & Beyond
Buffleheads are particularly common in coastal waters during the winter months. Like other diving ducks, these birds cannot take off directly from a sitting position in the water. Rather, they need to skitter a bit across the water's surface before taking flight.

Hooded Merganser
Lophodytes cucullatus

The hooded merganser is a hidden treasure of wooded wetlands, lakes, and bays, and is often spotted in small flocks skirting the back edge of fresh or brackish bodies of water. Of the three mergansers—ducks with narrow, serrated bills—the hooded is the smallest and has the shortest bill. Hooded mergansers occur in many areas also frequented by wood ducks.

All About
Both male and female hooded mergansers can be easily identified. The male is in gaudy plumage much of the year. Its head is an odd shape, either extremely round like a raised mushroom when its crest is raised, or bump-headed when its crest is relaxed. This shape influences the appearance of the dazzling white spot behind the bird's yellow eye. With raised crest, the white is like a fat inverted comma; with crest relaxed, it is like a horizontal blob. The male's bright coppery-orange sides contrast with a white chest pierced by two vertical black bars that bleed into the black back and head. The female lacks such bold coloration. A rich brown-rust on her head, she is an otherwise brown-gray. A dark bird, she lacks the white throat, bright orange bill, and gray to brown contrasts seen in female red-breasted and common mergansers.

Habitat & Range
Ponds, rivers, creeks, bays, and swamps are among the habitats used by this widespread species. Hooded mergansers breed from Canada to as far south as northern Florida and southern Louisiana. The situation changes during migration and winter, when many eastern hooded mergansers winter in the Southeast.

Feeding
While the other two mergansers are primarily fish-eaters, the hooded merganser has a more varied diet that not only includes small fish but also insects, crayfish, and other aquatic creatures. Like other mergansers, hoodeds dive for their food, apparently finding prey by sight.

Nesting
The female hooded merganser creates a shallow bowl at the bottom of a tree cavity or nest box, using whatever materials she finds there. She plucks down feathers from her undersides to line the nest. Up to a dozen white eggs are laid, which she incubates for up to 40 days. The young leave the nest at a day old and are attended by the female. Hooded mergansers often lay their eggs in the nests of other hooded mergansers and wood ducks, leaving their young to be raised by another mother.

Backyard & Beyond
The males of both hooded mergansers and wood ducks are equally gaudy in plumage, and both have odd head shapes. Look for "hoodies" in small flocks of males and females on freshwater lakes and ponds; they will often be hugging a wooded shoreline.

Turkey Vulture
Cathartes aura

Catharsis—a cleansing or purification—is the root of the turkey vulture's Latin name. It refers to this bird's invaluable service in ridding the landscape of animal carcasses—a necessity in the age of superhighways. The highway system, with its continual supply of shoulder fare, may have contributed to the turkey vulture's northward breeding range expansion.

All About
The tilting flight, with wings held in a shallow "V", immediately distinguishes a turkey vulture from most other large, dark birds in flight. At close range, the underwings appear two-toned, with the flight feathers having a reflective, pewter sheen. The small, naked head is red; the bill bone-white. On the ground, a turkey vulture appears to be all wing—a long blackish trapezoid, topped by a tiny red head. Hoarse hisses are their only sounds. Nestlings produce a continuous breathy roar when cornered in the nest.

Habitat & Range
Ranging widely as they search for food, turkey vultures prefer farmland pasture where carcasses might be found, and with nearby forests where they find nesting and roosting spots. Communal roosters, they may be seen warming themselves with wings spread open to the sun. Turkey vultures are migratory in the northern parts of their range, mingling with resident birds in the southern United States, some traveling as far south as Amazonia before returning in early spring.

Feeding
Powerful olfactory senses help the turkey vulture locate carcasses, and they may circle in groups, narrowing down the scent source, before spotting it. This allows them to find carrion in deep woods. One circling vulture brings sharp-eyed companions from miles around, and they share their plunder, rising with heavy flaps from roadsides when disturbed. Its bare head allows the vulture to reach into larger carcasses without fouling its feathers.

Nesting
Turkey vultures hide their nests on rock ledges, in hollow logs, under boulders, or in unused animal burrows. The female lays two eggs, which she and her mate incubate for around 28 days. The young are in the nest cavity and its vicinity for about 12 weeks, making first flights as early as 60 days of age. After a few weeks of exercising and being fed in the nest vicinity, they appear to be independent upon their first extended flight.

Backyard & Beyond
Turkey vultures have learned to exploit factory farms, especially chicken farms, for the inevitable carcasses they produce. They are closely attuned to spring calving and lambing times. Rather than being seen as harbingers of death, turkey vultures might be considered for their great beauty in flight and as a vital cleanup crew.

Black Vulture

Coragyps atratus

With its distinctive gray "light bulb head" and shorter, broader wings, the black vulture can easily be distinguished from the longer winged, more graceful turkey vulture. It makes smaller circles and flaps more, as if struggling to stay aloft. A long period of juvenile dependence and complex social structure also helps set it apart from the more aloof turkey vulture.

All About

Smaller and chunkier than the turkey vulture, the black vulture is also darker—a true soot-black. In flight, its extremely short tail and broad wings give it a distinctive headless and tailless silhouette. Labored, quick flapping is interspersed with gliding as the black vulture makes tight circles in the sky. A whitish spot at the base of the primary wing feathers is diagnostic. The voice is basic, with hisses, grunts, and low barks as a repertoire.

Habitat & Range

Black vultures are more common in flat, low-lying areas, especially agricultural areas with adjacent dense woodlands. They roost communally in isolated stands of trees, on utility towers, and on similar sites, where they are often persecuted by people who do not recognize their value as scavengers. Black vultures have expanded their range northward in recent years. They are migratory in the northern part of their range, resident in the southern.

Feeding

Lacking a well-developed sense of smell, this small cousin of the turkey vulture relies on its larger relative to find food. Black vultures fly higher than turkey vultures, presumably in an effort to keep them in view and hone in on their finds. Once there, black vultures will overpower turkey vultures and feed first. They primarily eat carrion, but they can kill small animals, including young pigs, calves, and lambs.

Nesting

Scattered, abandoned buildings provide nest sites for many black vultures, while others use caves, thickets, or hollow logs. The female lays two eggs, which she and her mate incubate for around 38 days. The young are in the nest cavity and its vicinity for about 90 days, when they are capable of following their parents. An extremely long juvenile dependency period follows. Young birds may be fed into the following spring, when it is time for the parents to nest once more. This long dependency period may contribute to the black vulture's complex social structure.

Backyard & Beyond

Black vultures use their communal roosts as an information-gathering tool. Birds that return from a successful day of feeding are followed the next morning by hungry birds. Black vultures associate primarily with "family," birds to whom they are related, and they frequently squabble with and oust unrelated individuals.

Cooper's Hawk
Accipiter cooperii

Cooper's hawks often perch in inconspicuous places, shooting through the branches or dropping from trees to nab unsuspecting prey. A flurry of fearful birds and a gray flash may mark the arrival of a Cooper's hawk to your backyard. Cooper's hawks are medium-sized hawks and formidable hunters that are usually seen singly except during migration, when they pass by in varying numbers at hawk-watching spots.

All About
Care must be taken to differentiate the Cooper's hawk from the similar sharp-shinned hawk. Adults of both species have similar markings, as do their brown-backed immatures and that of the northern goshawk (larger birds rarely seen south of Virginia, Indiana, and Missouri). Size is often not a trustworthy identification tool in the field—proportions and tail edges are more telling. Compared with the sharp-shinned hawk, the Cooper's has a proportionately larger head and neck and a rounded (not notched) or square-tipped tail (as does the sharp-shinned). Perched, adult Cooper's hawks often show a contrast between a blackish crown and gray nape and back. In flight, its head protrudes well beyond its often straight-held wings, and its tail usually looks rounded. Sharp-shinned hawks look like a capital "T" in flight, their shorter heads almost even with the leading edge of their wings.

Habitat & Range
In many areas, Cooper's hawks are uncommon nesters. Far-northern birds generally winter to the south. You can look for Cooper's hawks in any type of forest, along forest edges, and in woods near watercourses. But don't be surprised if you find one elsewhere, particularly in winter and fall. They seem to be adapting to suburban life, nesting near backyards or in city parks. During spring and fall, migrating Cooper's hawks gravitate toward ridges and coasts.

Feeding
These midsized hawks generally feed on midsized birds, including robins, flickers, and pigeons, but they also eat small mammals, including chipmunks and squirrels. Insects and reptiles sometimes feature on the menu.

Nesting
Cooper's hawks place their bulky stick nests high on horizontal branches in large trees, sometimes building them atop another large bird or squirrel nest. The female lays three to five eggs and incubates them for about five weeks. The male brings food, but the female feeds it to the young, which usually take flight about four or five weeks after hatching.

Backyard & Beyond
Cooper's hawks are attracted to what bird feeders attract—keeping intact natural predator and prey interactions, even in the suburbs. They will not scare birds from your feeders for long and, when successful, Cooper's hawks are usually weeding out the less-fit birds.

Red-shouldered Hawk
Buteo lineatus

The South is the heartland for this colorful raptor, which flourishes in swamps and along wooded riversides. Its strident KEEah, KEEah, KEEah call directs birders to soaring birds overhead or those coursing through the woods. Development strikes a blow to red-shouldered hawks, birds that normally shun the open habitats that are favored by the slightly larger red-tailed hawk.

All About
Robin-orange shoulder patches and breast barring are hallmarks of the adult red-shouldered hawk. Although chunky, the red-shouldered is slimmer than the red-tailed hawk, and its tail is comparatively longer and barred in black and white. In flight, especially while soaring or gliding, light or clear crescents can be seen at the base of the bird's flight feathers, areas called *windows* by birders. These windows are an important field mark to differentiate red-shouldered hawks from similar red-tailed and broad-winged hawks. The broad-winged hawk is also orange below, but its tail exhibits mainly one large, wide white band, while several bands are visible on the red-shouldered's tail. The red-shouldered hawk's underwings are darkish, contrasting with its light windows, while the broad-winged hawk's is almost all whitish underneath, bordered in blackish. Immature red-shouldered hawks are brown and white, with heavy teardrop streaks below and brown and whitish barred tails. Southern Florida adults are pale, with frosty heads and backs.

Habitat & Range
Red-shouldered hawks hunt in forests found near water. They nest throughout the eastern U.S. Many reside year-round, though some northern birds migrate south in winter. Red-shouldered hawks occupy the same habitats as barred owls—one hunting by day, the other by night.

Feeding
During warm months or in warm areas, red-shouldered hawks seek a variety of small animals, including various insects, frogs, snakes, and lizards. In colder weather, rodents and small birds play a larger role in their diet.

Nesting
The nest will most likely be located high in a mature tree in deciduous woods that do not have much undergrowth. The large stick nest is lined with softer materials, such as bark and grassy or leafy stems. The female lays two to four eggs, which she incubates for about a month. The male brings food. Young leave the nest after about six weeks, but parents feed them for two more months before they gain full independence.

Backyard & Beyond
Some suburbs sit within hearing or soaring range of red-shouldered hawks breeding in nearby woods; listen for their telltale scream. Migrating immatures often turn up in backyards, perching in large trees in wooded districts. Riverside walks will often yield sightings, as will trips to swamps.

Red-tailed Hawk
Buteo jamaicensis

This bird is the large raptor people most often see doing "lazy circles in the sky." The red-tailed hawk inhabits open terrain across the continent and south to Central America. It thrives in habitats opened up by human activities, such as farming or forest clearing. They are also the large raptor most commonly seen perched along roadways and power lines.

All About
Red-tailed hawks occur across the continent in quite a variety of plumage colorations. In the East, however, count on a few easy field marks to help identify adult birds: the reddish-orange tail, a dark-streaked belly band, and a white chest. This hat trick of field marks can easily be seen in many soaring redtails, as well as in perched birds. Additionally, two chocolate-colored bars adorn the leading edge of the underwing. Overall, soaring red-tailed hawks are bulkier and more formidable in general appearance than slimmer red-shouldered hawks and broad-winged hawks, which have shorter tails. Red-tailed hawks younger than two years old lack the telltale reddish tail, but they still exhibit the belly band and white chest.

Habitat & Range
Look for red-tailed hawks along highway edges, over farm fields and forest clearings, and in almost any other open habitat with at least some telephone poles or trees on which they can perch and scan for prey. From tundra to tropical forests, the red-tailed hawk is a formidable predator. They breed as far south as Panama and on various Caribbean islands, thus the species name *jamaicensis*. For nesting, they usually avoid areas with a lot of human activity, even though they nest in New York City's Central Park and pass through suburbs during migration.

Feeding
Many farmers appreciate seeing red-tailed hawks flap over their acreage, as they eat many voles, mice, rats, rabbits, squirrels, and other small mammals. Other prey can include a variety of birds and reptiles. Red-tailed hawks may glide down from a perch to grab prey, dive down, or hover and then drop on prey.

Nesting
Nests are usually found in tall trees, although these birds will nest on cliffs and sometimes even buildings. Both mates build the large stick nest, which they line with softer materials. The female usually lays two or three eggs, which both parents incubate for about a month. The male hunts for food, passing it to his mate, who feeds their young. Nestlings fly after about 10 weeks.

Backyard & Beyond
You may hear the red-tailed hawk's blood-curdling cry around its nesting grounds. Because they range widely and some populations migrate short or long distances, you may see red-tailed hawks soaring or gliding over your home.

Bald Eagle
Haliaeetus leucocephalus

The bald eagle barely edged out the wild turkey when our founding fathers were voting on a national symbol. Skilled fishing bird, scavenger, and pirate, the bald eagle is an opportunistic raptor that's been given a second chance thanks to improved conservation and bans on DDT, which dramatically impaired the birds' breeding and sent their population into steep decline in the decades following World War II.

All About
There is no confusing the adult bald eagle, with its huge size and gleaming white head and tail. Adult plumage is not attained until after the third year. Until then, immature birds are dark brown with varying degrees of white mottling on their backs, wings, bellies, and, in older birds, heads. Depending upon age, the large bill is blackish or accented in the bright yellow seen in adults. Immatures and adults have strong, bright yellow talons.

Habitat & Range
Water plays a strong role in where bald eagles hunt and nest. In the process of rebounding in many areas, bald eagles now nest in most states, where they are often local nesters tied to specific sites. They are particularly common from Florida to coastal South Carolina, but the largest breeding populations are in Alaska and western Canada. During winter, bald eagles often congregate at wetland areas, rivers, and dams, where fishing or carrion feeding is particularly productive.

Feeding
Bald eagles hunt from perches or swoop down after sighting prey during soaring. While fish are preferred prey (frequently grappled from the water in the eagle's mighty talons), eagles also eat a wide variety of other foods, depending upon individual, time of year, and location. Carrion—particularly dead fish, birds, and mammals—plays an important dietary role. Many live animals are also caught: muskrats, reptiles, amphibians, crustaceans, and birds—as large as great blue herons—have been documented. Bald eagles also steal fish from ospreys and other birds.

Nesting
Bald eagles usually nest high in large trees in huge, bulky stick nests that are often used again over the years. Both mates collect sticks, and nest building may take several months. The female usually lays two eggs, which she and her mate incubate for just over a month. Once the first chick hatches, both parents incubate and *brood*, or cover, the eggs and hatchlings. Both parents feed their young, which leave the nest between 8 to 14 weeks after hatching.

Backyard & Beyond
Recently, bald eagles have started nesting in closer proximity to human development, thanks to protection from disturbance. If you see a large, dark raptor soaring slowly in the sky, with flat wings, look for the other clues of the bald eagle's identity.

Osprey
Pandion haliaetus

- Spring/Summer
- Year-Round
- Winter

The bold chocolate and white "fish hawk," so familiar to boaters and fishermen, is happy to exploit artificial nesting platforms, from power poles to those built specifically for it. Though osprey populations declined by 90 percent from the 1950s to the 1970s (poisoned by persistent organochlorides), they have made a heartening rebound in recent decades.

All About
Chocolate-brown above and pure white below, the osprey is armed with long, pale green legs and grappling-hook talons for seizing fish. Fierce yellow eyes are ringed in black, making the bird look as though it is wearing aviator's goggles. A banded gray tail and ragged crest complete this gangly bird's unusual look. Females have streaked upper breasts and are larger than males. When disturbed, ospreys give a series of high, piercing, chicklike peeps and thin screams.

Habitat & Range
One of the most widespread species, the osprey inhabits rivers, lakes, and coastlines throughout much of the United States. It is still reclaiming territory in the interior United States, helped by osprey reintroduction programs. Lacking body down, ospreys must migrate to stay warm and to find sufficient food in unfrozen waters, traveling down both coasts of Mexico and Central America.

Feeding
The only North American raptor to feed exclusively on fish, the osprey soars and hovers over shallow, clear waters of estuaries, marshes, lakes, and rivers, searching for fish. Spotting prey, it folds its wings and plunges, feet first, often completely beneath the surface. Unique cylindrical, recurved talons and horny spikes on the soles of its feet hold the fish securely until the osprey reaches a "carving block," usually a dead snag, where it can eat. Fish are always carried with the head facing into the wind, and are sometimes eaten as a snack on migration, far from water.

Nesting
The huge stick nests ospreys build are a familiar site on channel markers, dead trees, and artificial nesting platforms along coasts. Nesting pairs add sticks yearly until the nests assume enormous proportions. In the soft, grass-lined center the female lays two to three eggs, which she and her mate incubate for around 37 days. The male provides all the female's food during this time. Chicks stay in the nest for about 55 days, taking short flights, and are fed on or near the nest for around two weeks after first attaining flight.

Backyard & Beyond
Though artificial nesting platforms have had a positive influence on osprey populations, they are by no means out of danger. Overfishing, pesticide contamination, and persecution on Latin American wintering grounds (where they are shot by the hundreds at fish farms) continue to limit populations.

American Kestrel
Falco sparverius

North America's smallest falcon is also the most familiar to many, hovering over farm fields and air strips, perching on telephone poles and wires, and nesting in boxes put out by concerned landowners, who welcome these insect and rodent eaters. In some regions, kestrel numbers have fallen in recent decades, probably due to large-scale landscape changes, as farm areas have reverted to forest and as cities and suburbs have stretched out to once-rural areas.

All About
In flight, the kestrel has sharp-looking, pointed wings and a slender, long tail. In comparison to the merlin and peregrine falcon, it is slim. Sharp-shinned and Cooper's hawks also have long tails, but their wings are broad, not pointed. While soaring, the kestrel's wings look more rounded and the tail fans. Adult males are brightly colored, with blue-gray wings and crown, rufous tail, and a rusty back embellished with black barring. Black spots speckle the underparts. Both sexes have two vertical stripes on the face and a black spot on the back of the neck. Adult females lack the male's blue-gray wings, have barred tails, and—instead of black spots—sport rusty lines of spots on their underparts.

Habitat & Range
The American kestrel is nrm bird, although many farms prhabitat for them. They also nesurban areas, open forest, clearings, and even deserts. They are truly American in the New World sense, nesting from Alaska to southern Argentina. In the South, numbers swell in the winter, when northern birds move south en masse to winter in warmer areas.

Feeding
Grasshoppers and other large insects are important prey to kestrels, but voles, mice, and other rodents also play a part in their diet, as do small birds, reptiles, and other small animals.

Nesting
American kestrels are cavity nesters. Females usually lay their four to six eggs in a tree hole or other cavity, sometimes in a crevice in a building or cliff or in a nest box. Both parents share the month-long incubation duties. Young fly about a month after hatching, and parents feed them until about two weeks after they leave the nest.

Backyard & Beyond
Provision of nest boxes in rural areas has helped American kestrel populations, and this is one potential way to attract kestrels to your property if you live in an open area. Kestrels also pass through suburban areas during migration. In the South, they may frequent open suburbs rich in grasshoppers and such prey as small birds and lizards. They will use snags placed in the middle of grassy meadows as hunting and eating perches.

Northern Bobwhite
Colinus virginianus

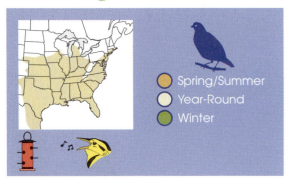

Conservationists are struggling to find out why the distinctive bob-WHITE call of the northern bobwhite no longer rings out in parts of its wide breeding range. Many suppose that large-scale landscape changes—such as the prevention of naturally occurring fires, which rejuvenate brushy fields—and the widespread use of herbicides have caused bobwhite populations to dive throughout much of the Southeast over the last three decades. In the northern parts of their range, hard winters often knock down populations.

All About
The bobwhite is the East's only quail. This plump, football-shaped bird more often runs than flies and, when not disturbed, picks at the ground for seeds like a chicken. Males have a striking head pattern, with white throat and supercilium (line above eye to back of head) cutting through an otherwise dark chocolate-brown head. Females are similarly marked, but have buff (rather than white) and rust (rather than dark brown) head coloration. Bobwhites have cinnamon-rust bodies embellished with long white streaks below, and they have very short tails.

Habitat & Range
Far more often heard than seen, the northern bobwhite occurs from Massachusetts west to Wyoming and south to the Mexico-Guatemala border. Some introduced populations inhabit western mountain states as well. Bobwhites feed and breed in a variety of open habitats. They favor farm fields and those just reverting to rank, weedy meadows; pastures; pine forests; and mixed pine and deciduous forests with undergrowth kept open by managed fire or regular cutting.

Feeding
Adult bobwhites are opportunistic seedeaters. Depending upon season and locality, they consume a wide variety of weed seeds, as well as agricultural seeds and those from various forest plants. They also eat some insects and berries, buds, and other plant foods. Until two months of age, young bobwhites mostly eat insects and other small invertebrates.

Nesting
During one breeding season, a bobwhite pair could ideally produce 25 or more young in several broods; however, they suffer high mortality rates and are rarely this productive. Bobwhite pairs build their grass or other vegetation-covered scrape nest in a well-camouflaged spot within their tangled habitat. There they incubate a dozen or more eggs for just over three weeks. Young hatch able to run and feed themselves. Parents usually loiter nearby.

Backyard & Beyond
Where prime habitat is carefully maintained, there are plenty of these quail left for hunters and birders. If you live on a large piece of land, you can make a bobwhite habitat by cutting (or with department supervision, burning) every three to five years.

Wild Turkey
Meleagris gallopavo

When restocking programs abandoned using farm-raised birds and turned to releasing wild-caught birds in the 1940s, the repopulation of wild turkeys into their former haunts took off. Today, the large dark forms of wild turkeys are a familiar sight along many highways, and the birds even come to backyard feeders.

All About
A tall, strong-legged bird, the wild turkey's feathers are iridescent with dark bronze, shot with hints of copper and acid green. Displaying in spring, the male erects its plumage in the strut posture, its enormous tail fanned, wings drooping, and wattles ablaze. A "beard" of wiry, barbless feathers sprouts from the center of his breast. Hens are visibly smaller and paler than gobblers, with a brown cast to their plumage and without distensible wattles. Along with the male's explosive gobble, turkeys employ a great variety of calls, including yelps and hollow *putt* sounds, in their intraflock communication.

Habitat & Range
Dense deciduous forests—either uplands or bottomlands—with some clearings are ideal turkey habitats. The nuts from oaks and other nut trees make up an important component of their diet. Some exploit agricultural fields for spilled grain. Wild turkeys are nonmigratory and may fast for more than a week in severe weather.

Feeding
The wild turkey's strong legs and feet help it scratch its way across the forest floor, raking away debris to uncover acorns, tree seeds, and invertebrates. Turkeys pluck buds and fruits as they walk or clamber through branches, and they strip grasses of their seeds by running stems through their bills. Young poults take a number of insects and invertebrates.

Nesting
Gobblers display—gobbling and strutting—in early spring to attract visiting hens. After mating, the hen lays about a dozen eggs in a feather-lined bowl in the ground at the foot of a tree or under brush. She incubates them alone for about 26 days. When all chicks have hatched and imprinted on the hen (from one to three days later), they leave the nest, following her every move. She feeds them for the first few days; after that they pick up their own food. She broods them on the ground until they are able to join her in a roost tree at night; she still shelters them with spread wings on the roost.

Backyard & Beyond
Wild turkeys may, in some rural and suburban situations, be attracted into yards with cracked corn spread on the ground. A small flock can consume as much as 50 pounds per week. Fascinating social behavior and courtship behavior is a rich reward. Rotate feeding areas to prevent the spread of disease.

American Coot
Fulica americana

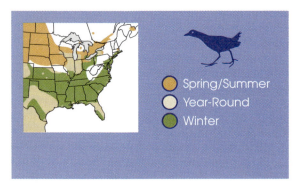

What looks like a duck and acts like a duck, but is not a duck? It's the American coot, of course. Coots are duck-like in many ways, but they are actually members of the rail family and are the most common (and most commonly seen) of all the rails. Like ducks, coots are excellent swimmers and use this ability to find and eat aquatic vegetation. However, coots are reluctant and awkward fliers—they must run, pattering across the water's surface and flapping madly to lift their heavy bodies into the air.

All About
Chunky and almost all black with a contrasting white bill and red eyes and forehead patch, the coot is hard to mistake for anything else. The common moorhen and purple gallinule are similar in shape, but both are more colorful (the gallinule much more so) and less common than coots. Coots swim using the lobed toes on their powerful feet, and when swimming they bob their heads back and forth with a "funky chicken" motion. Coots are raucous, loud birds that utter a variety of grunts, cackles, and croaks.

Habitat & Range
American coots are widespread across North America, especially in winter when they can be found in huge flocks on large bodies of water. They breed throughout the central and western portions of the continent, and they are year-round residents in spots in the South. During the breeding season, coots prefer ponds, lakes, and marshes of almost any size, provided that they have large stands of tall reeds, such as cattails.

Feeding
Finding most of their food on or below the surface of the water, coots dabble, swim, and dive when foraging. They are equally at home on land, grazing on the grass of city parks and golf courses. Their diet is largely vegetarian with the main menu items being duckweed, algae, and various pondweeds and sedges.

Nesting
The female coot builds a floating, basket-shaped platform of vegetation with a lined cup to hold the eggs. She lays up to a dozen eggs and incubates them for about 23 days. Young coots have shiny, bald, red heads and golden down, an adaptation that is thought to trigger feeding by the parents. Babies leave the nest after a day or so and are able to find food on their own shortly thereafter.

Backyard & Beyond
Though they may not be a backyard bird, coots should be easy to find in nearby parks and on golf course water hazards. In winter, look for flocks of coots on almost any body of water, from reservoirs to sewage ponds.

Killdeer
Charadrius vociferus

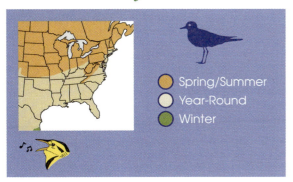

The killdeer is a large, double-banded plover that screams its name across farm fields and other grass- and dirt-covered habitats. If you see an orange-tailed, stripe-winged bird calling KILL-DEEE, KILL-DEEE, you can rest assured that it's this plover. Despite their lousy-tasting flesh, many killdeer were shot during the late 1800s, along with a wide range of other shorebirds. These species are now protected from harm by federal and state laws.

All About
On its white breast, two black bands stand out. Other plovers—such as the smaller but similar semipalmated plover—have only one band or none at all. Otherwise, killdeer are wet-sand brown above and clear white below, with white around the front of the face and eye. The killdeer is one of our largest and longest-tailed plovers, so even mixed with a few other species on a mudflat, they stand out, especially when you spot those two breast bands. Much of the tail is orange, except the tip, which is black punctuated with white dabs.

Habitat & Range
Unlike most other plovers, killdeer often forage or nest far from water. You may find them on ball fields and airport runways, on turf, in pastures, and in farm fields, as well as on mudflats. They are found throughout North America, but northern birds head south for the winter. In the South, only the Appalachians lose their killdeer during cold months.

Feeding
A farmer's friend, the killdeer spends its foraging time searching for beetles, grasshoppers, caterpillars, and other insects. Crayfish, centipedes, spiders, and other invertebrates are also eaten, as well as some seeds.

Nesting
A simple scrape in the dirt or gravel (including gravel-covered roofs) will do for a killdeer pair, although they sometimes add embellishments, such as a lining of pebbles, grass, or other small materials. Females lay three to five blotched eggs, which both parents incubate for just less than a month. Nesting in exposed habitats, killdeer rely on camouflage and deception to keep their eggs and chicks safe. If an intruder approaches the nest, an adult killdeer may feign injury—dragging a wing as if it is broken and exposing its bright tail—then lure the person or predator away from the nest. Adults watch over their hatchlings, little puffballs that can run around and find food by themselves shortly after hatching. They can fly before they reach one month old.

Backyard & Beyond
Killdeer are attracted to large areas of grass as well as to short-cropped fields, so you may see them on your property if it's relatively treeless and large. Their cries carry long distances, so you may also hear killdeer passing by or calling from nearby nesting grounds.

Lesser Yellowlegs
Tringa flavipes

Lesser yellowlegs is a tall shorebird commonly seen in a variety of saltwater and freshwater situations. It winters in the Gulf States and along southern seacoasts, both east and west, so wherever you live in North America you stand a chance of seeing this species at some time during the year. Lessers often travel in large flocks and may be found together with greater yellowlegs.

All About
True to its name, this bird has bright yellow legs, which really stand out against its dark back and speckled underparts. The sexes are alike. When alarmed, it will take flight with a loud *tu* or *tu-tu* call, trailing its long yellow legs behind. The only species the lesser yellowlegs is likely to be confused with is the equally common greater yellowlegs, a nearly identical, but larger, close relative. In flight, both show white on the rump. The smaller lesser yellowlegs has a shorter, straighter bill than the greater, and overall it has a much more delicate appearance.

Habitat & Range
During migrations, the lesser yellowlegs is more likely than the greater yellowlegs to visit fresh water. It occurs widely and may stop at small ponds or wetlands, temporary rainwater puddles, coastal marshes and mudflats, and flooded fields.

Feeding
Lesser yellowlegs feed in shallow water where they find their prey—aquatic insects, snails, small fish, and crustaceans—on or just beneath the water's surface. They sometimes swing their heads back and forth underwater in an effort to stir up food. On land, the lesser yellowlegs may snatch up terrestrial insects and worms from the ground, or pick flying insects out of the air.

Nesting
Breeding at the edge of the northern tundra, lesser yellowlegs nest in natural clearings with small clusters of vegetation. The nest is merely a scrape in the ground, softened with a few fallen leaves and placed next to a fallen log or under a low shrub, usually within 200 yards of a water source. Nesting starts as early as May, with the male calling loudly from the top of a tree or other elevated perch. The female lays three to four eggs, and both parents share the 18- to 20-day incubation. Within hours of hatching, the young are able to leave the nest. As soon as the chicks are self-sufficient—as early as July—the adults leave for the south. The youngsters start south a few weeks later.

Backyard & Beyond
Any marsh or wetland in your neighborhood might host lesser yellowlegs during migration. If you live in the winter range of this species, you should be able to find it easily at mudflats and marshes, mingling with other shorebirds.

Spotted Sandpiper
Actitis macularia

The spotted sandpiper is one of the easiest sandpipers to identify. Not only are its markings distinctive, but so are its mannerisms—the bird signals itself to birders by almost constantly bobbing its posterior. An inland nester across much of northern North America, the spotted sandpiper frequents waterways from creeks and streams to marshes, reservoirs, and mudflats during migration, and coastal areas during winter.

All About
The wood thrushlike breast spotting of breeding adult spotted sandpipers sets them apart from other sandpipers, but you can also easily identify spotless immatures (as shown in the photo) and non-breeders. For one thing, the spotted sandpiper's tail and rear end constantly bob up and down as the bird walks or pauses; this is true even in birds that have just left the nest. Also, look for a white crescent on the sides, which curls around the bend of the bird's folded wing, inching toward the back. Spotted sandpipers are about the length of a wood thrush and smaller than a robin—in other words, they are not the tiniest sandpipers, but they are rather small. Breeding individuals have bright orange bills; otherwise, spotted sandpipers have pale pinkish or orangish bills and legs.

Habitat & Range
Spotted sandpipers nest in freshwater habitats, both in forested and open settings across much of North America, except in the far South, where a good number winter. Find them at pools where rainwater collects, along lakeshores, and at streams, rivers, or marshes. Many winter far to the south, from Mexico and Central America to as far south as northern Chile and Argentina.

Feeding
As would be expected of a bird that frequents a mixture of habitats, the spotted sandpiper captures a variety of prey in diverse ways. Insects, crabs, worms, small fish, and other creatures may be picked from the water or shore, caught in quick flights, or chased.

Nesting
Parental care in spotted sandpipers differs from that in many other birds. Female spotted sandpipers often pair up with more than one male, laying two or more clutches of eggs. Both parents build the nest, a depression in the ground usually sheltered by some plant cover and lined with plants or moss. There the female usually lays four eggs, which may be incubated by the male or by both parents for about three weeks. The nestlings teeter as soon as they hatch and can almost immediately scamper from the nest. Usually the male watches over the young, which can fly when they are about 18 days old.

Backyard & Beyond
Any park or backyard with a large pond, stream, or lake is likely to host a migrating spotted sandpiper at one time or another.

Ring-billed Gull
Larus delawarensis

This gull might almost be called the inland gull. Though found in coastal areas like most gulls, it is also the most numerous and widespread gull away from the seacoasts, sometimes found in huge flocks. At first glance it looks like a slightly smaller version of the herring gull, but it has a personality all its own.

All About
The ring-billed gull is a medium-sized (19 inches long) gull, and in adult plumage it has a light gray back and wings on a pure white body. Its wing tips are black with white spots, and it has a black ring near the end of its yellow bill. Males and females look alike. Young ring-billed gulls take three years to mature, during which time their bodies and wings are varying shades of mottled brown and gray, with a white tail that has a prominent, black terminal band. These gulls are smaller, lighter, and more graceful-looking than similarly patterned herring gulls, and they have a more buoyant appearance in flight.

Habitat and Range
In addition to the beaches and bays of the seacoasts, ring-billed gulls may be found at large lakes and rivers, in newly plowed fields and pastures, and at sod farms, garbage dumps, and parking lots throughout their range.

Feeding
Ring-billed gulls are omnivorous, thriving on whatever food is on hand. Fish are a favorite item, but insects and earthworms are high on the list, along with grains, refuse, and even small rodents. They will eat the eggs of other species, and they are not averse to taking handouts from humans at parking lots and picnic grounds. (French fries, caught in midair, are popular. Ketchup is optional.)

Nesting
After a courtship routine by the male (which includes bowing, throat-puffing, and a ceremonial walk around the female, enlivened by many odd gesticulations), the mated pair will build its nest on the ground in a fairly open area near water. The ring-billed is colonial, so there are usually lots of similar nests nearby. Both sexes build the flimsy nest of grasses, sticks, and moss; and both take turns incubating the two to four eggs for up to four weeks until hatching. The downy young are tended by their parents in the general vicinity of the nest until they attain flight at about five weeks of age.

Backyard & Beyond
Look for ring-billed gulls in large, open fields after spring or autumn rainstorms, or watch for them anywhere there is an infestation of large insects, such as grasshoppers or locusts. If there is a landfill nearby, it may attract gulls from a wide surrounding area and can make for productive gull watching.

Herring Gull
Larus argentatus

Spring/Summer
Year-Round
Winter

This is the bird that most people think of when they hear the term *seagull*. Large, abundant, and widespread, the herring gull is an imposing bird—and, in its adult plumage, it is certainly beautiful. Picture a dozen or more sitting on a pier with ocean waves lapping below, and you have a perfect coastal postcard scene.

All About
Measuring up to 26 inches in length, the adult herring gull has silver-gray wings tipped in black and white, a dazzling white body, bold yellow bill, and pink legs. Males and females are alike, and they are considerably larger than similar-looking ring-billed gulls. Immature herring gulls wear varying shades of brown or gray-brown and are not fully mature until their fourth year. All ages join in making the yelping or trumpeting calls, which are a constant fact of life throughout the herring gull's entire range and which define the seacoast in the minds of anyone who's ever walked a beach.

Habitat & Range
Herring gulls are birds of shorelines, major lakes and rivers, garbage dumps, and, occasionally, farmlands—especially recently tilled fields. Their population, once confined to the northern states, has been spreading southward for decades and breeding birds may now be found as far south as Cape Hatteras, North Carolina.

Feeding
Herring gulls eat almost anything, which is one reason for their success. Fish, along with all manner of other seafood, are a staple of the herring gull diet, but they also eat the eggs and chicks of other bird species (they can decimate a tern colony if given the opportunity), all kinds of garbage, large insects and grubs, and even carrion. They are smart and have learned to drop clams onto rocks or pavement to open them. They are quite willing to steal food from other seabirds. In the gull world, there is no such thing as a guilty conscience.

Nesting
Herring gulls nest on the ground, preferably in the lee of a rock or some other natural feature. Both sexes help scrape out a site and line it with grass, weeds, and feathers. Many nests contain a ball of some kind—whiffle ball, tennis ball—which may be a courtship gift from the male. The usual clutch is three eggs, and both parents share the month-long incubation. The young, downy and active from the start, depend on their parents at least until they fly at about 50 days of age.

Backyard & Beyond
Check the range map above to see when herring gulls might be expected in your area, and then visit the nearest beach! These birds also hang out at sewage outlets, dams, or anywhere that human activity may generate a reliable food supply.

Mourning Dove
Zenaida macroura

Whether you regard them as songbirds or living skeet targets, if you feed birds, you probably have mourning doves as constant companions. These tapered, graceful brown and pinkish birds wholeheartedly embrace human alterations of the natural landscape, finding their greatest abundance in agricultural and suburban areas. Doves love water, but may foul birdbaths by sitting around the rim, tails in.

All About
The mournful *oooahh, oooh, ooh, ooh* song of the mourning dove is a song of the South, echoing from power lines and treetops in early spring. Mourning doves travel in flocks, breaking rank only to nest and raise young. Males defend their mates as a kind of mobile territory, defending her and the immediate nest site—but not much else—from other birds.

Habitat & Range
The only habitat shunned by mourning doves is deep, contiguous forest. They are most common in agricultural areas with hedgerows and shelterbelts. They are also abundant in suburban areas as well, where visits to feeding stations are an integral part of their daily routines. Mourning doves migrate, especially far northern populations, but some individuals are resident year-round.

Feeding
Streamlined, fast, and powerful flyers, mourning doves travel in flocks, descending to feed on a great variety of grains and weed seeds that they peck from the ground. They are often seen in ranks on power lines over farm fields. A capacious crop allows mourning doves to gorge—sometimes to the point of being misshapen—and then digest their stored food later when resting.

Nesting
Mourning doves may mate and nest in any month of the year, but males begin to tune up their songs in late winter. They have a production-line breeding mode, following one brood with another as often as six times in a season. The twig nest platform, placed in a wide variety of tree species, but frequently in a pine, is often flimsy enough so that eggs show through from beneath. Two eggs are incubated by both members of the pair, and they hatch in 14 days. Young doves are fed first on crop milk, a secretion unique to the pigeon family, and later on regurgitated seeds. Young remain in the nest for another 15 days but may fledge much earlier. The male feeds them until about day 30, while the female re-nests. Immature birds are visibly smaller and have fine, buff feather edges overall.

Backyard & Beyond
Mourning doves take any seeds that might be offered at feeders, preferring sunflower seeds, cracked corn, millet, milo, and other grains found in seed mixes. They become adept at emptying hopper feeders into their ample crops, and then sitting for long periods afterward to digest their food.

Rock Pigeon
Columba livia

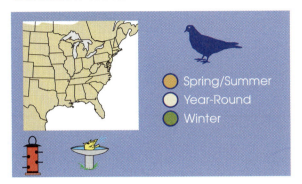

Originating in northern Europe, Africa, and India, rock pigeons—largely gone from their former wild haunts—have spread to cities and towns worldwide thanks to their domestication some five thousand years ago. Evidence of this domestication lies in their highly variable coloration; a flock may contain birds in every color from pure white to reddish to solid black.

All About
A substantial bird with a small head, deep chest, powerful wings, and a square tail, the rock pigeon is built for flight. Wild-type birds are slate-blue with a white rump, black terminal tail band, and two black bars on the secondary wing feathers. Pinkish green iridescence adorns the neck. Pigeons have short, reddish legs and a short, straight bill. Their song is a series of soft, resonant coos—*ooh-ga-rooogh*—and a harsh *Woogh!* serves as an alarm call. Pigeons can be found in flocks except when tending young.

Habitat & Range
It is rare to find rock pigeons in natural habitats, though there are still some cliff-nesting populations in North America. Most consider tall buildings, with their myriad ledges, to be ideal nesting grounds and are happy to take foods, such as bread and popcorn, from city sidewalks. Pigeons are nonmigratory, though their celebrated homing skills are exploited by pigeon racing clubs across the world.

Feeding
Walking and pecking with rapidly bobbing heads, pigeons find their preferred food—grains, seeds, and some fruits—on the ground. Urban birds have highly developed scavenging skills, raiding trashcans and fast food litter for high carbohydrate fare, such as bread.

Nesting
It's easy to watch pigeons display and even mate; the male's spinning, bowing, and cooing may be conducted underfoot on city sidewalks. Pigeons mate for life, guarding females zealously. They may lay eggs and raise young anytime. Building ledges, highway overpasses, barns, bridges, and other structures may be selected as the site on which to build a stick-and-grass nest and lay two eggs. Both male and female incubate for about 18 days. The rubbery, black-skinned squabs stay in the nest for a variable period of 25 to 45 days. Fat at fledging, they may be forced to shift entirely for themselves upon leaving the nest.

Backyard & Beyond
Thanks to the flocking habit of pigeons, most feeder operators are less than delighted when they descend. The most effective deterrents seem to be sturdy feeders enclosed by wire caging that excludes pigeons while admitting smaller birds. Some people opt to spread food at a distance to keep pigeons from overwhelming seed feeders. Pigeons will eat anything that might be offered, but millet and cracked corn are special favorites.

Yellow-billed Cuckoo
Coccyzus americanus

The yellow-billed cuckoo is a furtive, skulking bird of thickets and brushy woodland edges and, though it is fairly large, its retiring habits make it far more easily heard than seen. It often hides deep within the foliage and, when perching in the open, it tends to remain very still. The yellow-billed cuckoo makes a unique repetitive clucking sound that is a sure clue to identification.

All About
Slender and long-tailed, the yellow-billed cuckoo has a plain brown back and creamy white breast. The underside of the tail shows a pattern of bold white spots against a black background, and bright rufous wing patches are visible in flight. The lower part of the bill is yellow. Male and female yellow-billed cuckoos look alike. The only other species they are likely to be confused with is the related black-billed cuckoo, which lacks the rufous wing color and has a black bill, among other differences.

Habitat & Range
Yellow-billed cuckoos inhabit deciduous woodland edges, thickets and tangles along watercourses or roadsides, willow groves, and overgrown orchards. Yellow-billed cuckoos are not generally found in deep interior woodlands, as they prefer some kind of "edge" to their habitat.

Feeding
Yellow-billed cuckoos eat great numbers of hairy caterpillars and many large insects such as dragonflies, cicadas, grasshoppers, crickets, and beetles. Small fruits are a minor but regular part of their diet in summer. Most yellow-billed cuckoos forage by slowly and methodically exploring branches, twigs, and leaves for hidden insects, but they occasionally may act like flycatchers, darting into the air for a meal on the wing, or hovering to seize a caterpillar at the edge of a leaf.

Nesting
Once paired, cuckoos survey the surrounding area for a leafy and secluded nest site, five to ten feet off the ground. Both help build a loose shell of twigs and stems, lining it with fine grasses. Three to five eggs are laid, and both parents share the incubation and feeding of the young. The entire process, from egg laying to fledging, takes only 17 days, one of the shortest such periods for any bird species.

Backyard & Beyond
If you have mature trees rimming your backyard, you may have an occasional yellow-billed cuckoo stopping by on migration—listen for its patented clucking calls. An old folk name for the yellow-billed cuckoo is "raincrow," because these *kowp-kowp-kowp* calls are so often uttered on hot summer afternoons, when thunderstorms are likely to follow. Knowing the cuckoo's call will be helpful in finding this secretive bird; otherwise, check the thickets and edges of your local woodland or park for a chance to find this species.

Great Horned Owl
Bubo virginianus

Huge, powerful, and widespread across North America, the great horned is the king of all of our owls. Armed with incredible vision, the great horned sees and pounces on prey, using its powerful talons and bill to dispatch its victim. The deep, hooting call of the great horned—whoo-who-o-o-o-who-who—a staple of movie and television soundtracks, is most often heard in nature just after sunset.

All About
The great horned owl is named for its large size (up to 24 inches tall, with a wingspan of 44 inches) and its long feathered head tufts (horns). A deep rusty brown and buff overall, this owl has large, golden-yellow eyes. Its thick, soft feathers provide excellent insulation from either heat or cold, permitting the great horned to nest as soon as early to midwinter even in regions with harsh winter weather.

Habitat & Range
A nonmigratory bird throughout the Americas, great horned owls can be found as far north as the tree line, and as far south as South America—and in nearly every conceivable habitat and setting. Great horned owls are equally at home in urban and suburban settings, as well as in deep woodlands, grasslands, and deserts.

Feeding
Mammals (rabbits, hares, and large rodents) are the primary prey item of great horned owls. They also eat earthworms, fish, snakes, and even birds as large as great blue herons. They are one of the few predators that will readily kill and consume skunks. Within a great horned owl's territory, it's unusual to find other, smaller owls—they may have been eaten by the resident great horneds. Their primary hunting mode is to perch, watch, and pounce on prey.

Nesting
Great horned owls most often take over an old stick nest built by a hawk, heron, or squirrel, but they will also nest on cliff ledges, in tree cavities, and even on the ground. Two to four eggs are laid and incubation by the female lasts slightly more than a month. The male brings food to his mate on the nest each night. Six weeks or so after hatching, the young owlets venture from the nest to nearby branches. They remain dependent on the adults for many months, but leave the nest area before the next breeding season.

Backyard & Beyond
If you live in or near older woodlands, chances are good that great horned owls are your neighbors. Though there is little you can do to attract great horned owls to your property, listen just after dusk and before dawn for their deep hoots, which carry for great distances. Watch for the great horned's silhouette at dusk along woodland edges, especially in treetops and on power poles.

Barred Owl
Strix varia

Who cooks for you? Who cooks for you all? The wild hoots of the barred owl echo through swampy, deciduous woodlands throughout the South. Its dark, liquid eyes give it a deceptively gentle look, but this owl is a top-of-the-line predator, taking everything from fish to rabbits. Though it does some daylight hunting, most of the barred owl's foraging takes place at night.

All About
A rounded, earless outline, smoky gray-brown plumage that is heavily mottled and barred with white, broad brown streaks on a white belly, and dark eyes distinguish the barred owl. Its bill and feet are yellow. Its familiar eight-hoot call gives way to raucous and sometimes frightening caterwauling in breeding season. This species is more apt to call in daylight than any other; it may call all day during overcast conditions.

Habitat & Range
Like its famous endangered cousin the spotted owl, the barred owl prefers old forest, probably in part because the large nesting cavities it requires occur in trees of ample girth. It is commonly associated with lowlands, but occupies upland sites as well. The barred owl does not migrate, but may wander in harsh winters.

Feeding
Anything it can kill is fair game for this medium-large owl. Small mammals, as small as mice and up to the size of rabbits, make up at least half the barred owl's diet. It makes acrobatic strikes after squirrels, sometimes turning completely over in flight. Birds, amphibians, reptiles, insects, and other invertebrates compose the rest of its diet.

Nesting
Most barred owls select large nest cavities, such as those formed when a large branch breaks off a hollow tree. They will also use a hollow in a broken tree trunk, as well as the nests of other raptors or squirrels. Two to three eggs are incubated by the female alone. They hatch from 28 to 33 days later. The male feeds the family for the first two weeks of the chicks' life, after which the female leaves them and helps bring in food. Young owls, clothed in buff-colored down, begin venturing onto branches when they are around five weeks old, before they can fly. They give a hideous, rasping screech as a location call and may be found and observed discreetly from a safe distance. Fledglings are fed by their parents until early autumn, when they strike out to find new territory.

Backyard & Beyond
Surprisingly enough, the barred owl will accept nest boxes, because tree cavities large enough to contain them are hard to find. Plans for a wood duck nest box with a seven-inch entrance hole should accommodate them. This should be mounted as high as possible in a large tree.

Eastern Screech Owl

Megascops asio

Eastern screech owls are very acclimated to humans, but their nocturnal habits and cryptic coloration keep us from seeing them regularly. Even when perched in full view in daylight, screech owls have a remarkable ability to conceal themselves. Found commonly in cities and towns, the screech owl's success may be due not only to its secretive nature, but also to its ability to take a wide variety of small prey.

All About

A small bird (8½ inches long), the eastern screech owl occurs in two color variations: reddish and gray, with gray being more common. The screech owl's plumage appears very barklike. When a "screech" sits with its body elongated and ear tufts extended, it looks like a broken branch stub. This bird's name is misleading; a screech is rarely voiced. The call most bird watchers hear is a series of descending, whinnying whistles and tremolos on a single note.

Habitat & Range

A nonmigratory, resident bird throughout the eastern United States, the screech owl is found wherever woodlands are mature enough to have cavities. Unlike many other owl species, the screech owl is commonly found in urban parks and suburban backyards.

Feeding

Eastern screech owls will eat almost anything—from mice and voles to moths, earthworms, crawfish, frogs, and fish. In spring and summer, they prey upon small and medium-sized songbirds, but during winter small mammals are more common prey. Screech owls perch in a tree, waiting and watching for potential prey, most of which is captured with the owl's feet in flight or by pouncing on the ground.

Nesting

Screech owls nest in natural cavities and will readily use nest boxes. They begin nesting early, from mid-December in the South to late March in the North. From two to six eggs are laid and a month-long incubation period ensues. The female incubates the eggs and broods the young owlets, while the male delivers all the food. Owlets remain in the nest for a month before venturing into nearby trees. They remain dependent on their parents for two months.

Backyard & Beyond

You may very well already have eastern screech owls in or near your backyard. Spend some time outside at night—especially when the moon is full—listening for the screech owl's wavering calls. Check natural tree cavities during the day for roosting or nesting owls—they may be peering out of the hole. You can attract screech owls with an owl nest box. Boxes should be about 12 to 14 inches deep with an internal floor size of 7×7 inches and a 2¾-inch diameter entry. Place the box above 10 feet high in a shady spot on a tree trunk wider than the box's width.

Whip-poor-will
Caprimulgus vociferus

- Spring/Summer
- Year-Round
- Winter

Imagine sleeping all day and flying around the woods, singing all night. That's the life of the whip-poor-will. Like its relatives the common nighthawk and chuck-will's widow, the "whip" is most active at night and is often heard calling out its name repeatedly—whip-poor-WILL! whip-poor-WILL! In fact, whip-poor-wills have been known to give this call continuously, more than a thousand times in a row. Because of its nocturnal habits and cryptic coloration, many bird watchers never get a good look at a whip-poor-will.

All About
The whip-poor-will's body is just under 10 inches in length, and its wingspan is 19 inches—nearly 7 inches shorter than that of the chuck-will's-widow. The whip-poor-will's plumage is a subtle mix of charcoal gray, buff, black, and white. In flight, it shows prominent white corners on the tail. The large, dark eyes of the whip-poor-will are designed to function in the low-light conditions of dawn and dusk.

Habitat & Range
Whip-poor-wills prefer mixed woodlands with little underbrush or open farmlands, brushy fields, and rural roadways. These habitats all lend themselves to the pursuit of flying insects. Whips spend the winter in Florida, around the Gulf Coast, and into Mexico and Central America. They return each spring as early as March. In the Deep South, the whip-poor-will is replaced by the closely related chuck-will's-widow.

Feeding
The whip-poor-will is an insect specialist, perching and watching for passing prey, which it pursues in silent flight. Stiff bristle feathers line its wide-opening bill and funnel flying insects into its mouth as it flies along. Primary food items include mosquitoes, moths, beetles, and grasshoppers. Most foraging is done in the half-light of dusk and dawn, and on brightly moonlit nights.

Nesting
A ground nester, the whip-poor-will builds no nest. As early as mid-April, two eggs are laid in a concealed spot on the ground and incubated by both sexes for about 20 days. After hatching, the young birds remain with the parents for two weeks, with both parents sharing the brooding. Young whips are able move around on the ground within a few days after hatching; they are able to fly at about 16 days old. This early mobility helps young whip-poor-wills avoid predators.

Backyard & Beyond
Whip-poor-wills are declining in some parts of their range due to the effects of pesticides and the loss of breeding habitats. If you are close to a calling whip-poor-will, listen for the *cluck* sound that it makes just prior to the *whip*. Perhaps the best way to see whip-poor-wills is to watch for them at dusk as they make their silent, batlike forays after insects along woodland edges and over meadows.

Common Nighthawk
Chordeiles minor

Peent! *is the nasal flight call of the common nighthawk, a familiar sound in cities and towns, though it is usually mistaken for an insect call. This call accompanies the batlike flight of the nighthawk as it courses through the sky, hawking insects. Despite its name, the nighthawk is not a hawk and is active both day and night.*

All About
The common nighthawk is a long-winged, dark bird with characteristic white wing slashes. Its distinctive bounding flight can be used to identify it from a distance as it forages over fields, towns, and woods. Nighthawks belong to the goatsucker family, a name based on the old myth that they drank milk from livestock at night.

Habitat & Range
A common breeding bird throughout North America, nighthawks can be seen in flight over almost any habitat. In cities and towns, nighthawks are attracted to the insects around streetlamps. Beginning in late July, nighthawks can be seen at dusk in large migratory flocks, sometimes numbering dozens of birds. Nighthawks winter in South America, returning to the southern United States by early April.

Feeding
A specialist in catching flying insects, the common nighthawk's mouth opens wide to capture its prey. The nighthawk sees its prey—most often flying ants, beetles, moths, and mayflies—and pursues and catches it. When a nighthawk needs water, it swoops low over a lake or river and skims a drink from the surface.

Nesting
Historically, nighthawk nests were found on the ground in grasslands and in open patches of soil, gravel, or sand. The nest is a shallow depression near a log or stone that helps to shade and conceal it. Now, nighthawk nests are more commonly found on gravel roads or on flat, gravel-covered rooftops in urban areas. The female selects the nest site, lays two eggs, and handles the 18-day incubation. Young nighthawks are brooded by the female for 15 days, protecting them from sun and weather. The male feeds both his mate and the young in the nest. After 20 days, the young birds are able to fly, and the male then takes over their care while the female starts a second nest.

Backyard & Beyond
Nighthawks have good success nesting on gravel roofs, but not so on roofs lined with rubber or foam, materials that pool water and retain heat. Watch and listen for nighthawks in the sky at dawn and dusk. You may hear their *peent!* before you see them. During courtship, male nighthawks perform a diving display near females, swooping swiftly toward the ground. As the male comes out of the dive, he flares his flight feathers, creating a booming sound much like a large truck shifting gears.

Chimney Swift
Chaetura pelagica

- Spring/Summer
- Year-Round
- Winter

Known by bird watchers as "the flying cigar," the chimney swift is a familiar sight in the sky over cities and towns during the spring, summer, and fall. Its nickname aptly describes the swift's elongated flight silhouette. The twittering calls of chimney swifts are one of the most common bird sounds of summer. The chimney swift is named for its preferred nesting and roosting site—the inside of chimneys. This species spends much of its life on the wing, stopping only to sleep and nest.

All About
Chimney swifts are a dark charcoal-gray overall with a small black bill, eyes, and tiny feet. Indeed their feet are almost useless for walking, but are perfect for clinging to the inside of a chimney. The chimney swift is nearly all wing—with a 5-inch long body and a 14-inch wingspan. Four hundred years ago, all chimney swifts nested in hollow trees and caves, but the arrival of European settlers and their stone chimneys soon provided abundant nesting sites. Today most chimney swifts nest in chimneys and other human structures, such as unused smokestacks and abandoned buildings.

Habitat & Range
Widespread and common across the eastern half of the United States and southern Canada, the chimney swift is found wherever there are suitable nest sites. Fall migratory flocks of swifts are a magnificent spectacle as they form a swirling, chattering cloud descending to roost in a large chimney at dusk. In winter, this tiny bird migrates to South America, returning again in March to the southern United States.

Feeding
An all-insect diet is captured and consumed on the wing. Swifts often are seen flying high in the sky when foraging.

Nesting
A pair of swifts chooses a nest site—usually a chimney. The nest is a half-saucer shape made of sticks held together and made to adhere to the wall of cavity by the birds' saliva. Swifts break small twigs off trees, grabbing them with their feet as they fly past a tree. Two to five eggs are laid, and both parents share incubation (15 days) and brooding duties until the young swifts fledge at about 19 days after hatching.

Backyard & Beyond
Allowing chimney swifts to nest in your older, unused chimney is really easy—just let the swifts find it. They pose no danger and, if not for the sounds of hungry nestlings during a two-week period, you might not know they are there. If hosting swifts is not your cup of tea, check around your town or region for chimneys being used by swifts. Watch for them entering or leaving the large brick chimneys on schools and old factories. Modern chimneys with metal caps and flues are impossible for swifts to use.

Ruby-throated Hummingbird
Archilochus colubris

The only breeding hummingbird east of the Great Plains, the rubythroat enlivens many gardens and yards with its presence. Males are fiercely combative and will defend a single nectar source against all comers. Spectacular pendulum flights, constant chittering, the low hum of beating wings, and the occasional smack of tiny bodies colliding are familiar to anyone lucky enough to have rubythroats at their nectar feeders.

All About
Seen in direct sunlight, the male's ruby throat patch dazzles. Both male and female are iridescent green above. The female's underparts are white, and she sports white spots on her rounded tail. Males appear smaller and darker overall, with grayish-olive underparts and a slightly forked, all dark tail. A squeaky *chip* is uttered constantly while feeding. Males sing a seldom heard, monotonous song from exposed perches at daybreak.

Habitat & Range
Rubythroats prefer mixed deciduous woodlands with clearings, where wildflowers and abundant small insects can be found. They're fairly common in forested areas across the entire eastern United States, falling off abruptly at the Great Plains. Virtually all rubythroats leave for the winter, many making the arduous nonstop flight across the Gulf of Mexico on fat reserves alone. Rubythroats winter in Central America.

Feeding
Though they are usually regarded as wholly nectivorous, rubythroats take a great number of small insects, which they catch by gleaning or in aerial pursuit. They may even rob spider webs of their catch. They are strongly attracted to red or orange flowers, but rubythroats will take nectar from flowers of any color. They hover and probe rapidly, often perching to feed.

Nesting
Once a male rubythroat has mated, his investment in the offspring is over. The female constructs a walnut-sized, thick-walled cup of plant down and spider silk, bound tightly with elastic spider web and encrusted with lichens. This well-insulated nest protects the two lentil-sized eggs when she must leave to forage. The young hatch after about 13 days and remain in the nest for about 21 days. The female regurgitates small insects and nectar into their crops. They are fed for at least a week or longer after fledging.

Backyard & Beyond
Attract rubythroats with a 1:4 solution of table sugar (sucrose) and water. Wash feeders with hot soapy water every few days and replace the solution. Boiling the solution briefly helps it keep longer. Artificial coloring in the solution is unnecessary (feeders have ample red parts). To thwart a bullying male, hang several feeders within a few feet of each other. He'll be unable to defend them all.

Belted Kingfisher
Ceryle alcyon

The belted kingfisher is a bird many recognize but few know well. Kingfishers take wariness to new extremes, uttering a loud rattle of alarm and swooping off at the slightest disturbance. The belted kingfisher's piercing rattle call, usually given as it takes flight, is more often heard than this wary bird is seen. They are a thrilling presence on streams, rivers, lakes, and marshes—wherever clear water and small fish abound.

All About
Almost comical in proportion, the belted kingfisher has an oversized crested head and a heavy spearlike bill, but diminutive feet. It cannot walk, but only shuffle, and it relies entirely on flight for most of its locomotion. Slate-blue upperparts, a stark-white collar and underparts, and a bluish breast band complete the ensemble. The female wears a "bra"—another rufous breast band below the blue one.

Habitat & Range
Because it is a sight hunter, the belted kingfisher seeks out clear water. Most often found along clear running streams, lakes, and ponds, it will also hunt salt estuaries and marshes. Nesting requires an exposed earthen bank. Kingfishers are migratory in northern latitudes. Though they can survive winter temperatures, they require open water year-round; thus, southern birds may migrate only as far as they must to find open water.

Feeding
Most of its hunting is done from a perch, but the belted kingfisher also hunts on the wing. Suspended in midair like an angel, it hovers, seemingly weightless, over a riffle. Spotting a minnow, it closes its wings and plunges bill-first into the water. It carries the fish in its bill to a sturdy perch (usually a dead snag or partially submerged branch), where it subdues its prey by whacking its head against the perch with sideways flips of its bill. The fish is then swallowed head first. Belted kingfishers also take crayfish and (to a much lesser extent) amphibians, reptiles, small mammals, and young birds.

Nesting
Kingfishers occasionally are forced to commute, if they are unable to find a dry earthen bank near their chosen feeding territory. They may use sand and gravel pits, landfills, or road cuts. This species excavates, digging rapidly with tiny feet straight into the bank, creating a round entrance hole and an upward-sloping tunnel that may extend as much as six feet into the bank. A chamber at the end holds five to eight eggs, which both male and female incubate for about 22 days. Young stay in the burrow for up to 29 days and are fed by their parents for three more weeks.

Backyard & Beyond
Any clear body of water, including backyard ponds with plump goldfish, can host a hunting kingfisher.

Red-headed Woodpecker
Melanerpes erythrocephalus

A striking combination of red, black, and white, the red-headed woodpecker is our most easily identifiable woodpecker and a favorite of many bird watchers. Though the species was first described in 1758, Native Americans had long used skins of the red-headed woodpecker as a battle ornament. Sadly, the red-headed has suffered population declines throughout its range, but it remains locally common in the proper habitat.

All About
The red-headed woodpecker could be called the red-*hooded* woodpecker because the red on adult birds forms a complete hood. Some mistakenly refer to the red-bellied woodpecker (which has a Mohawk stripe of red) as a red-headed woodpecker. The red-head's black back and tail are set off by a bright white breast and belly and an all-white patch of secondary (inner) wing feathers. The effect of these contrasting colors is stunning in flight. Red-heads give a variety of *churr-churr* calls as well as a loud, throaty *Queeah!*

Habitat & Range
Prior to the 1900s, red-headed woodpeckers were common in cities and towns. Today, red-heads are sparingly distributed across most of the eastern United States, usually in woods with mature oaks or beeches, in isolated woodlots along rivers, or in dead trees along flooded river bottoms and beaver ponds. Habitats affected by humans—strip mines, clear cuts, tree plantations, and farmlands—may attract red-headed woodpeckers so long as there are scattered, standing trees.

Feeding
Red-heads have the most varied diet of all woodpeckers, but they seem especially attached to acorns and beechnuts. They are excellent flycatchers and are known to eat grasshoppers, fruits, corn, eggs, mice, and even bird nestlings. When nuts and insects are plentiful, red-heads will cache them for later consumption, hiding food items in bark crevices and knotholes. At bird feeders, red-heads eat sunflower seeds, peanuts, and suet, but they are particularly attracted to cracked corn.

Nesting
Avid excavators of nesting and roosting holes, red-heads thus provide homes for many other cavity-nesting creatures. Nest holes are almost always in dead trees or dead portions of living trees, though wooden telephone poles are also used. Five eggs are the normal clutch, and both parents share in the two-week incubation duties. Young birds spend three weeks in the nest cavity before fledging, and they emerge with gray, not red, heads.

Backyard & Beyond
Red-headed woodpeckers are very aggressive and can out-compete European starlings for nest cavities. Look for red-heads in large stands of trees (especially oaks) with little vegetation below them, as in a park or golf course. Reliable locations for seeing red-headed woodpeckers are becoming noteworthy as the species declines.

Red-bellied Woodpecker
Melanerpes carolinus

The red-bellied woodpecker is so common, vocal, and eye-catching that it might be elected "most familiar woodpecker" in a vote of bird watchers in the eastern United States. Although occasionally misidentified as a red-headed woodpecker because of the male redbelly's bill-to-nape stripe of bright red, the red-bellied woodpecker actually is quite different in appearance—and much more common—than the real red-headed woodpecker, which sports an all-red head.

All About

A medium-sized (9 1/4 inches long) woodpecker with a stout, chisel-shaped bill and a zebra pattern of black-and-white horizontal strips on the back, the red-bellied woodpecker is named for a feature we rarely see—a light wash of pink or red on its belly. Hitching up tree trunks with the aid of its strong feet and stiff tail, the bird's red belly is almost always obscured. Adult males have a solid strip of red from the top of the bill and head and down the back of the neck (the nape). Females have a red nape, but are brownish on the top of the head. The redbelly's loud, rich call sounds like *qurrrr*, and its longer version is more rattling and harsher—*chrr, chrr, chrchrchrchr*.

Habitat & Range

A year-round resident across the eastern United States, the redbelly is an adaptable bird, found wherever there are mature trees. They do not migrate, though some northern birds may move southward in winter.

Feeding

The redbelly is an expert at excavating insects from trees using its bill as a chisel and its long, barbed tongue to extract food items. It will also eat berries, fruits, nuts, tree sap, salamanders, mice, and even small nestling birds. At bird-feeding stations, redbellies relish peanuts, suet, sunflower seeds, and cracked corn.

Nesting

The male redbelly begins courtship by drumming (a rapid pounding with the bill) on a tree trunk or branch to attract the female's attention. Both male and female excavate the nest cavity, which is usually located in a dead tree below an overhanging branch. The 8- to 12-inch deep cavity will accommodate four eggs. Incubation duties are shared and last about 12 days. Nestlings are fed in the nest cavity by both parents for almost a month before they fledge; afterward, they remain near the nest and are fed by the parents for several more weeks. Nest hole competition from European starlings can be fierce and usually results in the redbellies being evicted and forced to excavate a new nest elsewhere.

Backyard & Beyond

Peanuts and suet are the redbelly's favored foods, but you can also offer apple halves stuck on a tree stub, sunflower bits, and grape jelly (in a small dish). Listen for the redbelly's loud, ringing calls and watch for its swooping flight.

Downy Woodpecker
Picoides pubescens

Downy woodpeckers are a favorite of backyard bird watchers because they are often the first woodpeckers to visit bird feeders. Common in any habitat with trees, downies are as equally at home in backyards as they are in remote woods. In all seasons, downy woodpeckers give a rattling whinny that descends in tone. They also utter a sharp pik! call regularly while foraging.

All About
The downy is the smallest ($6^{3/4}$ inches long), most common, and most widespread woodpecker. Its black-and-white plumage is similar to that of the larger ($9^{1/4}$ inches long) hairy woodpecker. In both species, the males have a red patch at the back of the head. Downy woodpeckers have an all-white breast and belly and a white stripe down the middle of the back. The wings and tail are black with spots of white.

Habitat & Range
A common resident of woodlands throughout North America, the downy is a habitat generalist—found anywhere there are trees or woody plants on which to find food. Though their population appears stable, downies suffer from nest site competition and from the removal of dead trees, which they need for nesting and feeding.

Feeding
Downy woodpeckers use their stiff tails and strong, clawed feet to propel themselves along tree branches or trunks. As they move along, downies probe and chisel at the tree's bark, searching for insects, insect eggs, ants, and spiders. They also eat fruits, such as sumac and poison ivy. At bird feeders, sunflower seeds and bits, suet, peanuts, and peanut butter are favorite foods.

Nesting
Like all woodpeckers, downies are cavity nesters. Each spring they excavate a new nest hole in the dead stub or trunk of a tree—usually one that is already rotting. The nest hole is placed underneath an overhanging branch higher than 12 feet above the ground. Excavation can take as long as two weeks—even with the male and female participating. Clutch size is usually four to five white eggs, with both sexes incubating. Hatching occurs at 12 days, and both parents feed the young for about three weeks until they fledge.

Backyard & Beyond
Telling the downy and hairy woodpecker apart can be difficult. A way to remember which is which is: *Downy is dinky; hairy is huge.* Downies have a small body, small head, and a small, thin bill. Hairies have a big body, a big head, and a large, chisellike bill. Though downies rarely nest in nest boxes, they readily use them for nighttime roosting, especially in harsh weather. Leave a dead tree or large dead branch on a tree in your yard (in a safe location), and you will be much more likely to attract woodpeckers.

Hairy Woodpecker
Picoides villosus

A *familiar visitor to bird feeders, the hairy woodpecker is named for the long, hairlike white feathers on its back. The hairy looks like a super-sized version of a downy woodpecker, but the best way to tell these two similar species apart is to compare the length of the bill to the length (front-to-back) of the head. The hairy's bill is always longer than the width of its head, and the downy's bill is always shorter than the length of its head. An easier way to remember is: Downy is dinky; hairy is huge.*

All About
Hairy woodpeckers are medium-sized woodpeckers ($9^{1}/_{4}$ inches long) with a long, sturdy, chisel-like bill that is used for finding food, for excavating nest holes, and for territorial drumming on hollow trees. Males and females look the same with white bellies, a white central back stripe, and distinctly patterned black and white on faces and wings. Adult males, however, have a red patch at the back of the head. Hairies utter a sharp *Peek!* call, as well as a loud ringing rattle on a single pitch.

Habitat & Range
Hairy woodpeckers are year-round residents across North America in mature forests and wherever there are large trees, including suburban backyards, urban parks, and isolated woodlots. They are one of our most widespread woodpeckers with a range extending into Central America.

Feeding
Using their bill, hairy woodpeckers can glean insects from tree bark or excavate them from beneath the bark's surface. Primary diet items include beetles, spiders, moth larvae, and ants, as well as fruits, seeds, and nuts. At bird feeders, hairies readily eat sunflower seeds, peanuts, suet, and cracked corn.

Nesting
It can take up to three weeks for a pair of hairy woodpeckers to excavate their nest cavity in the trunk or dead branch of a living tree. When completed, the nest cavity will have a 2-inch entry hole and will be 4 inches wide and as deep as 16 inches. Into this cozy space, four eggs are laid, and both parents share the roughly two-week incubation period. Less than a month after hatching, young hairies are ready to fledge from the nest, though the parents tend them for several more weeks. A new nest is excavated each spring, but old cavities are used for roosting at night and in winter.

Backyard & Beyond
If your neighborhood has large shade trees or mature woods, chances are good that you've got hairy woodpeckers nearby. Check large, dead snags and branches for woodpecker holes and listen for the birds' vocalizations and drumming in spring. Offer peanuts, sunflower seeds, or suet (in winter) in hanging feeders to attract hairy woodpeckers to your yard.

Northern Flicker
Colaptes auratus

A familiar and fairly large (13 inches long) woodpecker, the northern flicker is a distinctively marked bird that—unlike other woodpeckers—is often seen foraging on the ground. The eastern form of the flicker is known as the yellow-shafted flicker for its bright lemon-yellow underwing and tail color. A red-shafted form of the northern flicker occurs in the West. There are more than 130 different names by which the flicker is known, including high-hole, yellowhammer, and yawkerbird.

All About
The northern flicker is all field marks with its bright yellow wing flashes, white rump, spotted breast, and barred back. It is not easily confused with any other bird. In the East, both sexes have a red crescent on the back of the head, but only males show a black "moustache" mark on the cheek. The flicker has several calls including a single note *kleer*, a short *wickawicka* series, and a monotonous *wickwickwickwick* song. It also communicates by drumming on the resonating surface of a tree, pole, or even metal downspouts and chimney flues.

Habitat & Range
Widespread across North America, the northern flicker is found almost everywhere wooded habitats exist, though open woods and woodland edges are preferred. Flickers in the northern portion of the range migrate southward in winter, while southern birds are nonmigratory.

Feeding
Flickers feed on the ground where they specialize in eating ants. A flicker pokes its long bill into an anthill and uses its long, sticky tongue to extract the ants. They also eat other insects, as well as fruits and seeds. At bird feeders, they will eat suet, peanuts, fruits, and sunflower bits.

Nesting
Excavating a new nest cavity almost every year, flickers perform a much-needed service for many other hole-nesting birds—from chickadees to ducks—that use old flicker nests. Both sexes excavate the nest cavity in a dead tree or branch. The female lays between 5 and 10 eggs; both sexes share the 11-day incubation period. Young flickers leave the nest after about 25 days. Flickers will use nest boxes with an interior floor of 7×7 inches, an interior height of 16 to 24 inches, and a 2½-inch entry hole. Because excavation is a vital part of courtship, boxes packed full of woodchips are more attractive. Competition for cavities from European starlings is fierce and may be causing a decline in flickers.

Backyard & Beyond
Offering suet, corn, or peanuts and nest boxes in your wooded backyard is one way to attract flickers. Equally important is the presence of ground-dwelling insects (leave those non-threatening anthills alone!) and dead trees or dead branches. A large, dead tree branch placed vertically in your yard may entice a flicker to stop.

Pileated Woodpecker
Dryocopus pileatus

People who have never had a good close look at a pileated woodpecker invariably utter an exclamation when they finally see one. This is a magnificent, flashy, loud, but shy bird—the largest living woodpecker in North America. Its name is Latin for "capped," a reference to its crest. The pileated and its crazy laugh was the inspiration for Woody Woodpecker, but there the similarity ends.

All About
Both male and female pileated woodpeckers sport a red crest; the female's forehead is brownish and the male's is scarlet. A dull, dark charcoal-gray overall, pileateds reveal a large amount of white in the underwing when they take flight. Seen crossing high over a road, their wingbeats are slow and steady, the wings seeming to close between each beat. The call is a high, wild *yik-yik-yik-yik-yik*, suggesting a flicker, but not as monotonous. The pileated's hollow, sonorous drum roll fades away as it finishes.

Habitat & Range
Such a large bird needs large diameter trees because it roosts and nests in cavities that it excavates with its chisellike bill. Older-growth forests with standing dead trees, usually in bottomland or near watercourses, are preferred. In autumn, wandering pileateds may show up unexpectedly along roadsides and in yards, feasting on sumac, firethorn, dogwood, viburnum, or other fruits. Pileateds are resident throughout their range.

Feeding
Loud, chopping blows herald the presence of a feeding pileated woodpecker. They sometimes sound not so much like a woodpecker as a strong person wielding an axe. Palm-sized pieces of bark and punky (soft and rotted) wood fly as the bird strips bark or excavates to reach the ant galleries and beetle larvae it needs. It is a surprisingly agile fruit plucker, clinging like an overgrown chickadee as it eats small fruits. Pileateds also glean bark and branches for insect prey.

Nesting
Pileated pairs stay together year-round and presumably mate for life. Male pileated woodpeckers do most of the nest cavity excavation. The female lays four eggs, and both she and her mate incubate them; they hatch after about 16 days. Young remain in the cavity for up to 30 days, after which they have a long apprenticeship of learning to procure food with their parents.

Backyard & Beyond
People with heavily wooded yards are sometimes successful in attracting pileateds to raw suet or peanut butter suet mixtures offered in sturdy cages affixed to the trunk of a large tree. Having such an impressive bird in one's yard is an event; successfully feeding one is well worth the extra effort. These birds occupy the same territories throughout their lives, so it could be the start of a long relationship.

Eastern Wood-Pewee
Contopus virens

PeeUWEEE? *and* PWEE-eehr *are plaintive sounds familiar to many forest hikers, bikers, and birders. Eastern wood-pewees call their name time after time, but it often takes a little effort to see them—unless you happen to be standing under a branch from which one flaps out, snaps up an insect, and then returns to the same spot.*

All About
Compared with smaller *Empidonax* flycatchers, the eastern wood-pewee is more sturdy, longer-tailed, and longer-winged. It is also generally grayer in appearance, with gray washed across its entire breast (the Acadian flycatcher is mostly whitish below). The wood-pewee lacks the prominent eye ring present in the Acadian and some other *Empidonax* species. Unlike the eastern phoebe, the eastern wood-pewee has two prominent wing bars and a two-toned black-and-orange (not all-black) bill, and it does not pump its tail. It usually feeds higher up than the phoebe, sallying forth from bare branches to grab its prey.

Habitat & Range
Common nesters across the forested eastern United States and southeastern Canada, eastern wood-pewees reach their southern breeding limits from northern Florida west to central Texas. They nest in deciduous forests and mixed deciduous and coniferous forests; they are often active at the forest edge and in clearings.

Feeding
Eastern wood-pewees pick their insect prey from leaves while hovering, but they are most noticeable when they sally forth from an exposed perch to capture flying insects (often the snap of bill meeting bug is audible). After the capture, they often return to the same perch to repeat the entire process—after ingesting their latest meal. They are most active and most vocal early and late in the day.

Nesting
Eastern wood-pewee nests are shallow cups made of weeds, grasses, bark, and other materials; they are placed on tree branches above or well above head level. On the outside, the nest is often festooned with lichens; inside, it is lined with such soft materials as plant fluff, hair, and fine grasses. There, the female usually lays three eggs. She incubates the eggs for just under two weeks. Both the male and the female feed the young, which leave the nest about two weeks after hatching.

Backyard & Beyond
In many areas, eastern wood-pewees are common migrants. It pays to learn this bird's field marks rather than just memorizing its song because wood-pewees don't usually sing while migrating to or from their South American wintering grounds. By "planting" snags—dead trees or large dead tree limbs—in your garden, you can provide hunting perches for migrating wood-pewees and other flycatchers.

Acadian Flycatcher
Empidonax virescens

Most Acadian flycatchers nest south of the Mason-Dixon Line. They are, along with eastern wood-pewees, eastern phoebes, and great crested flycatchers, the most common and frequently heard woodland flycatchers of the humid Southeast. Where widespread forest clearance occurs, however, their populations usually decline, with populations only remaining in larger, less disturbed woodlands.

All About
Song is often an important clue in identifying the little gray and greenish flycatchers. In the South, the Acadian is the only one that nests outside of the Appalachians and the rolling Piedmont surrounding them. (Willow, least flycatchers, and alder flycatchers provide ample identification challenges in these areas.) From spring into midsummer, the Acadian flycatcher belts out its distinctive and loud *spit-ZEEP!* song, often from a partially hidden tree branch beneath the forest canopy. During migration, all five eastern *Empidonax* flycatchers may occur in one area. (See the profiles for eastern wood-pewee and eastern phoebe.) The Acadian and its *Empidonax* brethren (except willow) have bold or fairly bold, whitish eye rings. The Acadian has a greenish gray back and head, two bold white wing bars, and a mostly orange bill. It is mostly whitish underneath, with a faint olive wash on the breast.

Habitat & Range
Humid bottomland woodlands with ample shady undergrowth of young trees provide the ideal habitat. These birds also nest in other deciduous forests with young trees under the canopy, and they winter in the tropics in woodlands as well. Nesting occurs primarily in the South, into east Texas and east to central Florida. These birds winter from Central America to northern South America.

Feeding
Most of the Acadian flycatcher's varied insect prey is taken on the wing, either during quick flights from a regular perch or while hovering near leaves. Prey includes caterpillars, bees, wasps, beetles, and flies, but other small invertebrates (such as spiders) are eaten, as well.

Nesting
Acadian flycatchers often fasten their nests to forks of thin branches, usually well above head level. The female fashions the cup-shaped nest from twigs, plant stems, vines, grasses, and other materials, many of which raggedly hang from the nest bottom. Usually, the female lays three eggs, which she incubates for about two weeks. Both parents feed the nestlings, which leave the nest at about two weeks of age.

Backyard & Beyond
During migration, Acadian and other *Empidonax* flycatchers often use snags from which to hunt. Provide snags by "planting" large dead tree limbs or small dead trees in your garden.

Eastern Phoebe
Sayornis phoebe

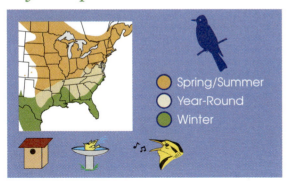

A very adaptable flycatcher, the eastern phoebe often nests on human structures, such as on building ledges, inside barns, under bridges, and in culverts. Nesting in such proximity to humans, phoebes are used to our activity and this apparent tameness allows us to think of them as "our phoebes." Many bird watchers consider the early spring return of the phoebe (and not the American robin) to be the most reliable sign of spring's arrival.

All About
The eastern phoebe, unlike most other flycatchers, is relatively easy to identify. A medium-sized bird that constantly wags its tail, the phoebe also gives a vocal clue to its identity by softly uttering its name—*fee-bee*. Phoebes are a dark, drab gray-brown on the back, with faint wing bars and a light breast and belly, often washed with yellow.

Habitat & Range
Wherever there is a suitable nesting ledge (with abundant flying insects nearby), phoebes may be found. Natural habitats include woodland edges and small streams. Common throughout most of eastern North America during the spring and summer (eastern phoebes breed far into northern Canada), in winter many phoebes migrate to the southern Atlantic Coast and along the Gulf Coast into Mexico.

Feeding
The eastern phoebe is a perch-and-wait hunter, watching for flying insects from an exposed perch and making short flying forays to nab its prey. Phoebes consume vast quantities of flying insects, but will also pluck food items from the ground or vegetation. Wasps, bees, flying ants, moths, and butterflies constitute much of their prey. In fall and winter, when insects are scarce, phoebes will eat small fruits and berries.

Nesting
Phoebes are early nesters throughout the breeding range, and nest building often begins almost immediately after a male attracts a mate to a likely site. Favored natural nest sites include rock ledges and caves, but they also nest in barns or outbuildings, and on handy ledges or sills on house porches. The female builds the cup-shaped nest out of mud, moss, and grass. Four to six eggs are laid and incubated by the female alone, for just over two weeks. Young phoebes, unless disturbed earlier, fledge after about 16 days.

Backyard & Beyond
Bird watchers love phoebes not only because they are common, but also because they are so full of energy and seem willing to make their nests in close proximity to humans. To attract phoebes to your property, place nesting shelves (about 6×8 inches in size) about a foot below the eaves of your house, garage, or outbuilding. Choose a site that is away from human activity and is as safe as possible from predators, such as snakes, raccoons, and cats.

Great Crested Flycatcher
Myiarchus crinitus

Although one of the largest and most common eastern flycatchers, the great crested is raucous enough that it is usually heard before it is seen. A loud, enthusiastic *wheeep!* or *whit-whit-whit-whit* call is most often heard in woodland clearings during the summer months. The great crested is unusual among eastern flycatchers in that it is a cavity nester, relying on old woodpecker holes, hollow trees, and even birdhouses for nest sites. Adding to this bird's preference for the unusual is its habit of using shed snakeskin in its nest construction.

All About
One of our larger flycatchers at 8 1/2 inches tall, the great crested is a pleasing blend of colors with a lemon belly and underwings and a rufous tail, set off by a gray head and olive back. Males and females are alike in appearance, and both will aggressively defend their nesting territory against trespassing birds of almost any species.

Habitat & Range
Great crested flycatchers can be found in open woodlands, forest clearings, and even in wooded city parks throughout eastern North America during the summer months. Winter finds most of them in southern Mexico and southward to South America, though some spend the winter in south Florida. Fall migration starts in late August, with spring migrants returning to the Gulf Coast by late March.

Feeding
Capturing flying insects is the great crested's main foraging mode, but it will also glean insects from vegetation and supplement its diet with small berries and fruits. Butterflies, moths, beetles, and grasshoppers are its most common foods. Great cresteds usually forage high in the treetops or from a high, exposed perch.

Nesting
A cavity nester that cannot excavate its own nest hole, it must rely on finding old woodpecker holes, naturally occurring hollows in trees, or human-supplied nest boxes. After inspecting possible nest sites with her mate, the female begins nest building using an incredible array of material, including animal hair, feathers, pine needles, string, cellophane, and shed snakeskin. Why great cresteds use such a variety of materials is a mystery. Five or more eggs are laid and incubated by the female for about two weeks. Two weeks after hatching, young flycatchers leave the nest.

Backyard & Beyond
Any backyard with large shade trees and adjacent woodland in the eastern United States has the potential to attract nesting great crested flycatchers. To encourage them, leave standing any dead or hollow trees, especially ones with knotholes or existing woodpecker holes. Nest box dimensions should be: interior floor of 6×6 inches, inside height of 12 inches, entry hole of 1 3/4 to 2 inches. Mount at a height of 10 to 20 inches.

Eastern Kingbird
Tyrannus tyrannus

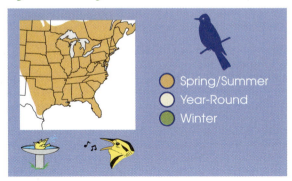

- Spring/Summer
- Year-Round
- Winter

High in the treetops a medium-sized, black-and-white bird flutters out to catch flying insects and aggressively attacks other birds in flight, all the while emitting a sputtery series of sharp notes that sound like the zapping of an electric current. This is the eastern kingbird, whose Latin name translates into "tyrant of tyrants," the most common kingbird found in the East.

All About
The eastern kingbird is an excellent flier, able to catch flying insects and aggressively defend its breeding territory with its aerial mastery. Both sexes are blackish above and white below. The female's chest is grayish. Male kingbirds have a small, red-orange patch of feathers on the crown, though this is rarely seen. A thin, white band on the tail margin clinches the identification.

Habitat & Range
Spending the breeding season in open areas with scattered trees, eastern kingbirds prefer locations near water, probably for the bounty of insects. Fairly common in agricultural areas, pastures, city parks, and suburban neighborhoods with large trees and open understory during summer, most eastern kingbirds migrate to Central and South America in winter. In migration, the kingbird travels in loose flocks, and it is not uncommon to see a dozen or more birds in one tree in spring or fall.

Feeding
The eastern kingbird, or beebird, is an insect eater, specializing in bees, wasps, moths, butterflies, and other large, flying insects. Sit-and-watch hunters, kingbirds find an exposed perch and wait for something edible to fly past. They then sally forth and grab the prey in their bill, returning to the perch to stun and eat the insect. Kingbirds also eat fruits at all seasons, including mulberries, cherries, and elderberries. Fruits make up the bulk of their winter diet in the tropics.

Nesting
The kingbird's nest is placed high in a tree and is a large, loosely woven cup of bark, twigs, and weed stems. Females do all of the nest building and incubation. A typical clutch is two to five eggs with a 15-day incubation period. Hatchling kingbirds spend about 16 days in the nest before fledging, after which they are attended to by both parents for several more weeks.

Backyard & Beyond
Kingbirds can often be seen perching high in a tree or along fences or power lines, hunting for insects. They are very active in their territories in summer, so watch for their fluttery flycatching flights and listen for their loud zapping calls. The old myth that eastern kingbirds prey primarily on honeybees resulted in many of these birds being shot. Studies have now shown that kingbirds eat relatively few honeybees, mostly drones.

Loggerhead Shrike

Lanius ludovicianus

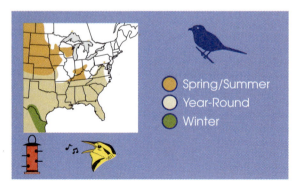

"Loggerhead" refers to this bird's large-headed appearance, but what really sets the loggerhead shrike apart is its hawklike feeding behavior. Its Latin name Lanius means "butcher," a reference to its habit of impaling prey on thorns or barbed wire to aid in carving them up. Look for signs of their presence by checking barbed-wire fencing for impaled insects, toads, or other prey items.

All About

With just a quick glance at a loggerhead shrike, you might mistake it for a mockingbird, as both birds are a blend of gray, black, and white. A closer look reveals the shrike's flesh-tearing bill (shaped like a falcon's bill), black mask, and its overall big-headed appearance and compact shape—quite different from the lanky mockingbird. In flight, loggerhead shrikes flash white wing and tail spots. Its song is a rich, burry warble, underscoring its standing as our only truly predatory songbird.

Habitat & Range

The loggerhead shrike is much more common in the southern portions of its range, where it is a year-round resident. In the Northeast, this bird has vanished as a breeder due to reforestation, competition from other birds, and the effects of pesticides. Loggerhead shrikes prefer open country, such as pastures and grasslands with short grass and scattered, thorny trees or fencerows with barbed wire. They perch—body horizontal—in the open on wires and fences.

Feeding

Grasshoppers are the loggerhead's primary prey, but small amphibians, reptiles, mammals, and birds are also taken. Lacking the strong talons of a hawk, the shrike carries prey items to a convenient thorny perch, where it impales its victim. This holds the food item in place, allowing the shrike to tear it apart with its sharp, toothed bill—hence the common name "butcherbird." When prey is abundant, the shrike will impale prey for later consumption. One such "larder" in North Carolina held 15 small snakes on a single, thorny bush.

Nesting

The female shrike builds the nest in a tree or thorny shrub from materials collected by the mated pair. The cup-shaped nest is woven from bark strips, twigs, and plant stems and is lined with soft animal fur, feathers, or grass. About five eggs are laid, and the female alone handles the 16-day incubation period, though her mate brings her food. Young loggerhead shrikes remain in the nest for up to 20 days, and then remain in the nest area for about a week after fledging.

Backyard & Beyond

In the Deep South, loggerhead shrikes can be found in almost any open habitat, including city parks, golf courses, and along mowed roadsides. But across most of their range, they are most commonly seen in open pasturelands.

Red-eyed Vireo
Vireo olivaceus

Easy to hear and hard to see, the red-eyed vireo is one of the most numerous summer birds of the eastern American woodlands. It arrives in April or early May from its South American wintering grounds, and its song rings out from every wooded tract. Foraging high in the emerging leaves, the vireo sings almost endlessly—one patient listener counted 22,197 songs from the same bird in one summer day!

All About
The red-eyed vireo is about 6 inches long—an olive-backed, white-bellied bird with a gray cap and bold white stripe over its bright red eyes. Males and females are similar. They have sharp, slightly hooked bills designed to catch insect prey. Despite their small size, they are strong fliers; their twice-yearly migration carries them to the Amazon and back. Red-eyeds, like all vireos, are more deliberate in their movements than warblers.

Habitat & Range
Red-eyes are usually found in open deciduous or mixed woodlands with a strong understory of sapling trees. They sometimes occur in large city parks, orchards, or even wooded suburban backyards.

Feeding
Like many small neotropical migrants, the red-eyed vireo feeds mostly on insects. It gleans its food from the upper story of tall deciduous trees, singing as it moves slowly along the branches, peering under and around the leaves. Occasionally, it hovers to snatch a bug from an otherwise unreachable surface. In late summer, the red-eyed vireo will supplement its diet with berries of many kinds.

Nesting
The female selects a suitable site, usually 5 to 10 feet off the ground on a horizontal forked twig. She builds a tightly woven nest of fine grasses and strips of grapevine, suspending it below the fork and decorating it with bits of lichen on its outer surfaces. Here she incubates her four eggs for 11 to 14 days. Both parents feed the nestlings for 10 to 12 days until they are ready to fledge. Red-eyed vireos are frequent victims of cowbirds and only rarely do they fight back by building a floor over the cowbird egg and laying another clutch. Most of the time they simply accept the cowbird chick, to the detriment of their own.

Backyard & Beyond
The best way to find a red-eyed vireo is to learn its song, then listen for it in the spring and summer woods. It is sometimes written as *Here I am, look at me, over here, here I am* sung over and over in a clear sweet voice, usually from high in a tree. Finding the singer will take some persistence and a good pair of binoculars. In fall, silent red-eyed vireos may be spotted in hedgerows and tangles, looking for berries.

White-eyed Vireo
Vireo griseus

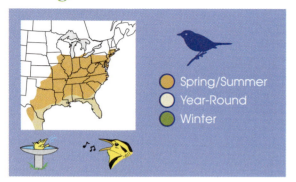

On a field guide page, the white-eyed vireo resembles other vireo species. In real life, however, this bird's voice, habitat, and perky habits set it apart from the rest of the pack. While red-eyed, yellow-throated, and warbling vireos winter in the tropics, many white-eyed vireos tough it out from southern Georgia across the edge of the Gulf of Mexico. In early spring, white-eyed vireos are usually the first of the vireos to return to their nesting grounds.

All About
The white-eyed vireo may at first appear nondescript, but this bird has field marks that will quickly set you on the path to its identification: the yellow that curls around the eye like spectacles, the white eye, and the yellow sides and flanks. Its head is mostly gray with whitish coloring on the throat, and you'll see two white wing bars on its darkish wings. The white eye is a useful field mark in adults, but immatures have dark eyes. You can easily coax a white-eyed vireo out of dense cover by making *spishing* noises or by waiting patiently to spot the bird as it sings its distinctive *Per-chick-a-WOW-chick!* song again and again.

Habitat & Range
The brushy edges of forests and waterways, along with old fields turning to young forest, are the domain of this common and very perky eastern songster. You will also find it in the brambly underbrush within open forests. In the Deep South, white-eyed vireos are present all year-round. Over much of the more northerly breeding range, birds retreat to the South and into the tropics for the winter.

Feeding
On their breeding grounds, white-eyed vireos eat insects, including butterflies, caterpillars, beetles, and many others. While migrating and wintering, they also eat berries.

Nesting
True to their habits and habitat, white-eyed vireos usually nest in shrubs or young trees, often not very high off the ground. Both male and female build the hanging cup nest, which is made of stems, bark, twigs, and other plant matter. The female usually lays three or four eggs. Both parents incubate the eggs for about two weeks, and young usually leave the nest before their twelfth day after hatching.

Backyard & Beyond
White-eyed vireos do pass through backyards during migration, and they often sing in spring while migrating. They are not, however, as likely to be found moving through suburbs as their red-eyed relatives. To be sure of a good look nearby, head to your favorite local park and seek out the more overgrown brushy corners. In the backyard, they will most likely turn up in dense shrubs, brambles, or young, leafy trees.

Blue Jay
Cyanocitta cristata

Blue jays are smart, adaptable, and noisy birds. They will often mimic the call of a red-tailed or red-shouldered hawk as they approach a bird feeder, in an apparent attempt to scare other birds away from the food. Sometimes persecuted by humans as nest robbers or bullies at the feeding station, blue jays are one of our most ornate and lovely birds. Bird watchers visiting the United States from abroad are astounded that such a beautiful bird is common in our suburban backyards.

All About
No other eastern bird is blue and crested, making the blue jay almost unmistakable. Males and females are similar. Besides the standard *jay jay* or *jeer jeer* call often used as a scold, blue jays also emit a variety of squeaks, rattles, and croaks, in addition to mimicking other birds' calls. If you hear a sound in the woods that is loud and unmusical, chances are good that it's coming from a blue jay.

Habitat & Range
Blue jays are common in wooded habitats, especially those with oaks. Indeed the blue jay has a special relationship with oaks, burying as many as five thousand acorns in fall caches for future consumption. Many of these acorns are never retrieved, so jays are credited with helping with forest generation. Resident throughout their range, especially in the Deep South, blue jays in northern latitudes migrate southward in early fall, traveling by daylight in flocks of 10 or more birds, many carrying acorns in their bills.

Feeding
Blue jays will eat almost anything. Grasshoppers and other insects, and acorns and other nuts are their primary foods. Bird eggs or nestlings, mice, frogs, and a variety of human-supplied foods are also eaten. When storing acorns, blue jays will carry as many as five acorns in the throat and bill to the cache site, drop them in a pile, and bury them one at a time. They will return to recover only some of these acorns.

Nesting
Males help gather nesting materials, but females do most of the building in a tree. The twig nest is woven into a cup and lined with wet leaves and rootlets. Suburban blue jays often incorporate string, plastics, and paper (human trash) into nests. The female lays four to six eggs and incubates them for 18 days, followed by about 20 days of nestling care before the young jays fledge.

Backyard & Beyond
A common feeder visitor, blue jays are attracted to suet, peanuts, sunflower seeds, and even dog food. A source of water is highly attractive to blue jays, too. Look for blue jays along woodland edges and listen for their raucous cries, almost always the first clue to their presence.

American Crow
Corvus brachyrhynchos

Noisy, sly, opportunistic, and ubiquitous, the American crow lives among us; yet, comparatively little is known about it. Like other bold, brash corvids (the blue jay being a prime example), the crow is downright sneaky where its personal life is concerned. Few people know that crows may breed cooperatively in groups of up to a dozen birds, helping tend the dominant pair's nest.

All About
An unrelieved glossy black from bill to toenail, crows are armed with a stout, strong bill that acts as a chisel, axe, shovel, or forceps, among other uses. Its distinctive wingbeats appear to row the bird through the sky. Crows are well known for their raucous *caw*. Evidence suggests that crows have different "words" for different situations (assembly, dispersal, mobbing); their language is complex, as is their social behavior. Few people are privileged to hear the crow's song, given by both sexes, which is a long recitation of rattles, coos, growls, and imitations of sounds.

Habitat & Range
Though they are strongly associated with agricultural areas, crows find perfect conditions in cities and suburbs, where they raid pet dishes, bird feeders, and garbage cans. In the northern part of their range, crows are migratory, but all spend the winter within the continental United States. Throughout their range, crows use communal roosts when not breeding, and these can swell to massive proportions by late winter.

Feeding
There's almost nothing edible an American crow will not eat. At roadkills, landfills, and compost piles, crows will load their distensible throat with food and fly heavily off, often caching it under leaves or sod for later enjoyment. Crows forage by walking slowly on the ground—hunting invertebrates and vertebrates alike—and are constantly scanning roadsides and fields as they fly, descending to investigate anything that might be edible.

Nesting
Crows stay in family units composed of a pair and their young from the previous year. These yearlings may help build the nest, incubate, or feed the incubating female or her young. Four or five eggs are laid in the bulky twig nest, which is usually hidden high in a pine. The female incubates for around 17 days, and young fledge at around 36 days of age. Their strangled, nasal calls sometimes betray the nest location.

Backyard & Beyond
Crows are always up to something, and feeding them gives us an opportunity to observe their always-intriguing behavior. To find something a crow might like, open the refrigerator. Freezer-burned meat is a favorite. Cracked or whole corn is irresistible as well. Neighbors may wonder, but crows are well worth watching.

Purple Martin
Progne subis

No other North American bird has a closer association with humans than the purple martin. For more than four hundred years, martins in eastern North America have nested in human-supplied housing, at first in hollow gourds offered by Native Americans and today in a variety of specialized housing. Generations of people and martins have grown up together. Even non-bird watchers can appreciate this friendly and familiar bird.

All About
Our largest swallow (at 8 inches), the purple martin is a graceful flyer with a bubbly, liquid song. The adult male has a deep blue body and black wings and tail. Females and youngsters are gray and black with some blue on the back. In flight, martins can be confused with European starlings, but martins have a notched tail and call out almost constantly.

Habitat & Range
Purple martins breed across eastern North America, except for the extreme north. They spend winters in South America but return to the southern United States in mid-January, their arrival eagerly anticipated by their human landlords. Because of their reliance on human-supplied housing, most martins are found around cities, towns, and settlements.

Feeding
Martins eat flying insects almost exclusively, but—contrary to popular opinion and marketing hype—martins do not eat many mosquitoes. Instead, their diet includes larger flying insects, such as beetles, flies, dragonflies, wasps, butterflies, and moths. In cold, rainy weather, martin landlords often resort to feeding them mealworms and bits of scrambled egg in an effort to keep their beloved birds alive. Some landlords even shoot mealworms into the air with a slingshot just so the martins can catch their food.

Nesting
Martins are rather selective in choosing colony nest sites, but one thing is certain: They like to be with other martins. Research has revealed that they prefer white housing with a large (8×8×8-inch) interior and an 1½-inch entry hole. The housing should be mounted near a human dwelling in an open area. Martins build a loose cup nest inside the cavity out of pine needles and grass, lined with green leaves (which limit parasites). The female lays four to six eggs and does most of the incubation, lasting about 16 days. Both parents feed the nestlings for the month-long period before fledging.

Backyard & Beyond
The most successful martin landlords are those willing to put in the extra effort to care for their tenants with predator-proof housing, elimination of competing house sparrows and starlings, and regular monitoring. Your chances of attracting martins are greatly enhanced if there is an existing colony within a mile of you.

Northern Rough-winged Swallow
Stelgidopteryx serripennis

For such a common species, the northern rough-winged swallow is not well known. In farm country it is often overlooked among the barn swallows, while anyone encountering it at a nesting site may be tempted to call it a bank swallow. Its rather nondescript plumage only adds to the confusion. But this little bird has characteristics all its own, and a very distinct personality that makes it worth knowing.

All About
Only 5 to 5 1/2 inches long, the northern rough-winged swallow is brown-backed with dirty-white underparts, a short notched tail, and narrow pointed wings. The rough-winged swallow lacks the distinct dark breast band of the bank swallow. Its legs are short, and its feet adapted more for perching than for walking. The rough-winged swallow is not very vocal at any time, but it does utter short, harsh *zeep* sounds in flight. The small serrations on its outer wing feathers, for which the species is named, produce fluttery noises during courtship displays.

Habitat & Range
Like all swallows, the rough-winged is a bird of open country. It may be found from sea level to 6,000 feet or more, and it is often (though not always) found near some kind of water. In all except the southernmost parts of the country, these are seasonal birds, arriving in early spring and departing by mid- to late fall.

Feeding
Its diet consists almost entirely of flying insects that are snatched in midair. Like other birds that catch their prey in flight, rough-winged swallows have wide gaping mouths to maximize their chances for success. Flies, wasps, winged ants, moths, and damselflies are favored items. They drink on the wing, barely breaking the surface of the water in a lake or pond to satisfy their thirst without wetting their wings.

Nesting
Rough-winged swallows breed in sandbanks or other vertical sites, such as road cuts or soft cliffs. Using their feet, they excavate a deep (up to six feet) burrow. Two or three pairs may nest in proximity, but this species does not breed in large colonies like the bank swallow. The pair constructs a twiggy nest at the end of the burrow. Five to seven eggs are laid, and incubation by the female takes 12 to 16 days. Both parents feed the nestlings, which leave the nest at about 20 days of age.

Backyard & Beyond
Look for rough-winged swallows in spring going into gravel banks or sandy road cuts, or near small bridges where they may nest in drainpipes. In late summer, they often perch with other swallows on roadside wires, and a careful observer can distinguish them clearly by their buffy, unbanded breast.

Barn Swallow
Hirundo rustica

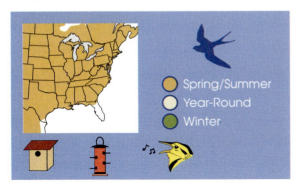

One early naturalist estimated that a barn swallow that lived 10 years would fly more than two million miles, enough to travel 87 times around the earth. This species seems to define what it means to be at home in the air, and it has been compared to an albatross in its ability to stay effortlessly aloft. One of the most familiar and beloved birds in rural America, the barn swallow is welcomed everywhere as a sign of spring.

All About
Glossy blue-black above and orange below, the barn swallow is the only American swallow that has a true "swallow tail," with an elongated outer pair of tail feathers. Males and females are similar, but females are not quite as glossy or highly colored, and the fork in their tails is not quite as pronounced. Like all swallows, they have short legs and rather weak feet used for perching, not walking.

Habitat & Range
A bird of rural areas and farmlands, the barn swallow may be found over any open area, such as pastures, fields, and golf courses, as well as lakes, ponds, and rivers. It has adapted well to humans and is not shy of people, nesting close to settled areas as long as it has open space for feeding. Barn swallows travel in great flocks during migrations, often in company with other swallow species. They arrive in most of their U.S. range in April and leave in early to midfall.

Feeding
Foraging almost entirely on the wing, the barn swallow takes a variety of insect prey from flies and locusts to moths, grasshoppers, bees, and wasps. Occasionally small berries or seeds are added to the diet, but this is uncommon. Only in bad weather will barn swallows feed on the ground.

Nesting
Nothing says "country" more than a pair of barn swallows zipping in and out of the open doors of a working barn, darting after insects and chattering incessantly. Sometimes two or three pairs will share a favored site. The nest itself is a cup of mud and grass, lined with feathers and placed on a rafter or glued under an eave. Besides barns, barn swallows may use other open buildings, covered porches, or the undersides of bridges or docks. During second nestings, immatures from the first brood help feed and care for their younger siblings.

Backyard & Beyond
During breeding season, you may bring barn swallows into close range by throwing feathers into the air near a flock of soaring birds; the graceful fliers will swoop in to snatch them up for nest linings. Barn swallows also enjoy eating bits of baked eggshells (crumble them first) during breeding season.

Tufted Titmouse
Baeolophus bicolor

From deep mixed woods to old orchards, from city parks to leafy suburban backyards, this friendly and active little bird makes itself at home throughout the year. It is noisy and sociable, quite tame in human company, and fearless among other small birds with which it associates. Its cheerful calls of peter, peter, peter ring out even in midwinter, chasing away the January blahs.

All About
The tufted titmouse is 6½ inches long and dressed primly across its upperparts in gray, with a creamy breast and rusty flanks. A black-button eye stands out against its white cheek, and a crest adorns its head. Its small, sharp bill is black, as are its legs and feet. Titmice are very vocal and, besides their signature *peter* calls, they have a variety of whistled notes—similar to those of the cardinal and Carolina wren. Their harsh, raspy, scolding notes are similar to the chickadee's.

Habitat & Range
The tufted titmouse was originally considered a southern woodland bird, but for the past 50 years it has been expanding its range northward. The species' affinity for bird feeders and nesting boxes has played a part in this expansion. Titmice are nonmigratory and able to survive harsh weather if sufficient food is available.

Feeding
Tufted titmice eat mostly insects and seeds, depending on time of year. Caterpillars are a popular item in summer, but they also take wasps and bees, scale insects, beetles, the larvae of many species, and, in winter, insect eggs. Acorns are a mainstay in fall and winter. At feeders, titmice relish sunflower seeds, suet, suet dough, and peanuts.

Nesting
The natural nesting choice of the tufted titmouse is a tree cavity—an abandoned woodpecker hole, or crack caused by a lightning strike. Other sites include rotted fenceposts, drainage pipes, and nest boxes. The female builds the nest of grass, moss, bark, and leaves, filling up whatever size hole they have adopted. When the main structure is completed, the birds line it with hair—often plucked from a living animal—woodchuck, rabbit, dog, or even a handy human. Five or six eggs are laid, incubated by the female for 12 to 14 days. Both parents feed the young, which fledge at about 15 days. The family group stays together, sometimes into the next year, and year-old birds may help their parents care for the nestlings of the newest brood.

Backyard & Beyond
Tufted titmice sometimes breed in nest boxes, especially those with an entrance hole in the 1½-inch range. In winter they travel in mixed flocks with chickadees, sparrows, woodpeckers, and kinglets. Tufted titmice are easy to locate in woodlands by their noisy scolding calls.

Carolina Chickadee
Poecile carolinensis

Gregarious and widespread, chickadees are just about everyone's favorite backyard birds. In the South, the resident chickadee is the Carolina, a slightly smaller but otherwise very similar cousin to the black-capped chickadee of the northern states. Chickadees travel in noisy little bands and draw attention to themselves with their frequent scolding chatter. Chickadees are often the first birds to discover a newly installed bird feeder.

All About
Only about 4½ inches in length, the Carolina chickadee has a black cap and bib with a white cheek patch; gray back, wings, and tail; and pale underparts with buff-colored flanks. The bill is tiny and dark, the legs and feet black. Males and females are alike, and there are no seasonal differences in plumage. The *so-fee, so-fay* song of the Carolina chickadee is longer than the black-capped chickadee's—four notes as opposed to two or three—and its *chick-a-dee-dee-dee* call is higher-pitched and more rapid.

Habitat & Range
The Carolina chickadee is resident (nonmigratory) and, through most of its range, it is the only chickadee present. It is generally replaced by the black-capped chickadee at elevations above 5,000 feet in the southern Appalachians, though. Where the two species overlap they may occasionally interbreed, so identifying individual birds under such circumstances is tricky.

Feeding
Carolina chickadees have a varied diet. Nearly half of the food taken in the wild consists of insects, such as aphids, ants, moths, and leafhoppers. They also eat spiders, weed seeds, and the seeds and small fruits of many trees and vines. At feeders they are partial to sunflower seeds, suet, and peanuts.

Nesting
Cavity nesters, Carolina chickadees seek out natural holes in woodland trees, often adapting old woodpecker holes. They readily accept not only nesting boxes, but also crevices under eaves or porch roofs, hollowed out fenceposts, or drainpipes. The nest (made by the female) is a thick mass of mosses, bark, and grasses, enclosing a cup of soft hair. One side is built up higher than the other and can be pulled down like a flap to cover the young when both parents are away. As many as eight eggs are laid and incubated by the female for 11 to 13 days; both parents then share the feeding of the young until they fledge after two weeks.

Backyard & Beyond
It is easy to lure chickadees into your yard by providing black-oil sunflower seeds in hanging tubes or hopper feeders, and by offering suet or other fats, such as a peanut butter-cornmeal mix or "bird pudding." To induce a pair to stay and nest, install one or more nest boxes with entrance holes that are 1¼ to 1½ inches in diameter.

White-breasted Nuthatch
Sitta carolinensis

Nuthatches are universally referred to as "upside-down birds," because they forage by probing the bark of tree trunks with their heads downward. During their journeys down the trunk of a tree, they often pause, and then raise their head so that it is parallel to the ground—an absolutely unique posture among birds. The most well-known member of the family is the white-breasted nuthatch, a bird of deciduous woods and well-treed backyards.

All About
At nearly 6 inches in length, the white-breasted nuthatch is the largest of its tribe. Males have gray backs with black caps, white underparts, and a beady black eye on a white face. Females are similar but wear gray, not black, on their heads. White-breasteds are thick-necked and short-tailed, with a stocky appearance. White-breasted nuthatch calls—uttered frequently in all seasons—are a nasal and repetitive *ank-ank*.

Habitat & Range
White-breasted nuthatches prefer deciduous woods, but are also found in large parks and leafy backyards. In northern coniferous woods, and at high elevations along the Appalachian chain, they are replaced by the smaller red-breasted nuthatch, while the brown-headed nuthatch displaces them in the dry pine woods of the South.

Feeding
The white-breasted nuthatch eats both insects and seeds, varying its fare with the seasons. Insects make up nearly 100 percent of their summer diet, with seeds being added in fall and winter. Autumn's extra seeds and nuts are sometimes stashed—or "hatched away"—in tree bark crevices, to be retrieved later—a habit that has given these birds their name. White-breasted nuthatches will come to feeders for sunflower and other seeds, or suet, but they tend to abandon backyard feeders almost entirely in spring and summer when insect prey is plentiful.

Nesting
Nuthatches maintain their pair bond and territory all year long. The nest is placed in a natural cavity, old woodpecker hole, or more rarely a nest box. Built by the female, it is a cup of grasses, bark strips, and twigs and is lined with hair. When the nest is finished, the nuthatches "sweep" the entrance with their bills, rubbing a crushed insect against the wood—the chemicals released may aid in repelling predators. The female incubates a clutch of eight eggs for two weeks. Both parents feed the young for at least two weeks until fledging.

Backyard & Beyond
Nuthatches are irregular feeder visitors, but they like black oil sunflower seeds and suet, peanuts, or peanut butter mix. In woodlands, listen for the nuthatch's nasal honking calls anytime. Male and female always forage near each other and, in winter, with other species in a mixed flock.

Carolina Wren
Thryothorus ludovicianus

Creeping and exploring around door stoops, garages, and tool sheds, Carolina wrens adopt a *mi casa, su casa* policy when it comes to nesting. If you find a nest cleverly hidden on a cluttered shelf or in a hanging flower basket, it's likely that of a Carolina wren. Their persistent songs, often given as a duet between pairs, brighten winter days and ring through the thick underbrush that they prefer.

All About
The Carolina wren is a rotund, warm-brown bird that often carries its tail cocked. Leading with its longish, curved bill, it resembles a little brown teapot. Reinforcing this impression is the phrase it often sings: *teakettle, teakettle!* The bright white line over its eye and its warm buffy underparts (paler in summer) help clinch the identification. Males and females are alike.

Habitat & Range
Wherever it occurs, the Carolina wren stays as a year-round resident. It's most common in swampy, mixed hardwood forests that are thick with vines, shrubs, and tangles, but it is happy in yards and gardens with plenty of shrubbery and outbuildings. Carolina wrens love poking about stacks of firewood, and they'll help themselves to the shelter of an open porch, garage, or shed, cleverly concealing their nests in our clutter.

Feeding
Insects and spiders make up virtually all the Carolina wren's natural food diet, which they capture while gleaning on or near the ground. At times, they will climb trees to glean insects hidden in bark or toss aside leaf litter while searching for prey. They'll bash large prey, such as katydids and moths, into manageable pieces and hunt cobwebby corners for spiders. In snowy winters, Carolina wrens resort to visiting feeders.

Nesting
Carolina wrens weave a surprisingly complex and bulky nest, hauling volumes of bark strips, fine twigs, leaves, grasses, green moss, and rubbish into a hidden nook, thick intertwining of vines, natural tree cavity, or cranny in an outbuilding. They often make a "porch" of such material leading to the nest. The entire affair is domed, and the finely-woven inner cup holds four eggs. The female incubates for 14 days, while the male feeds her. The young leave the nest from 12 to 19 days later.

Backyard & Beyond
Though they're unable to crack seeds with their fine, curved bills, Carolina wrens poke about for fragments of sunflower hearts and swallow white millet whole. They're most fond of peanut butter suet mixtures and mealworms, and they have been known to enter houses through open doors and windows to seek food. Highly intelligent, they easily find their way back out and make charming neighbors. Listen for their ringing whistles in any low-lying, tangled woods, and enjoy them in your yard.

House Wren
Troglodytes aedon

The rich and burbling song of the house wren is surprisingly loud for such a tiny (4 3/4 inches long) bird. House wrens are named for their preference for living in close proximity to humans, often in tiny houses we provide for them. This mostly plain brown bird makes up for its small size and drab coloration by being a fierce competitor for nesting sites.

All About
House wrens are notable for their lack of field marks—the warm-brown upperparts and tail are matched by a grayish breast. Look closely at the house wren, and you'll see a variety of small white and black spots, the only variation in the bird's plumage. Males and females look alike and both have the wrenlike habit of cocking their tails up when perched. The thin, slightly curved bill is ideal for capturing and eating the house wren's insect prey.

Habitat & Range
Spending the summers in thickets and brushy edge habitat adjacent to woodlands, the house wren is a familiar bird in parks, backyards, and gardens, often—but not always—near human settlements. Some house wrens winter in the southernmost states in the United States, but many travel beyond our borders farther south.

Feeding
Insects make up the house wren's diet (grasshoppers, crickets, spiders, and moths are on the menu), but they will also eat snails and caterpillars. Most of their foraging is done in thick vegetation on or near the ground.

Nesting
House wrens nest in a variety of cavities from woodpecker holes to natural cavities and nest boxes. Like Carolina wrens, house wrens will also nest in flowerpots, drainpipes, and other such sites. They are very competitive about nesting sites, often filling all or most available cavities with sticks. The male builds these "dummy" nests, and the female selects one in which to nest. The twig structures are lined with soft materials, such as grass or hair, and the female lays six to eight eggs. She performs the incubation duties, which last from 12 to 14 days. Fledglings leave the nest two or more weeks after hatching. House wrens are known to pierce the eggs of other cavity nesting birds in their territories.

Backyard & Beyond
House wrens will readily accept nest boxes with interior dimensions of 4x4 inches and entry holes of 1 1/4 inches in diameter. Nest boxes placed adjacent to brushy habitat or a wood's edge seem to be most attractive. The house wren's song and scolding calls are heard often wherever they are present. Nest boxes for bluebirds and tree swallows should be placed far from edge habitat, in the open, to avoid conflict and competition from territorial house wrens.

Golden-crowned Kinglet
Regulus satrapa

After various hummingbirds, the tiny, plump golden-crowned kinglet is North America's smallest bird. What it lacks in size, it makes up for in energy, constantly flipping its wings and flitting, tilting, and scooting across branches in search of even more diminutive prey. The golden-crowned's high pitched zeet-zeet-zeet call is easily learned and often heard before the birds are seen.

All About
A reasonably good look will reveal its striking face pattern, with its yellow (female) or yellow-and-orange (male) crown bordered in black and a black stripe through the eye. In contrast, the other North American kinglet, the ruby-crowned, has a bold, white eye ring and rarely shows its scarlet crown patch. Both kinglets flick their wings and have single wing bars, short tails, and tiny bills. In comparison, most warblers are longer and slimmer. Kinglets frequently associate with other small songbirds, including chickadees, titmice, and warblers, and you may find both kinglet species in the same flock.

Habitat & Range
The golden-crowned kinglet is primarily a northern nester, but its breeding range dips well south to the Appalachians and also includes western mountains and the Pacific Northwest. In the East, they commonly nest in mature spruce forests, including stands of tall Norway spruce, and their range has expanded somewhat in recent decades. In winter, golden-crowned kinglets are found across much of the United States in deciduous and mixed forests, as well as in coniferous forests. They often forage high in trees but can also be seen low down, at times even descending to tall-weed level.

Feeding
Golden-crowned kinglets feed on a range of insects and other invertebrates and their eggs. In the cold of winter, they relentlessly glean brittle twigs and branches, vines, and stems for dormant invertebrates and egg clusters. Summer finds them among spruces and pines, seeking a variety of spiders, gnats, and caterpillars. They tilt over to look under branches and hover briefly to seek or secure prey.

Nesting
The female golden-crowned kinglet knits together bits of bark, lichen, leaf fragments, and other materials to construct her cup-shaped nest, where she lays nine or so tiny pale eggs. She incubates her clutch for about two weeks. Both male and female feed the hatchlings, which leave the nest before they are 20 days old.

Backyard & Beyond
During migration and winter, watch out for golden-crowned kinglets in your backyard trees. These energetic balls of fluff often turn up in mixed flocks, so they may be drawn to your yard by chickadees and titmice dining at your feeders. They sometimes dine at suet feeders.

Blue-gray Gnatcatcher
Polioptila caerulea

The blue-gray gnatcatcher is the birder's "mini-mockingbird," always in motion and usually talking about it. This graceful, delicate, miniscule bird seems to arrive too early in spring, sallying into swarms of midges from still-budding branches. Its slender, elongated form and flashy black-and-white paneled tail are hard to mistake, though the gnatcatcher often goes unnoticed. It's most likely to be spotted on its early spring migration, for it is a woodland denizen, often hidden by foliage after the trees leaf out.

All About
It's often the gnatcatcher's twangy, whining call—like a miniature banjo being tuned—that alerts us to its presence. Its song is a sputtering, wheezy, petulant-sounding jumble, punctuated by mews. The blue-gray gnatcatcher has been recorded mimicking other species, a talent not widely appreciated, perhaps because its high, whispery voice is beyond the hearing register of many bird watchers. A white eye ring and neat black eyeline, blue-gray upperparts, and a long, slender tail edged in white distinguish this elegant bird. Females are similar, but lack the black eyeline.

Habitat & Range
Blue-gray gnatcatchers are strongly associated with oaks in a wide range of habitats, sticking to woodlands dominated by broad-leaved species. They are more often seen along woodland edges than in yards and gardens, except during migration. Gnatcatchers winter in the western coastal scrub of Mexico and Central America.

Feeding
Perching on the outer twigs in the mid- to high canopy, gnatcatchers go out after flying insects or glean the outer foliage for insects and spiders. As they forage, they flick their white outer tail feathers, which is thought to create bursts of light that startles UV-sensitive insects into flight. The bill is a fine black forcep, good for grasping tiny prey.

Nesting
Gnatcatcher nests are often mistaken for those of hummingbirds, being neat, compact cups of silk (often gathered from tent caterpillar nests), plastered with lichens. They are usually saddled on a horizontal limb. It is often possible to witness construction because the male gnatcatcher escorts the nest-building female with much fanfare and conversation. Both male and female incubate four eggs for 13 days, and young birds leave the nest 13 days after hatching. They are still being fed by their parents three weeks after departing the nest but gain independence soon thereafter.

Backyard & Beyond
This species has expanded its range explosively over the past three decades, pioneering into the Northeast and southeastern Canada. However, its range expansion cannot be attributed to feeding stations, as has been postulated for the northward movement of tufted titmice, northern cardinals, and red-bellied woodpeckers. The gnatcatcher relies solely on insects for sustenance.

Eastern Bluebird
Sialia sialia

The eastern bluebird is our most famous thrush, even more popular than its cousin, the American robin. Its beauty, its song, and its willingness to live close to us has inspired many poets, songwriters, artists, and bird watchers. You can attract bluebirds to your property if you have a large open lawn, especially if you provide housing. Thanks to a concerted effort by bluebird lovers to provide nest boxes, the eastern bluebird has rebounded from its low population in the 1960s.

All About
The sky-blue back and rusty breast of the male bluebird are echoed in the female's more muted tones. There are three bluebird species in North America, but only the eastern is commonly found in the South. Bluebirds are often seen perched along fence lines, on wires, or high in trees. They may appear all dark in bright sunlight, so many observers miss seeing them. During spring courtship, paired bluebirds can be seen fluttering their wings near a prospective nesting site, uttering their rich *turalee turalay* song.

Habitat & Range
Bluebirds are resident (nonmigratory) throughout the eastern United States in open habitats, such as pastures, grasslands, parks, and large suburban lawns (especially where bluebird nest boxes are available). The two habitat requirements of bluebirds are large, open, grassy areas for foraging and cavities for roosting and nesting. In harsh winter weather, bluebirds may migrate short distances to find food or shelter.

Feeding
From an elevated perch, bluebirds watch for moving insects and then drop to the ground to pounce on them or to capture flying insects in midair. They eat insects year-round and will shift to fruits and berries when insects are scarce. Bluebirds visit feeders for mealworms, berries, and suet or suet dough.

Nesting
Bluebirds are cavity nesters and will use old woodpecker holes or natural cavities in trees where available. Human-supplied nest boxes are an important resource for the eastern bluebird. The female bluebird builds the nest inside the cavity using bark strips, grass, and hair. She lays four to six eggs and incubates them for 12 to 16 days. Both parents care for the nestlings until fledging occurs after 14 to 18 days.

Backyard & Beyond
If you offer housing, it's important to monitor and manage it to keep non-native house sparrows and starlings from usurping it and to keep predators from accessing the eggs or young. Place the houses (with 1 1/2-inch entrance holes) on metal poles with a pole-mounted baffle beneath the house. House location should be in the middle of a large, open, grassy lawn or field. Bluebirds catch insects on the ground in grassy areas, so they are particularly vulnerable to lawn chemicals.

American Robin
Turdus migratorius

Almost all North Americans have grown up having a fairly intimate acquaintance with a thrush. The American robin, the largest and most widespread and most abundant North American thrush, has followed the watered lawn—with its plentiful earthworm prey base—westward across the continent. Only parts of Florida, Texas, and the Southwest, where the soil is too sandy to support the introduced common earthworm, lack robins.

All About
The robin's simple yet evocative *cheerily-cheerio* song meshes well with the thunk of basketballs and the drone of lawnmowers in suburban neighborhoods all across North America; yet, they also hide their nests in mountaintop spruce and fir forests, where they are as wary as any hermit thrush. Males sport brick-red breasts and black heads with broken white spectacles and a streaked white throat and lower belly. Females are paler.

Habitat & Range
The robin is primarily a bird of lawns with trees and shrubs, though it also breeds in high mountain forests near clear-cuts or openings. Few other species show its adaptability to diverse habitats, from landscaped parking lot islets to dense, secluded forests. Migration is marked in northern climes, but is less so in southern ones.

Feeding
Running, then standing erect and motionless on a lawn, the robin watches and listens for earthworms and other invertebrates crawling in the grass. A quick stab captures them, sometimes resulting in a tug-of-war with a recalcitrant night crawler. Robins flock in fall to exploit fruiting trees and shrubs, fluttering and giggling as they reach for food.

Nesting
Most bird watchers are familiar with the robin's sturdy mud-and-grass cup, often nestled in an evergreen, a climbing vine, on a horizontal branch, or even on a windowsill. The female incubates three to four eggs for 12 to 14 days. Adults can be seen foraging with bills full of earthworms as soon as the young hatch. Young leave the nest, barely able to flutter, on about the thirteenth day. They are distinguished by their spotted, whitish breasts and reedy, begging calls. The male feeds them for another three weeks, while the female usually starts a second brood.

Backyard & Beyond
By mowing the lawn regularly and planting dense evergreens and fruit-bearing shrubs and trees, we unwittingly provide perfect conditions for robins. Robins seldom visit feeders, but will take bread, chopped raisins, and crumbled moistened dog chow in severe winter weather. Oddly enough, the American robin is the only member of its genus, *Turdus*, that breeds in any numbers in North America. The closely related clay-colored robin, which looks like a washed-out, American robin, breeds sparingly in south Texas.

Wood Thrush

Hylocichla mustelina

The lilting flutelike song of the wood thrush inspires bird watchers, naturalists, poets, musicians, and humankind in general. Few things are more beautiful than the evening song of the wood thrush as it echoes from deep within the forest. However, this species has suffered severe declines in population during the past thirty years due to loss of habitat, forest fragmentation, and nest parasitism from the brown-headed cowbird.

All About

This medium-sized (7 3/4 inches in length) brown thrush has a bright rufous head and neck, olive-brown back and tail, and a white breast with large dark spots. Erect and robinlike in its posture, the wood thrush sings a multi-pitched and highly variable *eeeolay* song and utters a *whit-whit-whit* call when agitated. Wood thrush males do most of their singing at dawn and dusk, and usually from a midlevel perch in the forest.

Habitat & Range

Wood thrushes only spend their summers with us in eastern North America, arriving as early as April, but departing for the tropics by mid-August or later. Many make the flight across the Gulf of Mexico in both spring and fall. During the breeding season, they can be found in mixed deciduous forests with tall trees and a thick understory. Fragmented forest plots or those with cleared understory (due to deer browsing or human landscaping) are far less attractive to wood thrushes.

Feeding

Feeding much like a robin on the forest floor, the wood thrush sweeps aside leaf litter with its bill to uncover insects, larvae, millipedes, moths, ants, and even salamanders and snails. In fall, wood thrushes will feed in forest edge habitats to take advantage of fruits and berries.

Nesting

The female wood thrush builds a cup-shaped nest out of grasses, leaves, and rootlets, usually held together with mud, in the fork of a tree branch within 20 feet of the ground. She lays three to four eggs and incubates them for about 12 days before they hatch. Young wood thrushes are ready to fledge two weeks later. Wood thrush nests in fragmented forest habitats are more likely to be parasitized by the brown-headed cowbird, which does not build its own nest, but rather lays its eggs in the nests of other songbirds—often at the expense of the host species.

Backyard & Beyond

From spring through fall your best chance of locating a wood thrush is to listen for a male singing from patches of dense forest. Once you hear the song, patiently scan the upper, inner branches of the forest for this rusty-brown master singer. If you live in wooded habitat that is home to wood thrushes, be a good neighbor and keep pets restrained during breeding season.

Swainson's Thrush
Catharus ustulatus

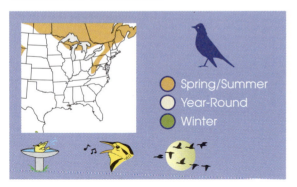

En route to or from wintering grounds, Swainson's thrushes are widespread migrants through the South that appear in a variety of shady migration stops, from local parks and backyards to mountain ranges and coastal migration hotspots. These birds—like many other neotropical, migrant songbirds—migrate at night. Listen for the peeping calls of Swainson's and other thrushes as they pass over.

All About
Swainson's thrush was once called the olive-backed thrush. The name changed in part because some Swainson's thrush populations have brownish backs and also because the olivelike tone seen in others—which varies with light conditions—is much like that of gray-cheeked, Bicknell's, and hermit thrushes. These species, however, lack the Swainson's buff-colored eye ring, lores, and breast. In addition, the hermit thrush has a rusty tail that contrasts with its back. Like the three other woodland thrushes mentioned, the Swainson's has dark brown spotting on its breast. This spotting differs from the sparse rusty flecks of the veery thrush and the larger black spots on the orangish brown-backed wood thrush. At times, migrating Swainson's thrushes sing their spiraling flute-like song; it resembles that of the veery, but slurs upward not down.

Habitat & Range
The Swainson's thrush nests sparingly in the Appalachians, but more commonly in western mountains and across much of Canada and central and southern Alaska. These birds primarily nest in coniferous forests in the East, but they migrate through all types of woodland. They winter in varied tropical forests, mostly in northern South America, but to a lesser degree from Central America north into Mexico.

Feeding
Swainson's thrushes feed on a variety of insects and berries, which they find on the forest floor or in trees. While wintering in the tropics, these birds disperse plant seeds by eating berries and then scattering the seeds in their droppings. During migration, you may find Swainson's and other thrushes doing the same thing as they dine on wild grape and other berries.

Nesting
In its forest breeding grounds, the Swainson's thrush builds sturdy cup nests using grass, bark, leaves, and other plant materials, lining these structures with softer materials. The female lays three or four eggs and incubates them for about two weeks. Both parents feed their young, which leave the nest before they are two weeks old.

Backyard & Beyond
During migration, Swainson's thrushes often show up and forage in shady backyards that have shrubs, young trees, and leaf litter. Focus your binoculars on a full or nearly full moon, and you may see the tiny silhouettes of these small travelers as they pass by.

Gray Catbird
Dumetella carolinensis

Named for its mewing catlike call, the catbird is actually a multitalented singer that is almost comparable to the mockingbird in its vocal versatility. Able to operate both sides of its syrinx, or vocal organ, independently, it can actually sing two different songs at once, and it's a mimic, too—not a bad resume for an otherwise plain gray bird.

All About
A slim, slate-gray bird about 9 inches long, the catbird is distinguished by a solid black cap and a bright chestnut patch under its tail. Because of its habit of cocking its tail, this patch is often visible. Catbirds are easy to recognize because—no matter what age, sex, or season—they all look the same. Very vocal, the male catbird makes an almost endless array of sounds, one after the other; some are his own and others are "stolen" from other birds or even from frogs, domestic animals, or mechanical devices heard in his travels. You can usually tell a catbird's song from that of other mimics, though, because each phrase is repeated only once, and the telltale *meouw* is thrown in from time to time.

Habitat & Range
In most of its U.S. range, the catbird is migratory, moving southward in winter, away from the coldest weather. Flying at night, migrant catbirds are often victims of collision, striking tall buildings or communication towers with distressing frequency. A few avoid the dangers of migration by remaining in their northern territories, a tactic that works if they are well fed and the season is not overly harsh.

Feeding
Foraging in thickets and brambles, the gray catbird eats mostly insects in spring and summer, adding small fruits as fall approaches. Favored insects include caterpillars, ants, aphids, termites, cicadas, and dragonflies. Among fruits it chooses grapes, cherries, and berries, followed by such late-lingering items as multiflora rosehips, catbrier, privet berries, bittersweet, and mountain ash.

Nesting
Singing from deep within a thicket, the male catbird courts his female in spring. After mating, she builds a bulky cup of twigs, weeds, and leaves, sometimes adding bits of paper or string and then lining it with fine grasses or hair. She incubates her three or four eggs for about two weeks; both parents then feed the nestlings for 10 to 12 days until they fledge. Two broods are common.

Backyard & Beyond
If a catbird remains in your neighborhood during winter it may be attracted by offerings of dried or fresh fruit, suet, doughnuts, peanut hearts, or table scraps. These birds are easily intimidated by other species, so they are more likely to respond to food scattered on the ground than concentrated in a small feeding dish.

Northern Mockingbird
Mimus polyglottos

- Spring/Summer
- Year-Round
- Winter

This formerly southern species has been expanding its range for a century and now covers nearly every corner of the United States. Its rich, warbling voice and uncanny ability to imitate the calls of other birds—not to mention rusty hinges, frogs, dogs, and squeaky wheels—make it a superstar in any avian chorus. Five different states have chosen this popular songster as their state bird!

All About
The mockingbird is fairly large (9 to 11 inches long) with medium-gray upperparts and a pale breast and belly. Its long tail is edged in white, and there are prominent white patches on the wings that are especially visible in flight. The bill and legs are black. The sexes are alike. This bird's voice more than makes up for its plumage. It is loud, clear and—in spring and summer—nearly incessant. When the moon is bright, mockingbirds will sing at night. The mockingbird tends to repeat each phrase three times before moving on to the next. Both males and females sing.

Habitat & Range
Mockingbirds like to feed in short-grass areas with shrubby edges, so they are common in suburban towns, open city parks, small family farms, hedgerows, backyards, and similar situations. They are nonmigratory, present year-round in the areas they inhabit.

Feeding
The diet of the mockingbird is composed of insects (spring and summer) and fruits (summer, fall, and winter). Earthworms, spiders, snails, and other small meaty prey round out the menu. Multiflora rosehips are a mainstay in winter, and the range expansion of the mockingbird may have coincided with the spread of this alien plant.

Nesting
During spring courtship, a male mockingbird sings almost around the clock, often from a high perch, all the while jumping up in the air and waving his wings. When a female responds, both partners build the nest, a bulky mass of twigs around a cup of softer plant material, lined with moss and animal hair. Three to four eggs are laid and incubated by the female for about two weeks. The nestlings are fed by both parents for 12 days until fledging, and for about two weeks after as they learn to fend for themselves.

Backyard & Beyond
Though mockingbirds do not eat the usual feeder fare they may be attracted, especially in winter, with offerings of suet, peanut butter, doughnuts, or small fruits. This is not always a good idea, however, for mockers are very territorial, and individual birds may defend a winter-feeding area against all other species. If this happens, the easiest solution is to hang feeders on all sides of your house, so the aggressive mockingbird cannot see and defend all of them at once.

Brown Thrasher
Toxostoma rufum

The brown thrasher has a lush resounding voice, and sings a seemingly endless train of melodies—its own and others'—from one end of a spring day to the other, and it may stay hidden in a deep shrub all the while. The state bird of Georgia, the brown thrasher is common throughout its range, but not as well known as it ought to be. This mimic is a cheerful and friendly addition to any backyard.

All About
Nearly a foot long, the brown thrasher is a strong and handsome bird, equally at home in woodland edges or shrubby backyards. Its upperparts are bright cinnamon, broken only by two, thin, white wing bars; its white breast is heavily streaked in brown. It has a long tail, a long slightly curved bill, and strong sturdy legs well suited to "thrashing" about on the ground. Beginning birders may confuse a thrasher with one of the thrushes, or perhaps a fox sparrow, but the thrasher is much larger, with a longer bill and tail. The thrasher's song is almost as rich and varied as a mockingbird's, and it is very similar in quality, but where the mocker usually sings its phrases three times each, the thrasher utters his only twice.

Habitat & Range
Often seen on the ground, the brown thrasher is a bird of woodland edges, thickets, hedgerows, brushy riversides and parks, and shrubby backyards. It retreats from the northern reaches of its breeding range to spend the winter in less frigid areas, usually returning sometime in April. In most of the South, it is a year-round bird.

Feeding
More than half the brown thrasher's diet consists of insects—beetles, grasshoppers, cicadas, and caterpillars—most of which it finds on the ground as it rummages with feet and bill among the leaf litter. Brown thrashers also eat fruits, nuts, seeds, and acorns.

Nesting
The male brown thrasher sings vigorously upon first arriving at its breeding grounds, both to establish territory and to attract a mate. The mated pair builds a large, twiggy nest in deep cover, usually quite close to the ground. Both parents incubate four eggs for nearly two weeks. Chicks are fully feathered and ready to fly in just nine days, an adaptation to avoid predators, which are especially dangerous to low-nesting birds. Two and sometimes three broods are raised each year.

Backyard & Beyond
Brown thrashers will visit feeding stations for seeds and grains that are scattered on the ground. Nuts are popular, as are suet mixtures, cornbread, doughnuts, and raisins. Thrashers are not particularly shy of humans, but do require some shrubs or hedges nearby where they can retreat if they feel threatened.

European Starling
Sturnus vulgaris

In 1889, there were no European starlings in North America, yet today—just over a century later—we have more than 200 million. Blame a fan of William Shakespeare. In 1890, a flock of a hundred starlings was released in New York's Central Park in an attempt to bring to America all the bird species mentioned in Shakespeare's plays. The adaptable starling soon spread westward in history's greatest avian population explosion.

All About
Glossy black overall, with a yellow bill during breeding season, the starling is one of the most familiar birds—not only because it is so common, but because it almost always lives close to human settlements. In winter, starlings are duller overall, covered with white spots (little stars, or "starlings") and with a blackish bill. In all seasons, starlings are very vocal, displaying an astonishing ability to mimic other bird songs, sirens, voices, barks, or mechanical sounds. In flight, starlings flap their triangular-shaped wings rapidly.

Habitat & Range
Starlings cover the entire North American continent year-round, except for the Far North in winter. In fall they form gigantic, noisy flocks roaming in search of food and roosting sites. Every habitat type can host starlings, but they prefer those altered by humans (farmland, urban, and suburban areas) and tend to avoid remote, pristine habitats except where humans are present.

Feeding
Insects, berries, fruits, and seeds are the starling's regular diet, but they are highly adaptable—as willing to eat French fries from a dumpster as they are to find bugs in our lawns or suet at our feeders. The starling's traditional foraging technique is to insert its long, sharp bill into the ground and then open it to expose beetle grubs and other prey.

Nesting
Starlings are cavity nesters that cannot excavate their own holes, so they use existing cavities, such as woodpecker holes, pipes, crevices in buildings, and birdhouses. Sites are often usurped from other, less aggressive cavity nesters, such as bluebirds or purple martins. Once a male has a site, a female will help finish the nest—a messy affair of grass, feathers, paper, and plastic. Between four and six eggs are laid and incubated by both parents for about 12 days. Young starlings leave the nest three weeks later.

Backyard & Beyond
Most Americans can see a starling simply by looking out their window. Many bird watchers consider them a pest at their feeders and birdhouses. To discourage starlings at your feeders, simply remove the foods they prefer: suet, peanuts, bread, and cracked corn. At nest boxes, an entry hole diameter of $1^9/_{16}$ inches or less will exclude starlings. Frequent removal of their nesting material will also discourage them.

Cedar Waxwing
Bombycilla cedrorum

A beady, insectlike trill first alerts many bird watchers to the presence of cedar waxwings, so completely do they blend into canopy foliage. These wandering fruit-eaters appear and disappear seemingly without rhyme or reason, descending to strip a tree of its fruits, then whirling off to parts unknown. Fermented fruits may cause entire flocks to stagger about on the ground until the intoxication wears off.

All About
"Sleek" is the word most often used to describe the silky fawn plumage of the cedar waxwing. A velvety-black bandit mask hides the eyes, and a bright yellow band tips the gray tail. Older birds have red tips on the secondary wing feather shafts, which look like shiny drops of sealing wax. Cedar waxwings are most often seen in flocks in fall and winter.

Habitat & Range
The cedar waxwing's only real habitat requirement is the presence of fruit-bearing trees and shrubs; thus, it can be found everywhere except grasslands, deserts, and deep interior forests. Thought to be nomadic, the species does make a poorly understood migration that takes it as far south as southern Central America.

Feeding
Cedar waxwings travel in tight flocks to locate and feed on small fruits. They may be completely hidden in leaves as they flutter and pluck fruit, only to explode out with reedy calls and a rush of wings when startled. In late summer, they may be seen in twisting, dodging pursuits of winged insects over water.

Nesting
Though they defend no territory and in some places are semicolonial, cedar waxwings are monogamous. Both sexes help build a bulky, cup-shaped nest in the outer canopy of a tree. Leaves, straw, twigs, and string, often in a trailing mass, comprise the nest. The female lays four eggs and incubates them for 12 days, while the male feeds her. Young are fed on insects for the first two days, then solely on regurgitated fruits, leaving the nest around 15 days later. This fruit-based diet ensures that any parasitic brown-headed cowbirds hatching in their nests do not survive. Large flocks of immature birds (identifiable by their yellowish, streaked bellies) linger near breeding grounds for one or two months after the adults leave.

Backyard & Beyond
Attracting cedar waxwings is best accomplished by planting the trees and shrubs they prefer—serviceberry, hawthorn, firethorn, dogwood, chokecherry, viburnums, native honeysuckles, blueberries, cedars, and others with small fruits. They may also visit birdbaths, especially those with moving water. Worldwide, there are only two other species of waxwing: the Bohemian and Japanese waxwings. Waxwings are related to silky flycatchers, a largely tropical family.

Tennessee Warbler
Vermivora peregrina

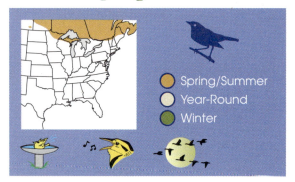

Legendary ornithologist Alexander Wilson first described and named the Tennessee warbler after shooting one on the shore of the Cumberland River in Tennessee. He must have thought this bird was not a nester because the scientific name he gave it means, roughly, "the wandering worm-eater." Wilson thought the bird was rare, but we now know that it is a widespread, common nester in a variety of woodlands across northern North America, mostly in Canada.

All About
The Tennessee warbler is very active, short-tailed, and nondescript. The male is most distinctive in spring, when its gray crown contrasts with its olive-green back. Females, fall males, and immatures have a yellow wash underneath. In all plumages, the white or whitish undertail contrasts with the bird's darker, grayish (adult) or yellowish (immature) breast. Females and immatures have two very faint wing bars, but you won't find much else in the way of distinguishing marks. The Tennessee warbler's chipping song has three parts, with the third part faster than the first two.

Habitat & Range
Tennessee warblers nest across much of Canada and in some northern U.S. states. During spring migration, Tennessee warblers are usually found high in deciduous trees, and they migrate mainly west of the Appalachians. In fall, southbound birds feed at various heights in shrubs and trees, and they appear most frequently *east* of the Appalachians. Tennessee warblers spend the winter from southern Mexico to northwestern South America. They just pass through the South during migration, and, depending upon location and season, can be easy—or hard—to find.

Feeding
On their nesting grounds, Tennessee warbler populations ebb and grow in rhythm with populations of spruce budworms—insects important to this and a number of other songbirds. During migration, you will find Tennessee warblers mixed with other warblers, chickadees, and other mixed flock feeders. They often feed on outer branches, but they can be seen low in shrubs and even in weeds. Insects form most of their diet, but in winter these birds eat some berries and probe tropical flowers for nectar.

Nesting
The female fashions her nest from grasses and other plant materials, on or near the ground, often in bogs. She lays between four and seven eggs, which she incubates for about 12 days. It's believed that young Tennessee warblers fledge from the nest before they are two weeks old.

Backyard & Beyond
Keep this drab songbird in mind while scanning mixed migrant flocks in your backyard or neighborhood park. Like ornithologist Wilson, you too may find the warbler far closer to Tennessee than to its wintering or nesting grounds.

Magnolia Warbler
Dendroica magnolia

A small and active bird, the magnolia warbler (or "maggie" as some bird watchers call it) is a frequently seen spring migrant because it forages low in shrubby vegetation. The striking magnolia warbler has no particular association with magnolias—it was named in 1810 by early American ornithologist Alexander Wilson when he saw them for the first time in a stand of magnolias in Mississippi.

All About
Magnolia warblers could be the poster bird for bird identification because they have one of everything: a dark mask, white eyeline, gray cap, white wing bars, a black necklace on a contrasting yellow breast, a yellow rump, and white tail panels. As they move about, magnolias almost seem to be trying to show you all of their markings. Adult males in fall plumage are a grayer version of their spring selves, but they retain the yellow breast and white tail panels. Male magnolias sing a highly variable song that sounds like *weeta, weeta, WEETA!* and is more recognizable for its soft delivery than for its rhythmic pattern.

Habitat & Range
During the breeding season, magnolias are found at high elevations or in the Far North in young scrubby pine, spruce, fir, and hemlock forests. In migration, magnolias can turn up almost anywhere, but they are most frequently seen in brushy areas with young deciduous trees. Because they are nocturnal migrants, magnolias are frequently seen first thing in the morning, actively feeding to refuel themselves after a night of travel.

Feeding
Magnolias glean insects, spider eggs, aphids, and beetles from trees and vegetation. As they hop through a sapling, they check the branches, bark, and undersides of leaves for food items. They will also catch insects in midair and will hover briefly to nab an otherwise hard-to-get insect from beneath a hanging leaf.

Nesting
In May and June, magnolia warblers are getting busy with breeding. Both sexes work to build the nest on the male's territory, and the site chosen is usually low and well concealed in a hemlock, spruce, or fir. The female lays three to five eggs and handles the 13-day incubation chores. Young magnolias leave the nest fairly soon—about 10 days after hatching—but the parents will continue to feed them for nearly a month after fledging.

Backyard & Beyond
Magnolias are one of our most common warblers, perhaps due to their preference for habitats with young trees. Finding a maggie in spring is as easy as getting out during the peak migration period in late March, April, and May. Once the breeding season starts, you'll either need to visit high elevation coniferous forests or head north to the heart of the breeding range.

Yellow-rumped Warbler
Dendroica coronata

One of the best-known warblers in the United States—and easily the most widespread and numerous in winter—the yellow-rumped warbler is a paradox: Its plumage and its habitats are very variable; yet, it is relatively easy to identify whenever you find it. Eastern birds of this species used to be called "myrtle" warblers, while their western counterparts were known as "Audubon's" warblers. They are now all yellow-rumped warblers, despite differences in plumage and habitat. Trendy birders stick to their own favorite name: "butterbutt."

All About
The yellow-rumped warbler is 5 to 6 inches long, with a sharp thin bill and slightly notched tail. In breeding plumage, the eastern male is blue-gray with a white throat and belly, black streaking on the back, a black face patch, two white wing bars, black bib, and yellow spots on the crown, shoulders, and rump. Spring females are browner and duller than their mates. Immatures and fall adults are brown above, with brown-streaked underparts and little or no yellow visible. The one constant in all plumages is the bright yellow rump. That, along with a frequent and distinctive *check!* note, will quickly identify these birds.

Habitat & Range
Breeding in the far north, the eastern race of the yellow-rumped warbler is known in most of the country only as a migrant or winter resident. Migrants can be found in woodlands, hedgerows, thickets, and even along beaches as they stream through in large flocks. Winter birds congregate wherever they can find berries, their principal cold-weather food. In Florida, yellow-rumps are known to drink the juice of broken or fallen oranges, and throughout their winter range they will consume weed seeds large and small. Some yellow-rumps come to backyard feeders where they eat a variety of fare.

Nesting
For nesting, the yellow-rumped warbler selects conifer forests, generally spruce, pine, or cedar. The female builds the nest on a horizontal branch, anywhere from 5 to 50 feet high in the tree, using bark, twigs, weeds, and roots to create an open cup that is then lined with hair and feathers. The female incubates the four or five eggs for 12 to 13 days. When the chicks hatch, both parents feed them for 10 to 12 days until fledging, and then the male feeds them for a time afterward. There are usually two broods per year.

Backyard & Beyond
In winter, yellow-rumped warblers may visit feeders to eat suet, hummingbird nectar, orange halves, or grape jelly. It is possible to lure them with sprigs of bayberry or other wild fruits. Away from home, look for them where natural foods are plentiful, such as in bayberry thickets or stands of wax myrtle.

American Redstart
Setophaga ruticilla

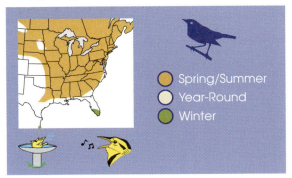

If you make *spishing* or pishing *noises around a mixed flock of migrating warblers, one of the first birds to pop up for a closer look may be this flashy little bird. The American redstart is a wood warbler that was named after a European member of the thrush family. But the American redstart is a true American original, even if its name derives from elsewhere.

All About
Like Europe's redstarts, the American flashes not red but orange in its tail, as well as on its wings and the sides of its breast. Otherwise, this warbler is black with a white belly. Birders call females and immatures "yellowstarts" because of similarly distinctive flashes of yellow (or in first-spring males yellow-orange) on the tail, wings, and the sides of the breast. Even seasoned birders can be thrown by the redstart's high-pitched, variable song, although some versions are easily recognized, such as *sweet-sweet-sweet-sweet-WHERE*.

Habitat & Range
Within its extensive breeding range across eastern and northern North America, American redstarts nest in a variety of wooded habitats (deciduous or mixed) with an understory of young trees. In mountainous areas, they are common nesters in regrowing forests or at the forest edge. In much of the lowland South, they nest in lush forests bordering river courses and are uncommon. During migration, American redstarts are among the most visible migrating warblers. They primarily winter from Mexico south to northern South America and in the Caribbean, although small numbers winter in Florida and more rarely in Texas and Louisiana.

Feeding
Spiders, caterpillars, and a wide variety of other small invertebrates wind up between the thin mandibles of the flittering redstart. The birds mostly seek insect prey, which they pick off leaves or capture in midair sallies, but redstarts also sometimes eat berries and seeds.

Nesting
The female redstart twines together grasses and other plant materials and spider webs to make its cup nest, which is placed in young trees, often no higher than 15 feet above the ground. The female usually lays four eggs, which she incubates for about 12 days. Both parents feed their young. Before they are 10 days old, the young leave the nest but are attended by either parent.

Backyard & Beyond
Among the most common migrant warblers, American redstarts frequently turn up in backyard trees during spring and fall. You can increase your odds of finding them at home by planting native small trees or shrubs where these insectivorous birds can seek insects. Shallow birdbaths or pools attract redstarts and other warblers; take care to situate water sources near shady cover that will still allow birds to see approaching cats.

Ovenbird
Seiurus aurocapilla

The ovenbird is a warbler that looks like a small speckled thrush. This deep forest bird only thrives where forests remain in large blocks, probably because if clearings are nearby, there are more nest predators and parasitic brown-headed cowbirds. Although spotting the forest-dwelling ovenbird takes patience, the bird's TEAcher-TEAcher-TEAcher-TEAcher song is distinctive and rings through the woods in spring and summer.

All About
A good look at the ovenbird's head will help you differentiate it from larger thrushes and same-sized waterthrushes. The wide, white eye ring is the first clue. The waterthrushes lack this, having instead a white stripe (*supercilium*) running from above the eye to the back of the head. Several species of brown-backed thrushes have eye rings that are not as pronounced. These birds are also much larger and have heavier bills than the ovenbird. Thrushes hop and feed, at one moment still, then dashing; the ovenbird walks methodically. The ovenbird has neat "stripes" of spots running down its breast, while the thrushes are more randomly speckled underneath. While not always visible, the ovenbird's black-bordered, orange crown patch is a diagnostic field mark.

Habitat & Range
Ovenbirds nest in mature deciduous or mixed deciduous and pine forests in the northern part of the Southeast, but they appear throughout the region during spring and fall migration. Most winter in Mexico, Central America, and on Caribbean islands. Forests that host nesting ovenbirds have a thick layer of dry leaf litter beneath them, providing the birds with feeding and nesting opportunities.

Feeding
The ovenbird quietly chugs along the leafy forest floor, walking and looking for insects, spiders, and other invertebrates (such as earthworms and snails) among the leaves littering the ground.

Nesting
This bird is named for its domed nest, which usually sits on the ground and is so well camouflaged with dead leaves that you can easily walk past without noticing it. Although leaves help conceal the nest, the female ovenbird constructs this structure using grasses, bark, and other materials. There is a side entrance for stealthy exit and entry. Inside, the female lays four or five eggs and incubates them for up to two weeks. Both parents feed the young. They leave the nest after about a week, but they are still fed by the adults for about two weeks afterward.

Backyard & Beyond
If you have a well-treed backyard with ample leaf litter, you may spot a foraging ovenbird walking in your woods during migration. If you hear the ovenbird's loud song, watch for it on a low- to midheight perch or foraging on the ground.

Common Yellowthroat
Geothlypis trichas

This charming bird may be the most popular warbler in North America. It is certainly one of the most widespread and well known. Its repetitive song, written as *witchety-witchety-witch* actually does sound like that, and beginners trying to learn bird songs find that the yellowthroat's is one of the easiest to master.

All About
Averaging about 5 inches in length, the common yellowthroat packs a lot of personality into a very small frame. Males are olive on top with a lemon-yellow throat and upper breast, white belly, yellow patch under the tail, and a bold black mask across the eyes, thinly bordered in white on top. The female is similar, but lacks the black mask. These are very active little birds and seem to be less timid than most warblers, possibly because they are nearly always low to the ground and therefore relatively easy to view. Their distinctive song continues well into the heat of summer.

Habitat & Range
Only in the dry southwestern states is the common yellowthroat hard to find during the breeding season. Everywhere else this little bird has no trouble locating the moist, shrubby, brushy conditions it needs for nesting. Even a relatively small patch of suitable habitat will do for a single pair, while large areas may host many nests. In winter and on migration, yellowthroats extend their interests to include shrubby backyards, dry woodland edges, and similar sites.

Feeding
Yellowthroats are almost exclusively insect-eaters, though they will add a few small seeds to their diet from time to time. Some favored insects are moths, aphids, leafhoppers, small caterpillars, mayflies, grasshoppers, and grubs. Foraging is done low to the ground, in dense cover.

Nesting
Female yellowthroats build a bulky cup nest quite low to the ground in thick weeds, using grasses, sedges, and other materials taken from the surrounding area. After lining it with fine grasses and hair, she lays three to five eggs and incubates them for 12 days. Her mate will bring her food during this time, and will then help her feed the nestlings for up to 10 days until fledging. The family stays together longer than most warblers, as the adults continue to feed the dependent young. Common yellowthroats are frequent victims of cowbird nest parasitism and do not seem to have an adequate defense against it.

Backyard & Beyond
In breeding season, thickets, hedgerows, marsh edges, and abandoned and overgrown farm fields are good places to look for common yellowthroats. Listen for their *witchety* song from spring through fall. In their southern winter homes, they may be harder to find, but their loud, scolding *chuck* notes will often give them away.

Hooded Warbler
Wilsonia citrina

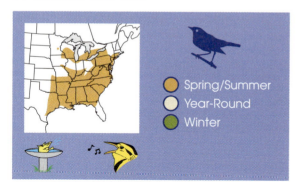

If you want to see a tropical bird without visiting the tropics, head out to a lush forest or swamp with dense undergrowth. There, you may hear the sweet, rich weeta-weeta-wiTEEoh of the dazzling hooded warbler. With luck, you may soon catch a glimpse of this "delicious" bird. Its species name citrina means "lemon colored," and no North American bird is more rich in yellow than a male hooded warbler.

All About
Like many wood warblers, flycatchers, vireos, and other neotropical migrants, the hooded warbler spends half or more of its year in the tropics, returning to eastern North America to breed. Yellow, black, and white are the hooded warbler's signature colors. All are bright yellow below, have blackish *lores* (areas between the eyes and bills), and large black eyes. Males have distinctive black hoods running around their yellow cheeks, from crown to throat. Females have variable versions of black or blackish hoods, while immatures have yellow heads with olive on their crowns. Hooded warblers flick their tails to flash their white, outer tail feathers—another identification clue.

Habitat & Range
Hooded warblers are common in many parts of the Southeast, both in lowland areas, such as cypress swamps, and in hilly deciduous forests. In some areas, they also nest in pine woods. One of the most important habitat requirements is dense undergrowth, with bushes that provide cover for these low-feeding, low-nesting birds. In late summer, hooded warblers migrate south to winter in southern Mexico and Central America.

Feeding
Much of a hooded warbler's feeding time is spent low in the bushes, picking caterpillars, spiders, moths, beetles, flies, and other invertebrates from the leaves. These very active birds dart out to grab prey in flight, briefly hover to grab insects off leaves, or move through the branches, grabbing food as they go.

Nesting
Hooded warblers usually nest in shrubs between 2 and 6 feet above the ground. There, the female usually constructs a cup nest of dead leaves, bark, grass, and plant fluff. Dead leaves decorate the outside of the nest, camouflaging it—although cowbirds often find hooded warbler nests and lay their eggs there. Snakes and other predators take many of the young as well. The female hooded warbler lays four eggs, which she incubates for about 12 days. Both parents feed the young, which can fly about 10 days after hatching.

Backyard & Beyond
During migration, look for hooded warblers along densely wooded waterways and swamps, areas where they may also breed. The birds are silent during the fall, but are much more easily detected in spring and early summer by their penetrating song.

Yellow-breasted Chat
Icteria virens

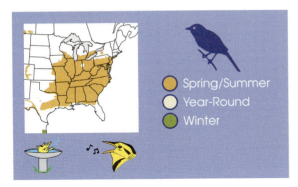

By far our largest warbler, the yellow-breasted chat inhabits the shrubby transition between field and forest. Its ratchety song often reveals this skulking bird rather than its bright colors, but the patient observer will often be rewarded with at least a glimpse of this impressive bird.

All About
The yellow-breasted chat is probably our most unusual warbler, with its distinctive, raspy, rich song; its odd behavior; and its unusual long-tailed, thick-bodied form. The chat has a heavier bill than other warblers, and its combination of field marks—rich lemon-yellow below and smooth olive above, with a white spectacle, moustache, and undertail—sets it apart at a glance. Male and female chats cannot be separated in the field, but males are most easily seen in spring, when they sing from perches overlooking their tangled, mostly low habitat. Male chats also sing during short, vertical display flights—their loud, peppy song incorporating harsh *ret, ret, ret* notes and smoother *chu, chu, chu* notes. Outside of breeding and chick raising, chats are solitary.

Habitat & Range
Yellow-breasted chats inhabit tangles of shrubs, vines, and young trees, a habitat that in the East usually lasts less than a decade before turning to shady forest. Due to urbanization and forest maturation, yellow-breasted chats have lost ground in many parts of their wide range. They remain common in much of the South, especially where forest clearings or fields are allowed to regrow naturally. Yellow-breasted chats spend their winters in Mexico and Central America.

Feeding
During much of the year, yellow-breasted chats eat insects plucked from leaves low in their densely vegetated habitat. Near summer's end and during fall migration, they feed on berries.

Nesting
Yellow-breasted chats place their well-hidden nests low, from just above the ground to 6 or 7 feet up. The female builds the leafy nest, lining it with grasses and bits of bark. She usually lays three or four eggs, incubating them for about 10 days. Both parents feed their young, which fly off just over a week after emerging from their eggs. This speedy time from hatching to fledging is an adaptation to help fledgling chats avoid nest predators.

Backyard & Beyond
Chats breed in wild, tangled, transitional areas, such as farm fields overgrown with shrubs and young trees. Backyard birders seeking to attract them as nesters will need to have wild areas adjacent to their property or large open acreage where nature can take its course, turning from field to shrubby pre-forest. After five to eight years, thickets often turn to forest and no longer attract chats, so cover will need to be cut and allowed to regrow.

Summer Tanager
Piranga rubra

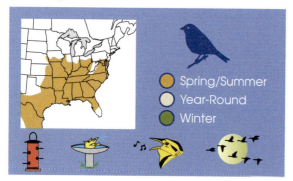

This trim and elegant neotropical migrant is sometimes called the "summer redbird" to distinguish it from the South's other "redbird," the familiar cardinal. It is shy and deliberate in its movements and, for such a colorful bird, can be surprisingly difficult to find. Luckily for the birder who seeks it, the summer tanager has several easily learned vocalizations, and it utters them often.

All About
Only the male summer tanager is red; the female is olive-backed with yellow-orange underparts. The male can be differentiated from the male cardinal by its more slender bill shape and lack of a crest on its head; it can be distinguished from a male scarlet tanager by its red (not black) wings and tail. Unlike the male scarlet tanager, the male summer tanager retains its red coloration throughout the year. The summer tanager is $7^{1}/_{2}$ to 8 inches in length and sings a rich, warbling song that is similar in phrasing to a robin's. Its call is an explosive *perky-tuck-tuck!*

Habitat & Range
The summer tanager arrives on its U.S. breeding grounds sometime in April and departs, as a rule, by midfall. During migration the species covers a wide front; many birds fly nonstop across the Gulf of Mexico on their journeys north and south. Its preferred habitat is dry, open woods of oak, hickory, or pine, but many nest in wooded residential neighborhoods, as well.

Feeding
Summer tanagers are insect-eaters, and they are noted for their fearless predation on wasps, bees, and other stinging creatures. Beetles, caterpillars, cicadas, flies, and other insects are also taken, and in summer small fruits are eaten. Summer tanagers normally creep along tree branches scanning for insects, but they can also hover to glean insects from hanging leaves or capture flying insects with short flights from a perch.

Nesting
The nest of a summer tanager is a rather shallow, flimsy cup of weed stems, leaves, and fine grasses, built by the female on a horizontal branch well away from the tree trunk. The usual clutch of eggs is four, incubated by the female for 12 days. Both parents feed the nestlings until they leave the nest at about two weeks of age.

Backyard & Beyond
Look for summer tanagers near wasp nests in late summer—both adult wasps and larvae are favored food sources. Bee concentrations may also attract this species. You will improve your chances of finding a summer tanager if you learn to recognize both the warbling, robinlike song, and the *perky-tuck-tuck* call unique to this species. Summer tanagers are not generally attracted to bird feeders, but a few have been reported to eat orange halves or a peanut butter-cornmeal mix.

Scarlet Tanager
Piranga olivacea

The male scarlet tanager in spring plumage ranks among the most stunningly beautiful birds in North America. One glance at his neon-bright plumage can turn even the most disinterested person into a confirmed bird watcher. Oddly, this dazzling bird's song has been compared to "a robin with a bad cold." A distinctive chick-burr call is often the first clue of a scarlet tanager's presence.

All About
The male scarlet tanager in spring plumage has a solid red body and jet-black wings and tail, with a black-button eye and bone-gray bill. The female is dull olive above with dark wings and pale yellow underparts. Immatures resemble females, and in late summer the adult males take on the muted olive-yellow plumage. In all plumages, the scarlet tanager's wings are darker than those of the summer tanager. At just 7 inches long, scarlet tanagers are the smallest of the four North American tanager species.

Habitat & Range
Preferring deciduous forests with oaks, maples, and beeches, scarlet tanagers generally inhabit areas farther north (or, in the South, at higher elevations) than summer tanagers. They arrive in April or May and depart by midautumn. Flocks of early migrants are sometimes decimated by sudden late-spring snowfalls or ice storms, which cause them to starve or freeze to death. Sometimes being the early bird is not such a good idea.

Feeding
Basically insectivorous, the scarlet tanager moves quietly about in the upper canopy of deciduous trees in search of prey. Small summer fruits—such as blueberries and mulberries—are also taken, as are fall staples, such as poison ivy berries and sumac fruits. Scarlet tanagers occasionally engage in flycatching, or hovering behavior, to obtain food. Early or late in the season, cold weather may force them to the ground to forage for bugs in sheltered microhabitats.

Nesting
Typically, the scarlet tanager nests in a large, unbroken, wooded tract and high in a deciduous tree—often, but not always—an oak. It will be situated well out from the trunk on a horizontal limb. Made by the female alone, it is shallow and loosely constructed of twigs, rootlets, weeds, and other plant material. Three to five eggs are laid, and the female incubates them for up to two weeks until hatching. Both parents feed the young during the 9- to 14-day nestling period and for two weeks more after fledging occurs.

Backyard & Beyond
Scarlet tanagers are not common at bird feeders, but they do—on occasion—respond to offerings of bread, doughnuts, orange halves, or a peanut butter-cornmeal mixture. They will also eat small fruits and, in fall migration, may be a regular sight along tangled hedgerows overrun by poison ivy or multiflora rose.

Northern Cardinal
Cardinalis cardinalis

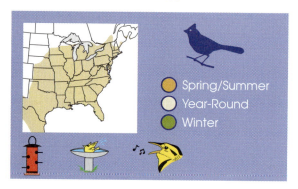

Cardinals are the familiar and beloved "redbird" found all across the eastern United States. This bird's popularity is such that seven U.S. states and countless sports teams have chosen the cardinal as their official emblem. In spring and summer, cardinal pairs can be found together, often with the male perched high above, singing his *what-cheer-cheer-cheer* song. In fall and winter, cardinals can be found in large loose flocks, especially during harsh weather.

All About
A black face and a long red crest smartly set off the bright red plumage of the male cardinal. Females are a muted, brownish version of the male. Strongly territorial, mated cardinal pairs will vigorously defend their nesting turf from rivals, even going so far as to attack their own reflections in windows, mistaking the image for another cardinal. One of the cardinal's most notable behaviors is the "courtship kiss" in which a male feeds a bit of food to a female he is wooing.

Habitat & Range
Found in a variety of habitats—from deserts to wetlands to manicured backyards, cardinals prefer an *edge habitat*—a place where woodland and open space meet. They are resident (nonmigratory) and thriving throughout their range, which has expanded northward in recent decades—thanks in part to the availability of food at bird feeders.

Feeding
Cardinals forage on or near the ground. During warm weather, insects, berries, buds, and seeds are their primary diet. Gardeners appreciate cardinals for eating grubs, beetles, caterpillars, and other garden pests. In winter, cardinals shift to a greater reliance on seeds, nuts, and wild fruits. At bird feeders cardinals prefer sunflower seeds, but will also eat mixed seeds, suet, fruits, and peanuts.

Nesting
Female cardinals choose thick cover—vine or rose tangles or shrubs—in which to weave their shallow, cup-shaped nests out of grasses, rootlets, twigs, and bark strips. Into this nest, the female will lay three to five eggs and incubate them for nearly two weeks before they hatch. Both parents feed the youngsters for about 10 days before they fledge. In summer, young cardinals can often be seen following a parent around, begging to be fed. Males will take on this duty while the female starts a second brood.

Backyard & Beyond
You can enjoy cardinals all year long in your backyard by offering them the four things they need to survive: food, water, a place to roost, and a place to nest. A few bird feeders, a chemical-free lawn and garden, and some thick brushy cover will suit their requirements nicely. Watch for cardinals early and late—they are often the first birds active at dawn and the last ones to "turn in" at dusk.

Indigo Bunting
Passerina cyanea

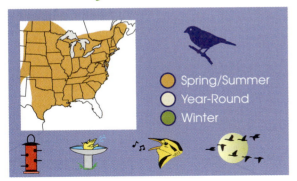

Appearing all black against the light, a male indigo bunting properly lit is an unforgettable sight. A persistent late-season singer, he sings a jingly song comprised of paired notes that are often described as: *Fire! Fire! Where? Where? Here! Here! Put it out! Put it out!* Much of what we know about celestial navigation in songbirds derives from work with captive indigo buntings at the Cornell Lab of Ornithology.

All About
The breathtaking, all-blue male indigo bunting, with his silvery conical bill, is unmistakable. Females and immatures are a warm cocoa-brown overall. This bunting has a habit of twitching its tail to the side, and its *spit!* note is characteristic. Males change their blue feathers for brown in autumn, which makes for some interestingly mottled specimens. They molt again on the wintering grounds and return in spring, blue once more.

Habitat & Range
This species is common on roadsides and disturbed areas where "trashy" vegetation flourishes. Power line cuts, old fields, landfills, railroads, and hedgerows ring with the songs of indigo buntings, especially as summer reaches its fullest. Indigo buntings are strongly migratory, wintering in Central and northern South America.

Feeding
The indigo bunting takes insects when they are available, especially to feed its nestlings. Weed seeds are its mainstay, supplemented by berries and small fruits. It forages on or near the ground, as well as in low shrubs and trees. Watch for them in autumn, bending grass stems and flicking their tails side to side as they forage in weedy patches.

Nesting
Indigo buntings have a rather loose definition of monogamy, with extra-pair copulations being quite frequent. Males visit females in neighboring territories, and females visit males. Males vary in their tendency to feed young; some are attentive parents, whereas others leave most of the chick rearing to their mates. The nest is bulky but compact, cup-shaped, and constructed of bark strips, grass and weed stems, and skeletonized leaves, all bound with spider webs. It's often low in blackberry, sumac, or other brushy vegetation. These birds nest quite late in the season, reflecting their dependence on late-maturing weed seeds. Three to four eggs are incubated by the female for about 12 days, and the young leave the nest from 8 to 14 days later.

Backyard & Beyond
Lucky is the one who hosts indigo buntings! Spring arrivals are most often first seen feasting on dandelion seeds. Later, black-oil sunflower seeds and millet mixes prove attractive. The growing popularity of "meadows in a can" make for rich feeding grounds for indigo buntings, which flock to coneflower, Mexican hat, cosmos, coreopsis, and especially foxtail grasses.

Eastern Towhee
Pipilo erythrophthalmus

Drink your TEA! *sings the towhee throughout the brushy woodlands of the eastern United States. Formerly called the rufous-sided towhee (a much more descriptive name), this large (8½ inches long) sparrow is boldly patterned and spends nearly all its time on the ground scratching among the leaf litter, looking for food. The name towhee comes from the bird's call, which has also been transcribed as* chewink. *Many people know this bird as the chewink instead of towhee.*

All About
Clean, flashy colors have given the towhee the nickname "Hollywood robin." In flight, the bird's white wing and tail spots are noticeable. Female eastern towhees replace the male's black plumage areas with chocolate brown. Towhees' preference for thick cover and brushy habitat make them harder to see than other common species. The loud scratching of a foraging towhee sounds like a large animal walking through dry leaves; this is often your first clue to a towhee's presence.

Habitat & Range
Widespread across the eastern half of the United States and southern Canada, towhees in the northern part of the range are migratory, but those in the southern half are resident (nonmigratory). During mild winters, towhees may linger until harsh weather forces them to migrate or to seek the cover of wooded valleys and hollows. Brushy woodland thickets and edge habitats are preferred, but towhees are also found in older woodlands and suburban backyards.

Feeding
Towhees eat just about anything found on the woodland floor, including insects, seeds, fruits, and even snails, spiders, and millipedes. They prefer to scratch the ground under feeding stations for mixed seeds, cracked corn, and sunflower seeds (which they crack with their powerful bill).

Nesting
Towhees nest on or near the ground in a well-concealed spot. The female weaves a cup-shaped nest out of rootlets, bark strips, and grass. She also handles all the incubation duty, which typically lasts about 12 days. Normal clutch size is three to four eggs; young towhees fledge in about 10 days. Both towhee parents feed the youngsters, which allows the female to start a second—and sometimes a third—brood.

Backyard & Beyond
Spring is the best time to find an eastern towhee. Male towhees are especially vocal during the breeding season and will leave deep cover to sing from a high perch within their territory. Make your feeders much more attractive to towhees by adding a brush pile nearby to help these shy birds feel more at home. In summer, recently fledged towhees can be confusing and hard to identify with their streaky, gray-brown coloring. Their white tail spots and ground-scratching habits will give them away.

Field Sparrow
Spizella pusilla

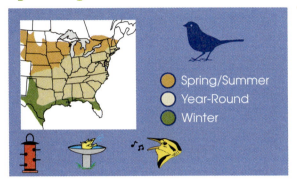

The field sparrow's clear whistled notes on a single tone is an easy bird song to learn and remember. Listen throughout the day, even in summer, for this persistent singer. Its rhythmic pattern resembles a ping-pong ball being dropped onto a table. A subtly beautiful sparrow of farm pastures and shrubby old meadows, the field sparrow is familiar to bird watchers in rural habitats.

All About
The field sparrow is a small bird (5 3/4 inches long) with a biggish bill and long tail, but the first field marks most birders notice are the pink bill, plain face, and white ring surrounding the dark eye. Telling the field sparrow apart from chipping or tree sparrows is a matter of noting the field's unmarked buffy-gray breast and indistinct head stripes of brown and gray.

Habitat & Range
As its name suggests, the field sparrow is found in fields, but it prefers brushy, older fields that have the beginnings of reforestation—saplings, small shrubs, and large thick clumps of grass. Field sparrows are found all across the eastern United States, but—unlike many of our migrant songbirds—they may only migrate a few hundred miles to spend the winter. In spring and summer, males do their singing from an exposed perch within their territories.

Feeding
Throughout the year, the field sparrow's diet is grass seeds and other small plant seeds; in spring and summer the diet shifts to insects. Moths, grasshoppers, flies, and other grassland insects make up half of their summer diet, with most of the insects being found on or near the ground. In winter, as flocks of field sparrows forage together, a single bird will perch on top of a tall grass stem, letting its weight bend the stalk to the ground where the seeds can more easily be eaten.

Nesting
In early spring (April to May) field sparrow nests are built on the ground, near a grass clump or small shrub. Later nests (June to July) may be in taller shrubs or vegetation, but the construction is the same—a loosely woven outer cup of grass lined with fine, soft grasses, all built by the female. Three to six eggs are laid and incubated by the female for about 12 days. Like other ground nesters, young field sparrows develop quickly and may leave the nest within a week. Flight is attained in two weeks and independence from the parents two weeks later.

Backyard & Beyond
Within the breeding range, any older farm field should host field sparrows. Look for males perched on top of saplings or fenceposts. Field sparrows will come to cracked corn, mixed seeds, and eggshell bits scattered on the ground beneath bird feeders.

Chipping Sparrow
Spizella passerina

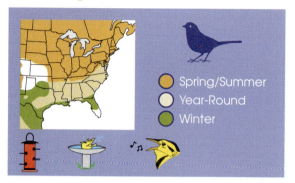

A close look at this natty little bird reveals much to admire in its quiet and confiding ways. As common as it is around dooryards and gardens, we know surprisingly little about the chipping sparrow's mating systems. One Ontario study showed males not to be monogamous, as assumed, but to mate freely.

All About
A rusty beret and bold, white eyeline are the best field marks of this slender little sparrow. Plain gray underparts, a streaked brown back, and a small, all-black bill set off its striking head markings. It is an under-appreciated bird, perhaps because it is so small and unobtrusive. Rather dry, monotonous trills, as well as its signature chipping notes, are the ambient sounds of a chipping sparrow's territory.

Habitat & Range
Before the massive expansion of suburbs, the chipping sparrow was limited to open, grassy coniferous forests and parklike woodlands with shrubby understories. Our suburban habitats have just the right mix of short grass, shrubbery, and conifers that chipping sparrows need, so we enjoy their company on doorsteps and sidewalks. Although northern populations are strongly migratory, southern birds flock up but tend to stay near their breeding grounds.

Feeding
Chipping sparrows forage primarily on or near the ground, feasting on weed and grass seeds and some smaller fruits. They feed insects to the young, however, sometimes flycatching on the wing. Winter flocks of up to 50 birds perch in trees, descending en masse to the ground to peck for seeds, then adjourning to treetops before the next feeding bout. At feeding stations, they'll peck on the ground or perch on hopper feeders.

Nesting
Female chipping sparrows weave lovely little nests of thin twigs and weed stems, with a center composed of animal hair. These are often concealed in low trees and shrubs, but are easily located by the shrilling of older nestlings. Females incubate the four eggs for around 12 days, and the young leave the nest about 9 to 12 days later. Streaky, brown, and nondescript, they're fed by their parents for three more weeks before forming juvenile flocks.

Backyard & Beyond
Chipping sparrows eagerly accept mixed seeds and suet dough mixtures offered on or near the ground. They're fond of rolled oats, and live mealworms will be taken straight to the young. They greatly appreciate baked and crushed eggshells strewn on a sidewalk. But it's most fun to offer them human or pet hair clippings. A trip to any salon can net a season's worth, and you may have the pleasure of finding a used nest lined with your own hair—the ultimate vanity piece for the discerning gardener.

White-throated Sparrow
Zonotrichia albicollis

Old Sam Peabody, Peabody, Peabody is the sweet whistled song of the white-throated sparrow. In Canada, where this species spends the breeding season, the song is transcribed as Oh sweet Canada, Canada, Canada—*but there's no arguing that the white-throated sparrow's song is easy to recognize. From September to March these northern breeders are with us, in loose flocks with other sparrows, brightening winter days with their cheery sounds.*

All About
The first field mark most bird watchers notice on the white-throated sparrow is not the white throat, but the black-and-white striped head pattern with a yellow spot between the eyes and bill. Even at a distance this striking pattern is obvious. Some white-throated sparrows have tan-striped heads and a tannish throat. These belong to the tan-striped variety of the species, though many ornithologists formerly thought these were young birds not yet in adult plumage. This medium-sized (6 3/4 inches long) sparrow has a gray breast and a brown, lightly patterned back.

Habitat & Range
Spending most of the summer in the boreal coniferous forests of the far north and New England, the white-throated sparrow spends fall and winter far to the south, where it is a regular at bird feeders and in brushy edge habitat. It prefers a habitat with thick underbrush and is found near the edge of the woods, along hedgerows, and in brushy thickets in parks and backyards.

Feeding
White-throated sparrows prefer to feed on the ground. In spring and summer, the white-throated sparrow's diet is focused on insects—ants, grubs, and spiders—that it uncovers as it scratches through the leaf litter, much like a towhee does. In fall the diet shifts to include berries; in winter it includes mostly seeds from grasses. At bird feeders they are attracted to mixed seed, cracked corn, and sunflower or peanut bits offered on the ground or on a platform feeder.

Nesting
White-throated sparrows nest on or near the ground in a well-concealed spot. The cup-shaped nest is built by the female from grass, pine needles, and twigs and lined with soft material, such as rootlets or fur. The female incubates the four to five eggs for about two weeks; the male assists her in feeding the nestlings for the nine days prior to fledging. The young birds rely on the parents for food for about another two weeks.

Backyard & Beyond
Look for white-throated sparrows on the ground beneath your feeders from late fall through early spring. If your feeders are some distance from cover, consider moving them closer to the woods' edge, or add a brush pile nearby to make woodland birds (such as white-throated sparrows) feel more at home.

Song Sparrow
Melospiza melodia

Persistent singing, often year-round, makes this a well-named species. If there's a resident song sparrow in your yard, you'll probably hear its cheery notes at first light—as reliable as, but more pleasant than, a rooster's. One of the best-studied birds in North America, the song sparrow was the subject of Margaret Morse Nice's groundbreaking behavioral study in the 1930s. Much of what we understand about songbird territoriality began with this study.

All About
The classic "little brown job," the song sparrow has a heavily streaked white breast marked with a messy central spot. A grayish, striped face and crown and warm-brown upperparts complete the description. Flight is low and jerky, with the tail twisting distinctively. Three introductory notes leading to a variable jumble of trills and chips distinguish its song. Males and females look similar.

Habitat & Range
Though song sparrows occupy a wide range of habitats, they are most often found in shrubbery near water, from small streams to beach habitats. Song sparrows tend to be migratory in northern climes and year-round residents in the southern United States; this varies by population. The song sparrow is one of the most variable songbirds known. Populations in the Pacific Northwest, for example, are larger, darker, heavier-billed, and virtually unrecognizable compared to Southeastern coastal populations.

Feeding
The song sparrow's diet varies seasonally, with insects being its primary prey in spring and summer and with seeds and fruits dominating in fall and winter. Most of the song sparrow's foraging takes place on the ground, where it will scratch and kick about in leaf litter and grasses for weed seeds and insects.

Nesting
The persistent singing of song sparrows is linked to strong territorial behavior; where they are resident year-round, they tend to defend territories year-round. Territory boundaries are quite stable from year to year. Both sexes defend their territory, and they tend to stay with one mate. Females construct a bulky nest of bark strips and weed and grass stems, well hidden deep in a dense shrub. Small, ornamental evergreens are irresistible to song sparrows. The female incubates three to five eggs for about 13 days. Young leave the nest at only 10 days and may be fed by the parents for the next 20 days before they are fully independent.

Backyard & Beyond
Song sparrows readily visit feeders for sunflower seeds, cracked corn, and mixed seeds, preferring to feed on the ground. Peanut butter-based suet mixes are a favorite food, and song sparrows will appear to beg at windows for such fare. They are fond of water and will often nest near a water garden or backyard pond.

Dark-eyed Junco
Junco hyemalis

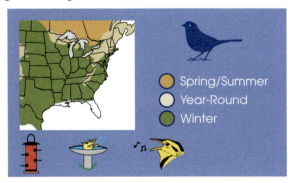

The dark-eyed junco is often called the "snowbird," because it seems to show up at our feeders and in our backyards at the same time as the first snows begin falling over much of the country. But even in the Deep South, this member of the sparrow family is a familiar winter visitor to backyards, gardens, parks, pastures, and feeding stations.

All About
Juncos are medium-sized (6¼ inches long) sparrows, but unlike most sparrows, their plumage lacks streaking. Dark-gray above and white below (or "gray skies above, snow below"), the junco has a conical, pinkish bill and flashes its white outer tail feathers in flight. Male juncos in the East are a darker gray than the brownish-overall females. Western junco forms show a variety of plumage colors, and many of these color forms were considered separate species until recently. Now they are all lumped into a single species: dark-eyed junco. Juncos make a variety of sounds, all of them high-pitched tinkling trills, especially when flushed from cover.

Habitat & Range
Few bird species' ranges cover North America more thoroughly than that of the dark-eyed junco. In winter it can be found in every state. Spring migration begins as early as March and continues through early June. During breeding season, juncos retreat to the far north woods and to coniferous and mixed woodlands at high elevations. Fall migration begins in mid-August through October. Their winter habitat preferences run to brushy edge habitat along woods, fields, and suburban backyards and parks.

Feeding
Juncos find their food on the ground. They are often seen scratching through the leaf litter, grass, or snow when foraging. In spring and summer the junco eats mostly insects, including spiders, caterpillars, ants, grasshoppers, and weevils, but it will also eat berries. In fall and winter the diet shifts to grass and weed seeds, along with birdseed gleaned from the ground beneath feeders.

Nesting
The junco's nest is a simple, open cup of grasses and leaves, loosely woven and lined with finer grasses, fur, or feathers. Nests are normally located on the ground in a concealed spot and built by the female. She incubates her three to five eggs for almost two weeks; the male helps with feeding chores once the young hatch. Within two weeks the young birds leave the nest, and the parents are free to start another brood if the season permits.

Backyard & Beyond
Where there is one junco, there is almost surely a flock. Seek them along the edges of woodlots, old pastures, and in areas with a thick growth of underbrush. Watch for the flashing white in the tail and listen for the juncos' trilling calls.

Eastern Meadowlark
Sturnella magna

The eastern meadowlark's sweet whistled song—spring of THE year!—is a sign of spring's arrival, as is its lemon-yellow color, adding a brightness to the most dreary of spring days. Ironically, this beloved "country" bird of open farmland is actually a member of the blackbird family, a clan that gets little affection from farmers. Echoes of the meadowlark's blackbird relatives can be heard in the bird's chattering scold calls given by territorial males in spring.

All About
A familiar bird of rural farm fields, meadows, and grasslands, the eastern meadowlark is known by its distinctive field mark: a bright yellow breast with a "V" of black. Meadowlarks will sing from the ground and in flight, but they often use an elevated perch, such as a fencepost, tree, or power line. In flight, the meadowlark looks chunky and shows white outer tail feathers. A series of shallow, stuttering wingbeats followed by a short glide (sometimes accompanied by a song or chatter) is the typical flight pattern.

Habitat & Range
Eastern meadowlarks prefer grassy meadows, prairies, and pastures with good grass cover. They can also be found along golf courses, in hay fields, and in the grassy margins of airports. Found year-round across most of the eastern United States, this species is declining slowly across its range, especially in areas with growing urbanization and heavy agricultural use. As abandoned farm fields grow up into shrubby woodland, they become less suitable habitats for meadowlarks.

Feeding
The meadowlark is a ground feeder that searches vegetation in spring and summer for insects, such as crickets, grasshoppers, grubs, and caterpillars. In winter, the diet shifts to seeds, grains, and some fruits. In fall and winter, eastern meadowlarks often form large flocks, with dozens of birds foraging together in the same field.

Nesting
Meadowlarks nest on the ground in thick grass. The nest is well concealed in a depression on the ground and is woven out of dried grasses. Two to six eggs are laid and incubated for about 14 days. Youngsters fledge about 10 days later. Both parents feed the young. For nesting, meadowlarks seem to prefer grasslands that are cut only once every three to five years. Even so, many meadowlark nests are lost to agricultural activity, to predation, and to pesticides.

Backyard & Beyond
To find a meadowlark, you must locate a suitable habitat, which usually means locating a rural spot with hayfields and pastures. During spring and summer, meadowlarks sing throughout the day, but do so most actively early in the morning. Listen for the slurring whistled song and the sputtering blackbirdlike calls. Scan the wires, treetops, and fenceposts for the singing adult bird.

Brown-headed Cowbird
Molothrus ater

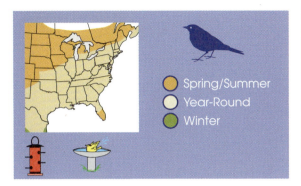

The cowbird's habit of laying its eggs in the nests of other, smaller songbirds makes the brown-headed cowbird a nest parasite. Cowbirds learned this behavior over centuries of following roaming herds of buffalo. The buffalo stirred up insects, the cowbird's main food. But all the movement made it impossible to stop, build a nest, and wait for the young to grow. So the cowbirds did the most convenient thing—laid their eggs in any nest they could find along the way.

All About
The cowbird is a small (7 1/2 inches long) blackbird. Males have a glossy black body and a dark brown head, while females are a dull gray-brown overall. The short, conical bill and pointed wings help to distinguish the brown-headed cowbird from larger blackbirds. The cowbird's song is a series of liquid gurgles followed by a high, thin whistle.

Habitat & Range
Cowbirds are found in a variety of habitats, but they prefer woodland edges, brushy fields, and old pastures, though they are equally at home in city parks and suburban backyards. Forest fragmentation has allowed the cowbird to parasitize the nests of woodland species, such as thrushes and vireos. In winter cowbirds often join flocks of other blackbirds—red-winged blackbirds, grackles, and European starlings—foraging in fields and grasslands and roosting en masse in large woodlots.

Feeding
The diet of the cowbird consists of weed and grass seeds, along with insects, especially grasshoppers and beetles. Nearly all food is taken from the ground.

Nesting
Male cowbirds court females with a variety of songs, bows, and sky-pointing displays. When she is ready to lay an egg, she finds a nest that often already contains the eggs of the nest's owner. This "host" nest is most frequently that of a smaller songbird—yellow warblers, song sparrows, red-eyed vireos, and chipping sparrows seem to be frequent victims—and the female cowbird may even remove one of the host's eggs before depositing her own. Hatchling cowbirds are almost always larger than their nest mates, and are able to out-compete them for food, enhancing the cowbird's chances of survival. Some bird species have evolved to recognize cowbird eggs and will build a new nest on top of the old one or will remove the cowbird egg.

Backyard & Beyond
Finding cowbirds is almost never a problem, but limiting their impact on our songbirds can be problematic. One way to discourage cowbirds is to stop offering mixed seed and cracked corn during spring when they show up at bird feeders before many migratory songbirds return. If you see a songbird feeding a fledgling that is larger than itself, the fledgling is likely a cowbird.

Red-winged Blackbird
Agelaius phoeniceus

The red-winged blackbird's name succinctly describes the male's handsome plumage; yet, the females of this ubiquitous species have baffled many a bird watcher. Their streaky brown plumage is confusingly sparrowlike. Studies have shown that one dominant male red-winged blackbird may have many adult females nesting on his territory.

All About
The *conk-a-ree* call of the male red-winged blackbird fills the air over marshes and fields all across North America. As he gives this call, announcing himself loudly to rivals and potential mates alike, he spreads his shoulders just so, showing bright red and yellow epaulets against his black wings. Redwings are medium-sized (8 3/4 inches long) blackbirds with an all-black body, an orange-red and yellow patch on the shoulder, and a nearly conical black bill. Females are streaky brown overall, but their longer bill helps separate them from the sparrows (which have stouter bills).

Habitat & Range
Wet meadows, cattail marshes, upland grasslands, and pastures are all breeding habitat for red-winged blackbirds. In fall and winter, they may join with other blackbird species to form huge flocks. Northern nesting redwings migrate (starting in September and October) to the southern U.S., while southern nesting birds are nonmigratory. Fall blackbird flocks move during the day in oblong, loose clouds of birds. These flocks forage by day in agricultural fields and are often persecuted as a nuisance species for the crop damage they inflict. Spring migration begins in mid-February and continues through mid-May.

Feeding
The red-winged blackbird's diet is mostly plant matter—weed seeds, grain, sunflower seeds, and tree seeds—along with some insects, all of which are gleaned from the ground. They will also visit feeding stations for sunflower seeds, cracked corn, peanuts, and suet. Surprisingly, they are able to use a variety of feeder types.

Nesting
Nesting starts early for the red-winged blackbird, with males singing from an exposed perch on their territories as early as February in the South, later in the North. Females choose a nest site on a male's territory and build cup-shaped grass nests that are suspended from vertical supporting vegetation. Mud forms the foundation of the nest and soft grasses are the inner lining. Clutch size is three to four eggs, and the female alone incubates them for 10 to 13 days. Both parents care for the nestlings for about two weeks, until they are ready to leave the nest.

Backyard & Beyond
Red-winged blackbirds are present continent-wide for most of the year. Wet meadows, swamps, and salt marshes are common habitats for these birds, especially in spring and summer. Listen for the male's loud *conk-a-ree* song.

Common Grackle
Quiscalus quiscula

Grackles are large, conspicuous, and noisy birds that are equally at home in a town or country setting. This species benefited greatly from the European settlement of North America as forests were turned into farm fields and new feeding and nesting opportunities emerged for the common grackle. Residential areas and farmland are particularly attractive to grackles.

All About
Nearly half of the common grackle's 12½-inch length is its tail. The grackle's black plumage is glossy and can show bright purple, bronze, or green highlights, especially on the head. Adult common grackles show a pale yellow eye, contrasting sharply with the dark head. The powerful bill is long and sharply pointed. In flight, grackles hold their long tails in a "V", much like the keel of a boat. Males and females are very similar in appearance. Grackles utter a variety of harsh, metallic tones.

Habitat & Range
Common grackles are found in almost every habitat in eastern North America; though, in winter the population is more concentrated in the eastern and southern United States. Grackles prefer edge habitat and open areas with scattered trees or shrubs. From late summer to early spring, grackles gather in large roosts with other blackbirds. These roosts can contain as many as half a million birds, and are notable both for their noise and their droppings. Spring migrants may reach breeding territories as early as mid-February. Fall migration begins in September and peaks in October.

Feeding
During breeding season, grackles eat mostly insects, but they are opportunists and will take nestling birds or eggs, small fish, mice, and frogs. In winter the diet shifts to seeds and grain. The impact of foraging winter flocks on crops has earned the common grackle a reputation as an agricultural pest. Most of the grackle's foraging is done on the ground, where the birds toss aside leaves and rubbish to uncover their food.

Nesting
Grackles prefer to nest in dense conifers, close to rich foraging habitat. The large, open, cup nest is built by the female from grass, twigs, and mud and is lined with soft grass. She incubates the four to five eggs for about two weeks. The male joins her in feeding the nestlings an all-insect diet until fledging time arrives about 20 days later.

Backyard & Beyond
Look for long dark lines of migrating common grackles during the day, especially in fall. Migrating flocks can contain thousands of birds and may stretch from horizon to horizon. At feeders grackles relish cracked corn and sunflower seeds most of all. Grackles are also known to take hard, stale pieces of bread and dunk them in a birdbath to soften them up.

Orchard Oriole

Icterus spurius

The smallest oriole in North America is also the darkest, with a designer color scheme of chestnut and black that is rarely seen in songbirds. Look for it along watercourses, on farmsteads, and in orchards. In suitable habitats, the orchard oriole may nest semicolonially, with several nests to a tree. This raises interesting and as yet unanswered questions about its mating system and social behavior.

All About

The male's deep orange-chestnut underparts are set off by a black hood, back, and tail. The female is an even olive-yellow overall, with whitish wing bars. She is small enough to sometimes be mistaken for a warbler. Newly fledged young are olive-yellow, and males in their second spring are similar, but for a striking black "beard." This plumage can confuse the beginning bird watcher. The orchard oriole's song is rich, fast, and varied, with chatters and metallic notes pouring out in a jumble. The alarm call is a dry *check!*

Habitat & Range

The orchard oriole is strongly associated with watercourses and inhabits areas with smaller, denser trees than does its larger cousin, the Baltimore oriole. Farmyards and gardens and some yards with scattered trees are graced with its dynamic presence. Orchard orioles spend a relatively short time on the breeding grounds, often departing for Central America as early as July, after raising a single brood.

Feeding

This oriole eats primarily insects, but it is fond of nectar and fruits as well, taking whatever is available. Blooming black locust trees, rich with sweet nectar, are irresistible, and it will slit the sides of trumpet vine flowers to access the nectar. Orchard orioles glean tree leaves for insects and sometimes hunt grasshoppers near the ground in agricultural fields.

Nesting

A master weaver, the orchard oriole makes a neat, round basket of green grass leaves that slowly dries and shrinks to a pale, densely woven ball. Though it is similarly suspended, its nest is not long-necked or pendulous like the Baltimore oriole's; instead, it is a deep cup. Four to six eggs are incubated by the female. Young fledge about 11 to 14 days later. They are fed by both the male and female until the male departs for the wintering grounds.

Backyard & Beyond

This oriole is not particularly attracted to feeders; however, fruit or nectar feeders might lure the occasional patron. Orchard orioles migrate in segregated flocks, with adult males departing suddenly in late July. Females and similarly plumaged fledglings flock together and forage for another four to six weeks before starting south.

House Finch
Carpodacus mexicanus

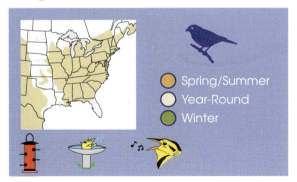

Bird watchers who rely on an eastern field guide that is more than thirty years old may be forgiven for some confusion. This bird won't be in it! The house finch, native to the West, is a well-established, but recently arrived resident of the eastern United States. Released upon the passage of protective legislation forbidding trade in native wild birds, a small population of the so-called "Hollywood linnets" began breeding on Long Island in 1940, and they have now blanketed the eastern United States with their progeny.

All About

People who feed birds are familiar with the house finches that sometimes cover feeders with fluttering, tweeting flocks. It's easy to see why they were kept as cage birds; the male's cheery, rich song, marked by a few harsh notes, tumbles brightly down the scale. Females are streaky, pale brown birds with white undersides; males have a rich pinkish-red rump, head, and upper breast. By comparison, male purple finches have an overall "dipped in wine" look, with a reddish suffusion to their back and wings, while female purple finches are much more boldly streaked with brown and white than are female house finches.

Habitat & Range

As its name suggests, the house finch prefers nesting and feeding near homes. It's a thoroughly suburban bird in the East, but in its native West, it is found in undisturbed desert habitats as well. This species appears to be developing migratory behavior in the East, with a general movement toward the South in winter.

Feeding

Most of the house finch's diet is vegetarian, and it spends a great deal of time feeding on the ground. Weed seeds, buds, and fruits are its mainstays away from feeding stations.

Nesting

House finch nests are shallow twig platforms with a finely woven inner cup composed of rootlets, grass, feathers, and string. They are tucked into dense ornamental evergreens, hanging baskets, ledges, ivy-covered walls, and other nooks where there is an overhanging structure. Two to five eggs are incubated by the female, while the male feeds her. Young are fed regurgitated seeds and fledge from 12 to 16 days later.

Backyard & Beyond

For most feeding station proprietors, the question is not how to attract house finches, but how to discourage them. Even attractive birds with pleasant songs wear out their welcome when they descend in dozens, monopolizing feeders. Black-oil sunflower seeds are a favorite, closely followed by Niger and mixed seeds. Some people resort to removing perches from tube feeders, thus discouraging house finches, which are poor clingers.

American Goldfinch
Carduelis tristis

The bright canary-yellow and black plumage of the breeding male American goldfinch has earned this species the nickname "wild canary." It is a familiar visitor to bird feeders at all seasons, especially in winter. The goldfinch's undulating flight is accompanied by a twittering call of perchickoree or potato chip!

All About
American goldfinches appear very different in summer and winter. The male's brilliant yellow body and black cap in summer give way to a drab, olive-brown plumage in winter. Female goldfinches, though never bright yellow, also lose most of their color. Both sexes retain their black wings and tail year-round. The sweet, high-pitched, warbling song of the male is often given in early spring, just as these small (5 inches long) birds are beginning to show their first bright yellow feathers.

Habitat & Range
Weedy fields, brushy woodland edges, and open habitats with scattered shrubs are the American goldfinch's normal habitats. In the breeding season, they prefer weedy fields with thistles and other seed-producing plants. In winter, goldfinches roam in noisy flocks, seeking food in fields, gardens, and at feeding stations.

Feeding
Goldfinches are seedeaters in all seasons, consuming a huge variety of weed, grass, and plant seeds as well as tree buds. In goldfinch nests parasitized by brown-headed cowbirds, young cowbirds are unable to survive the all-seed diet fed to nestling goldfinches. Goldfinches are agile birds, able to exploit seed sources that other finches cannot, by hanging upside down from seedheads, plant stalks, and bird feeders.

Nesting
Goldfinches' nesting season begins late, an adaptation to time so that nesting occurs when there is the greatest natural abundance of seeds, as well as the soft thistle down that goldfinches use to line their nests. Late June is the earliest nesting time, but peak nesting season is late July, though some nesting occurs as late as September. The site is in a shaded spot in a sapling or shrub and is selected by the pair. The female builds the open cup nest from twigs (attached with spider web), rootlets, and plant stems, and she lines it with soft thistle down or a similarly soft material. Four to six eggs are incubated by the female for about two weeks, with the male bringing food to her on the nest. Both parents tend the nestlings for 12 to 17 days before they fledge.

Backyard & Beyond
The twittering calls of goldfinches will alert you to the presence of these energetic songbirds. At bird feeders, goldfinches especially like thistle seeds (sometimes called Niger seeds), sunflower seeds and bits, and peanut bits. Goldfinches love to drink and bathe in shallow birdbaths and are especially attracted to moving water.

House Sparrow
Passer domesticus

Introduced to North America in the early 1850s from England to help control wireworms, the house sparrow population spread across the continent in just 50 years. The house sparrow enjoys a close association with humans, almost always nesting and living in proximity to our settlements. It is one of the world's most successful and widespread species.

All About
The chunky little house sparrow is known for its constant *cha-deep, cha-deep* calls and for the male's black bib in breeding plumage. Breeding males have a black bill and a contrasting black, gray, and brown head and face pattern. Winter males are a muted version of the breeding plumage. Females are drab gray-brown overall and lack the bib. House sparrows are constantly chirping and are aggressive competitors at feeders and nest sites.

Habitat & Range
House sparrows are year-round residents. It's easier to describe where you *won't* find house sparrows because they are utterly ubiquitous. Pristine natural habitats—forest, grassland, or desert—that are lacking human development will also lack house sparrows. Historically, the house sparrow associated with horses (and the seeds and insects in their droppings) and other livestock. Today, house sparrows are found in the most urban of habitats, living on food scraps and nesting in building crevices—though they are still a common inhabitant of horse barns, farmyards, and feedlots.

Feeding
Seeds and grains will be on the house sparrow's normal menu throughout the year. In spring and summer, they take advantage of bountiful insect populations. At any time, house sparrows are quick to take food at bird feeders or scraps of food offered directly or indirectly by humans in parks, picnic areas, fast food restaurants, and strip malls. Cracked corn, sunflower seeds, peanut bits, and bread products are favorite foods.

Nesting
Males choose a cavity and sing by it to attract the female. Both build the messy nest of grass, weed stems, feathers, paper, and string. House sparrows will appropriate nest boxes from bluebirds, swallows, and purple martins (forcing many nest box landlords to use controls and special housing to discourage house sparrows), and they may even kill nest box competitors. The female lays between three and six eggs, which are incubated by both parents for 10 or more days. The parents share feeding duties until the nestlings are ready to fledge at about two weeks.

Backyard & Beyond
House sparrows are feeding station regulars, especially in towns and cities. To discourage house sparrows from dominating nest boxes, use boxes with interiors less than 5 inches deep, remove their nesting material regularly, and place nest boxes far from buildings and thick shrubbery.

Solutions for Common Feeding Problems

Lack of Birds
- During spring and summer, the diet of many of our seed-eating feeder visitors shifts to a greater reliance on insects, fruits, and other natural, abundant food sources. Even during the traditional fall and winter bird-feeding seasons, birds may not immediately find a feeding station. Once the first chickadee, goldfinch, or titmouse "tunes in" to your feeders, the word will spread quickly and other birds will show up. Temporary loss of birds at a feeder can be caused by the presence of a hawk, a cat, or stale birdseed.

Discouraging Squirrels
- It is a battle that has been going on for nearly a century: humans trying to keep squirrels from getting to bird feeders. There are many squirrel-proof feeders available, but squirrels figure out many of these after a time. Placing your feeders on baffled poles far from any tree, deck railing, or other potential launching pad that a squirrel could use seems to be the most successful strategy. Alternatively, offer the furry menaces some cracked corn (or ears of field corn) far away from your feeders. Keep squirrels happy elsewhere, and you may keep them off your feeders.

Blackbirds, Pigeons, Jays, and Sparrows
- Certain birds can hog all the space and food at your feeders to the exclusion of the smaller, less aggressive species. You can limit the impact of these "feeder hogs" by removing their preferred food from the menu. For blackbirds, pigeons, and doves, limit the cracked corn and mixed seed; for jays and crows, limit the suet, peanuts, cracked corn, and table scraps; for sparrows, limit the cracked corn and do not feed bread. Larger birds (such as grackles, rock pigeons, and blue jays) can also be discouraged through the use of small tube feeders with short perches—small birds can use 'em, but big birds can't.

Hawk at Feeders
- Cooper's hawks and sharp-shinned hawks are songbird specialists that can be attracted to the bird activity at your feeders. Their tactic is a quick surprise attack, scattering the feeder visitors and perhaps catching a slow, sick, or unwary individual. As unpleasant as it may seem, it is perfectly natural and is an important aspect of nature's balance.

Cat at Feeders
- Place your feeders a short distance away from thick cover where hunting cats might lurk. Mount your feeders high enough (above 4 feet) that a leaping cat cannot reach feeding birds. A circle of short (1-foot) wire fencing can make it more difficult for charging cats to catch birds.

Night Marauders
- If your feeders empty out overnight, you probably have a mammal making nocturnal visits to your feeder. This furry critter could be a raccoon, an opossum, a flying squirrel, deer, or even a bear! Feed only as much seed as can be eaten by your birds during a single day, and you'll discourage these late-night diners.

Sick Bird at Feeders
- Sick birds often show up at feeders, desperate for an easy meal, and they usually succumb to their illness within a short while. Although most bird illnesses are not transferable to humans, it pays to be cautious. Contact your local wildlife officials about any sick birds you see at your feeders—they often monitor wildlife health trends. If you find a dead bird, avoid making direct contact with it (wear gloves or use a plastic bag to pick it up), and bury it or discard it in the trash. Clean your feeders thoroughly and consider halting your feeding for a few days to allow the healthy birds to disperse temporarily.

Food and Feeder Chart

Species	Food
Quail, pheasants	Cracked corn, millet, wheat, milo
Pigeons, doves	Millet, cracked corn, wheat, milo, Niger (thistle seed), buckwheat, sunflower, baked goods
Roadrunners	Meat scraps, hamburger, suet
Hummingbirds	Plant nectar, small insects, sugar solution
Woodpeckers	Suet, meat scraps, sunflower hearts/seed, cracked corn, peanuts, fruits, sugar solution, mealworms
Jays	Peanuts, sunflower, suet, meat scraps, cracked corn, baked goods
Crows, magpies, nutcrackers	Meat scraps, suet, cracked corn, peanuts, baked goods, leftovers, dog food
Titmice, chickadees	Peanut kernels, sunflower, suet, peanut butter, mealworms
Nuthatches	Suet, suet mixes, sunflower hearts and seed, peanut kernels, peanut butter, mealworms
Wrens, creepers	Suet, suet mixes, peanut butter, peanut kernels, bread, fruit, millet (wrens), mealworms
Mockingbirds, thrashers, catbirds	Halved apples, chopped fruit, mealworms, suet, nutmeats, millet (thrashers), soaked raisins, currants, sunflower hearts
Robins, bluebirds, other thrushes	Suet, suet mixes, mealworms, berries, baked goods, chopped fruit, soaked raisins, currants, nutmeats, sunflower hearts
Kinglets	Suet, suet mixes, baked goods, mealworms
Waxwings	Berries, chopped fruit, canned peas, currants, dry raisins
Warblers	Suet, suet mixes, fruit, baked goods, sugar solution, chopped nutmeats
Tanagers	Suet, fruit, sugar solution, mealworms, baked goods
Cardinals, grosbeaks, pyrrhuloxias	Sunflower, safflower, cracked corn, millet, fruit
Towhees, juncos	Millet, sunflower, cracked corn, peanuts, baked goods, nutmeats, mealworms
Sparrows, buntings	Millet, sunflower hearts, black-oil sunflower, cracked corn, baked goods
Blackbirds, starlings	Cracked corn, milo, wheat, table scraps, baked goods, suet
Orioles	Halved oranges, apples, berries, sugar solution, grape jelly, suet mixes, soaked raisins, dry mealworms, currants
Finches, siskins	Thistle (Niger), sunflower hearts, black-oil sunflower seed, millet, Canary seed, fruit, peanut kernels, suet mixes

Nest Box Chart

Species	Interior Floor Size of Box (inches)	Interior Height of Box (inches)	Entrance Hole Diameter (inches)	Box Mounting Height (feet)	Habitat for Box Placement
Chickadees	4x4	9–12	1 1/8 – 1 1/2	5–15	Open woods and edges
Prothonotary Warbler	4x4	12	1 1/4	5–12	Wooded areas, swamps and streams
Titmice	4x4	12	1 1/2	5–12	Wooded areas and edge habitat
White-breasted Nuthatch	4x4	12	1 1/2	5–12	Wooded areas and edge habitat
Carolina Wren	4x4	9–12	1 – 1 1/2	5–10	Old fields and thickets
Eastern Bluebird	4x4	12	1 1/2	5–6	Open land with scattered trees
Tree Swallow	5x5	10–12	1 1/2	5–10	Open land near pond or lake
Purple Martin	6x6	6	2 1/8	15–25	Open country near water
Great-crested Flycatcher	6x6	12	1 3/4 – 2	6–20	Open woods and edges
House Finch	5x5	10	1 1/2	5–10	Backyards and porches
Downy Woodpecker	4x4	12	1 1/2	5–20	Forest openings and edges
Hairy Woodpecker	6x6	14	1 1/2	8–20	Forest openings and edges
Red-bellied Woodpecker	6x6	14	2	8–20	Forest openings and edges

Nest Box Chart

Species	Interior Floor Size of Box (inches)	Interior Height of Box (inches)	Entrance Hole Diameter (inches)	Box Mounting Height (feet)	Habitat for Box Placement
Red-headed Woodpecker	6x6	14	2	8–20	Forest openings and edges
Northern Flicker	7x7	16–24	2 1/2	10–20	Farmland, open country
Pileated Woodpecker	12x12	24	4	15–25	Mature forest
Bufflehead	7x7	17	3	5–15	Wooded lakeshores, swamps
Wood Duck	12x12	24	3 x 4 oval	5–20	Wooded swamps, bottomland
Hooded Merganser	12x12	24	3 x 4 oval	5–30	Wooded swamps, bottomland
Goldeneyes	12x12	24	3 1/4 x 4 1/4 oval	15–20	Wooded lakeshores, swamps
Common Merganser	12x12	24	5 x 6 oval	8–20	Wooded lakeshores, swamps
Saw-whet Owl	7x7	12	2 1/2	8–20	Forest clearings and edges
Screech-owls	8x8	18	3	8–30	Farmland, orchards, woods
Barred Owl	14x14	28	8	15–30	Mature bottomland forest
Barn Owl	12x36	16	6 x 7 oval	15–30	Open farmland, marshes
American Kestrel	9x9	16–18	3	12–30	Farmland

A Glossary of Common Bird Terms

- **Avifauna:** The community of birds found in a given region or habitat type.

- **Cavity nester:** A bird that nests inside an enclosed area such as a hollow tree, an old woodpecker hole, or a bird house.

- **Crown:** The top of a bird's head.

- **Diurnal:** Active during daylight hours.

- **Edge habitat:** A place where two or more habitats come together, such as where woodland meets an old meadow. Edge habitat typically offers a rich diversity of birds.

- **Endemic:** A breeding species that is unique to a given geographical region.

- **Extinct:** A bird that no longer exists in the wild. The Carolina parakeet is an example of an extinct species.

- **Extirpated:** A bird that once was present in a given area but no longer is. It does exist in other areas, however. For example, the red-cockaded woodpecker has been extirpated from much of its original range throughout the South, but remains in small pockets of its former range.

- **Eyeline:** Refers to a line of contrasting colored feathers over or through a bird's eye, often used as a field mark for identification.

- **Field mark:** An obvious visual clue to a bird's identification. Field guides are based on describing field marks of birds.

- **Fledgling:** A bird that has left the nest, but may still be receiving care and feeding from a parent.

- **Hotspot:** A location or habitat that is particularly good for bird watching on a regular basis.

- **Juvenile/Juvenal:** *Juvenile* (noun) refers to a bird that has not yet reached breeding age. *Juvenal* is an adjective, referring to the plumage that a juvenile bird wears.

- **Life bird:** A bird seen by a bird watcher for the first time is a life bird. Life birds are usually recorded on a birder's life list, a record of all the birds he or she has seen at least once.

- **Lores:** The area between a bird's bill and its eyes.

- **Migrant:** A bird that travels from one region to another in response to changes of season, breeding cycles, food availability, or extreme weather. Many of our warbler species that spend the spring and summer in North America *migrate* to Central or South America for the winter.

- **Mimic:** A term used to describe birds that imitate other sounds and songs. Three common bird species are mimics: the northern mockingbird, gray catbird, and brown thrasher.

- **Nape:** The back of a bird's neck, often referred to in reference to a field mark for identification.

- **Neotropical migrant:** Refers to migratory birds of the New World, primarily those that travel seasonally between North, Central, and South America.

- **Nestling:** A bird that is still being cared for in the nest.

A Glossary of Common Bird Terms

- **Peeps:** A generic term for groups of confusingly similar small sandpipers.

- **Pishing (or spishing):** A sound made by bird watchers to attract curious birds into the open. Most often made by repeating the sounds *spshhh* or *pshhh* through clenched teeth.

- **Plumage:** Collective reference to a bird's feathers, which can change both color and shape through the process of seasonal molt. During a molt, a bird loses some or most of its old worn-out feathers and grows new healthy feathers to replace them. Breeding plumage is worn by birds during the breeding season and this is often when a bird is at its most colorful. Non-breeding or winter plumage is worn during fall and winter, generally, and is often less colorful than breeding plumage.

- **Primary feathers (primaries):** The long flight feathers originating from the "hand," or end, of a bird's wing.

- **Raptor:** A term used to refer to a bird of prey, including hawks, owls, osprey, and vultures.

- **Resident:** A non-migratory species—one that is present in the same region all year.

- **Spotting scope:** A single tube optical device mounted on a tripod and used to look at distant birds. Most birding scopes are between 15x and 60x in magnification power.

- **Suet:** The large chunks of hard, white fat that form around the kidneys of beef cattle. Suet is used by bird watchers as a high-energy winter food for birds.

- **Tail spot:** Spots, usually white, on a bird's tail, often used as a field mark for identification.

- **Underparts:** A term referring to the lower half of a bird (breast, belly, undertail), often used in relation to a field mark.

- **Upperparts:** A term referring to the upper half of a bird (crown, back, top of tail), often used in relation to a field mark.

- **Vagrant:** A bird that wanders far from its normal range.

- **Wing bars:** Obvious areas of contrasting color, usually whitish, across the outer surface of a bird's wings.

Frequently Asked Questions

General

Q. There is a bird in my backyard that not only sings throughout the day, but also *all night long!* This particular bird has many, many songs. Do you have any idea what kind of bird this is?

A. Your bird is most likely a northern mockingbird. Don't worry, male mockingbirds only perform this nocturnal singing in the spring and summer, during the time of the full moon. Try running an electric fan (to create a buffer of sound) or using your earplugs on those nights when the male mockingbird is singing. Having a mocker around is a good thing—some would even consider you lucky!

Q. A female robin recently built a nest in a tree on my patio. On May 10, she started laying her eggs—four in total. How long before they hatch, and how long after that do they still need the nest?

A. Robins incubate their eggs for 12 to 14 days. Once hatched, the nestlings remain in the nest for another 14 to 16 days before fledging. Two weeks is normally the incubation period for most songbirds. Another two weeks is an average time before the young leave the nest.

Q. Many times I have seen hawks being mobbed by American crows or other blackbirds. Is this a common phenomenon, and why does it occur?

A. Mobbing behavior by crows is common. The crows are reacting to the potential threat that the hawk poses as a predator to the adult crows and their offspring. The mobbing often serves to harass the hawk into leaving the area. Occasionally, a mobbed hawk will turn the tables and attack and kill a crow.

Q. A woodpecker is pecking holes in my house siding. Is there anything I can do to get it to stop?

A. A woodpecker drilling on your wooden house is only doing what comes naturally—drilling into wood in search of shelter or food. Most house-wrecking woodpeckers do their damage in fall, which is when they begin making their winter roost holes. Try mounting a nest box with an appropriately sized hole over the drilled area. Fill the house with wood chips, and you may divert the bird's attention and gain a tenant.

Woodpeckers also use wood and sometimes metal parts of houses as drumming sites. They drill their bills against the surface in a rapid staccato beat. This drumming noise is a territorial announcement and a method for attracting a mate. Drumming happens most regularly in spring. There are several things you can try; one of them may work.

1. Place some sheet metal or heavy aluminum foil over the area the bird is using.
2. Hang some aluminum pie plates around the affected area. Make sure they move in the wind (to scare the bird away).
3. Place a rubber snake near the drilling area (to scare the bird away).
4. Repeatedly scare the bird when it lands on your house.
5. If nothing else works, call your local wildlife official to see if someone can come to your house to remove the offending bird.

Frequently Asked Questions

Q. Is seeing a robin a true sign of spring's arrival? Where do they go in winter?

A. American robins are surprisingly hardy as long as they have access to their winter food sources: fruits. They switch over in winter from their mostly insect-based summer diet. As such, robins are *facultative migrants*. This means that they will migrate only as far south as they need to or are forced to by bad weather or food shortages. During ice storms, when fruits are covered in a thick coating of ice, many robins flock together and move south. In the same way, if a robin spends the winter in your region, it's probably because there's enough food to see it through.

The idea that robins are the first true sign of spring is somewhat mythical. In much of northern North America, a few robins overwinter, but they stick to woods and thickets where they can find fruit. Most backyard bird watchers do notice the robins' return when these birds appear on lawns with the onset of warm weather, seeking their warm-weather food: earthworms, grubs, caterpillars, and other insects.

Q. Do all birds mate for life?

A. No. Some species have unusually strong pair bonds between mated birds. These species include some eagles, cranes, swans, geese, and ravens. Being mated "for life" means, really, for as long as both birds are alive. When one of the pair dies, the other will take a new mate. Most North American bird species pair up primarily to reproduce, and then go their separate ways soon after they have nested. In some species, the pair bond is brief. In the case of ruby-throated hummingbirds, the pair bond lasts only as long as courtship and copulation. The male has nothing to do with the incubation or raising of the young birds.

Q. Do all birds migrate?

A. Not all bird species migrate, but most do. Migration in North America is defined as the seasonal movement of birds, northward in spring from the wintering grounds, and southward in fall from the breeding grounds. Among the birds that are *resident*, or that do not migrate, are many grouse, ptarmigan, and quail species; many owl species; pileated, red-bellied, downy, and hairy woodpeckers along with white-breasted nuthatch, Carolina wren, northern cardinal, wrentit, ring-necked pheasant, Townsend's solitaire, common raven, gray jay, and northern mockingbird.

Bird Care

Q. Is it true that if you find a baby bird out of the nest, you should not touch it because the parent birds will detect your scent and abandon the nest?

A. No, most birds do not have a well-developed sense of smell. However, most mammalian predators (skunks, foxes, raccoons, weasels, and so forth) do have a good sense of smell and may follow your scent trail to a bird's nest. If you are going to handle a baby bird be sure to place it out of harm's way, back in the nest or in an open-topped cardboard box propped in a tree. Many bird species are equipped to survive outside the nest at a very young age. These species include many shorebirds, gamebirds, and birds such as robins and wrens.

Q. If I find a baby bird that has fallen from a nest, what should I do?

A. Try to place the nestling back in its nest if at all possible. This will be the baby bird's best chance at a normal life. If you can't find the nest or a place to put the nestling out of harm's way, you will need to get the bird to a licensed rehabilitator as soon as possible.

Frequently Asked Questions

Baby birds are unable to *thermoregulate* (regulate their body temperature), and so must be kept in a protected area with a heat source. A soft nest made of tissues inside a small cardboard box, placed on a heating pad set on LOW temperature, is a good example of a temporary home. A moist sponge placed in the box will add a touch of desired humidity. This will warm the bird.

Try to contact a wildlife rehabilitator as soon as possible. Your state fish and wildlife officers are responsible for licensing and regulating the activities of rehabilitators and have listings for those in your region. Make sure anyone else giving you advice is familiar and current with the specialized needs of wildlife.

Q. I found an injured bird. What should I do with it?

A. A person must have special permits from the federal, state, or provincial government to handle injured or dead non-game bird species. While your first instinct may be to call your local veterinarian, many vets are unwilling to care for "wildlife cases." In many situations, the best thing to do is to let nature take its course. Birds and other creatures are part of nature's natural cycle of life and death. An injured or dead bird may be a meal for another animal. If you feel you *must* do something to help an injured bird, call your local wildlife office, department of the environment, fish and game, or extension office. Your local vet may take rehabilitation cases—or may know of a licensed rehabilitator in your area.

Window Strikes

Q. A bird is flying from window to window, butting its head against the glass while looking into the house. Can you explain this behavior?

A. Your bird is fighting its reflection in the windows, thinking that the reflection is a rival bird. The behavior will last through the breeding season. One solution is to place screens over the outside of the window. Plastic wrap stuck to the outside will also work—anything that will break up the reflection will do. You may also offer your bluebirds places to perch, such as snags and posts, far from windows. Bluebirds love a perch in the middle of a lawn or field. This has worked to distract the birds from windows.

Q. How can I keep birds from flying into my windows?

A. Silhouettes of flying hawks or falcons do work, but they perform best when applied on the outside of the glass. Hanging ornaments such as wind chimes, wind socks, and potted plants also helps. Misting the outside of the window with a very weak detergent or soda solution will eliminate the reflection, but will also impair visibility for you. Awnings, eave extensions, and window screens will eliminate reflection and stop the collision problem. Plastic cling wrap applied to the inside or outside of the window can also be effective. One of the most effective solutions we have found is FeatherGuard, a series of bright-colored feathers strung on fishing line and hung over the outside surface of the glass.

Bird Feeding

Q. What is the best seed to offer birds?

A. Black-oil sunflower seed is the most universally eaten seed at bird feeders. But there are many other seeds and foods to offer birds. What is most popular with your birds depends on where you live and what birds are present.

Frequently Asked Questions

Q. What is the best feeder for bird feeding?

A. There is no single best feeder for bird feeding. A well-rounded feeding operation will include a platform feeder, a tube feeder, a hopper feeder, a suet feeder, and a peanut feeder. And don't forget the birdbath!

Q. I recently purchased a bird feeder, but have yet to see any birds. What am I doing wrong?

A. You're not doing anything wrong. It takes time for birds to locate a new feeding source. A spell of bad weather always drives birds to concentrate at feeders. Try putting your feeder in a new location far from your house and the portion of your yard where you are active. Put the feeder in or near a tree that the birds regularly use.

Q. Do birds that eat at feeders lose their ability to find food naturally? If I stop feeding them, will they starve?

A. No. Birds are not totally reliant on the food offered at your feeding station. Birds are programmed by instinct to forage for food, and they have evolved over millions of years to be very mobile in their food-finding habits. Because they can fly, birds are efficient at going to where the food is. Though feeding stations have been linked to slightly improved survival rates for birds in harsh weather conditions, overall bird feeding does not drastically affect the birds' survival. Also, when warmer weather comes, many of the seed-eating birds that frequented your feeders during winter switch to an insect-based diet in spring.

Q. How do I keep squirrels away from my bird feeders?

A. Baffling your feeders (preventing squirrels from gaining access to the feeders) is the best way. Feeders can be strung from a thin wire, far from any object from which the squirrels can leap. String the wire with empty 35mm film canisters (with the lids on), which will spin and dump the squirrels off. There are many squirrel-proof feeders on the market. These may give the squirrels a small electric shock, may prevent them from reaching the seed, or may rotate or bounce to dump the squirrels off. But be forewarned: Squirrels have been known to outsmart the most ingenious of the squirrel-proof inventions.

And if you can't beat 'em, join 'em! Feed squirrels ears of dried corn, but place the corn away from your bird feeders. Given the choice, squirrels will always go for the easiest food, and they *love* corn.

Q. What can I do to protect the birds in my yard from cats?

A. Hang feeders at least 5 feet above the ground. For ground-feeding birds, arrange ornamental border fencing in two or three concentric circles about 16 inches to 2 feet apart, to disrupt a cat's ability to leap at feeders or to spring on birds. Harass offending cats with a spray of water to train them to avoid your yard. If all else fails, use a live trap to catch the cats and take them to the local animal shelter. If the cats belong to your neighbors, ask them to restrain their pets from accessing your yard.

Frequently Asked Questions

Hummingbirds

Q. What is the best ratio of water to sugar to use for feeding hummingbirds?

A. Four parts water to one part sugar (a 4:1 ratio) has been shown to be the closest to the sucrose content of natural flower nectar. Concentrations stronger than this (such as a 3:1 ratio or stronger) are readily consumed by hummers, but no scientific evidence exists regarding the potential helpful or harmful effects on hummingbirds.

Q. Can I use molasses or honey instead of sugar to make my hummingbird nectar?

A. No. White table sugar is the only human-made sweetener that, when mixed with the right amount of water, closely resembles natural flower nectar. Resist the urge to use other sweeteners, which spoil quickly and may not be good for hummingbirds to consume.

Q. Is the red dye found in premixed solutions bad for hummingbirds?

A. Though no conclusive scientific evidence exists showing harmful effects of red food dye on hummingbirds, this chemical additive is certainly not a necessary ingredient in hummingbird solution.

Many commercially available brands of hummingbird solution contain red food coloring that is meant to be attractive both to hummingbirds and to shopping bird watchers. Brightly colored flowers are nature's way of attracting the eye of a foraging hummingbird, so the red solution in feeders is aimed at attracting hummingbirds. Bright red feeder parts (which most hummer feeders have) or a bright red ribbon hung near the feeder can be just as attractive as red-dyed solution. Red dye or food coloring may or may not be harmful to hummingbirds, but it is completely unnecessary.

Q. How do I foil a "bully" hummer?

A. Many hummingbird species defend feeding territories, and assemblages at feeders usually develop hierarchies. The behavior exemplifies natural selection at work, and you should do nothing except enjoy it.

If you're worried about hungry hummers, put up several more feeders near your original one. The bully will be overwhelmed by the sheer numbers of other birds and will quit being so territorial.

Q. Do hummingbirds migrate on the backs of Canada geese?

A. No. This is either a Native American myth or just an old wives' tale. Hummingbirds are excellent, strong-flying migrants. A healthy ruby-throated hummingbird can easily handle the 500-mile flight across the Gulf of Mexico.

Q. Is it true that hummingbirds at my feeder will not migrate if I leave my feeder up in the fall?

A. No. This is another in a long line of bird myths. Birds are genetically programmed to migrate when their internal "clocks" tell them to do so. They will depart when the time is right—whether your feeders are up or not. However, leaving your feeders up in fall, and getting them up early in spring may help early or late migrants that are passing through your area.

How to Build a Simple Birdhouse

These plans are designed to help you build a simple birdhouse—one that is easy to put together and will attract a number of species. The $1^1/2$-inch entrance hole will allow birds as large as bluebirds to enter the house, but even tiny house wrens and chickadees will find this house appealing.

Before you begin the building process, read through this entire plan. This will make the building go more smoothly and should prevent costly, frustrating errors. Study the instructions and drawings together. The letters in the instructions refer to the drawing that illustrates a particular section of directions.

Now, let's look at materials. Cedar will last, but it can be expensive. Pound for pound, cedar is the most durable, weather resistant, and provides the best insulation—so if your budget permits it, cedar is the best wood to use for birdhouses. After years of weather, nails in cedar can become loose, so I suggest using screws in place of nails for cedar construction. Pine is easy to nail and does not split easily, but it will decay unless preservatives are used (on the outside of the box only).

An excellent alternative material is $5/8$-inch thick exterior plywood. It is tough, weathers well, and will not split along the edge if you use nails of the proper size, usually four-penny galvanized box nails. Called T 1-11, this wood has vertical grooves to resemble boards and is often used for exterior siding on homes. Most lumber yards and home centers sell T 1-11 in large 4-x-8-foot sheets. When assembling a birdhouse using exterior plywood, always remember to keep the weather surface of the wood on the outside of the birdhouse. It is an obvious point, but one that is easily forgotten in the midst of the building process.

Unless otherwise instructed, use four-penny galvanized box nails for nailing house parts together. Remember to use screws when using cedar or pine or when you feel extra strong binding is necessary.

It's impossible to predict which bird species is most apt to settle in your new birdhouse. Half a dozen cavity-nesting birds prefer a box with a single slant roof and a $1^1/2$-inch-diameter entrance. Depending on your location, it could be tree swallows, hairy or downy woodpeckers, or perhaps titmice, chickadees, Carolina or house wrens, or even bluebirds.

Good luck with your building—and with being a landlord to the birds!

Materials:

western red cedar, exterior plywood, or T 1-11 siding scraps ($5/8$ inch thick, 31×14 inches), which will be cut into the following pieces:

bottom: 5×5 inches
sides (cut 2): each $10 \times 9 \times 5$ inches
back: $12 \times 6^1/4$ inches
front: $9^1/2 \times 6^1/4$ inches
roof: $8^1/4 \times 8^1/4$ inches
four-penny galvanized box nails
right-angle screw hook, about $1^1/2$ inches long
caulking compound
sixteen-penny galvanized framing nails
2 galvanized siding nails (or wood screws), $1^3/4$ inches long

Tools:

square	2 C clamps (optional)
ruler	rasp
pencil	hammer
saw	wood blocks of
plane	various sizes
brace, with $1^1/2$-inch expansion bit and $1/2$-inch diameter bit	drill, with assorted small bits

How to Build a Simple Birdhouse

Instructions:

A

1. On the weather surface of the plywood, measure and mark with a pencil the exact outlines of each piece. Be sure the grain of the wood runs vertically on the two side pieces, the back, and the front. The T 1-11 siding has a vertical groove running down it. This won't hurt anything—but when laying out the parts, keep the groove away from the edge of each piece to avoid problems with nailing later on.

2. Lay out the two side pieces with a common line along the 9-inch dimension so that the tops angle toward the center line, making a shallow V. In this way, when you assemble the house, the weather surface will end up on the outside.

3. After checking the measurements once more, carefully saw or cut out all the parts. Trim the rough edges with a plane to knock off splinters. You won't need to sand anything—this is going to be rustic!

4. Lay the parts on the workbench and mark them, just to keep track. There are six parts—two sides, a roof, a bottom, a front, and a back.

5. To accommodate the roof slant, you will need to bevel the top edges of the front and back panels with a plane. Set the two pieces in front of you, just as they will be when assembled. On the weather surface of the front panel and on the inside surface of the back, draw a horizontal line $1/8$ inch down from the top. Then bevel off $1/8$ inch from each piece individually.

6. On the front panel, center a vertical line running 3 inches down from the top. Put a cross mark on the line, $1^{3}/4$ inches from the top. Open the expansion bit to precisely $1^{1}/2$ inches, then test it on a scrap board and measure the hole. Now, to ensure a clean cut, clamp the panel tightly to a board. Center the bit on the cross mark and drill the hole. (If you have no C clamps, lay the panel on a board and drill halfway. Turn it over and drill through the other side.) Round off the sharp edges with a rasp.

7. On the bottom piece, measure $3/8$ inch in on each side of each corner and mark. Place a ruler diagonally across each corner and connect the two marks. Saw off the four corners at these points. The resultant openings in the finished house will allow adequate drainage and air circulation for the birds.

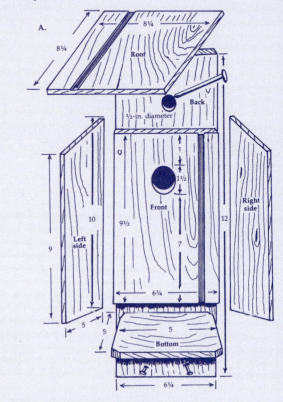

A Simple Birdhouse

Note: Dimensions are in inches

How to Build a Simple Birdhouse

8. On the back panel, with the weather side up, center a vertical line—2 inches long—down from the top. At the bottom of the line, drill a 1/2-inch hole.

9. Mark a line across the weather surface of both side panels, 1 inch up from the bottom. On the right panel, extend the bottom line across the edges. Mark a line across the face of the front panel, 1 inch up from the bottom. It, too, should extend across the edges.

10. Now, mark a line across the weather surface on the back panel, 2 1/2 inches up from the bottom, and extend it across the edges.

B

1. You are now ready to start putting things together. Lay the right-hand side panel (the one on the right when the entrance of the completed birdhouse faces you), weather surface up, on the bench. Start two nails, each 1 1/2 inches in from the edge and 1/4 inch below the bottom line. Drive them in until they barely peek through the other side. Be sure they are straight.

2. Place the bottom panel (weather side toward you) on edge and at a right angle to the bench, against a flat wall or solid surface. (When the corners are cut off, it is easier to get the side and bottom flush when both are pressed against a flat wall.) Lay the right side panel (weather side out) across the upper edge of the bottom piece, matching the line on the side panel with the interior surface of the bottom. (Place a block under the other end of the right panel.) Drive the nails in part way—just enough to hold.

C

1. Turn the assembled pieces over so the right side faces you. Place two nails in the weather surface of the back panel, 1/4 inch below the line you marked earlier and 1 1/2 inches from the ends of the bottom panel. Drive them in until they begin to show on the other side.

2. Put the back piece on the two pieces that you assembled. Make sure that the lines marked on the bottom match, and that the edges are flush with the outside of the side panel.

B.

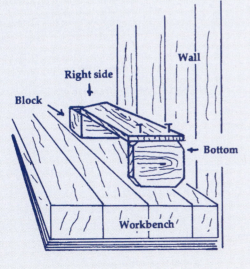

C.

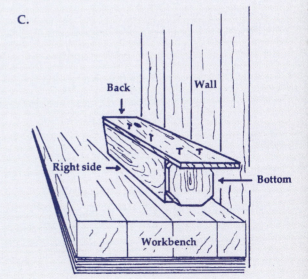

How to Build a Simple Birdhouse

D.

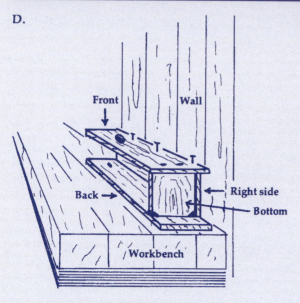

3. Drive the nail into the bottom, nearest the side panel, enough to hold. Start another nail along the edge of the back panel, 2 inches down from the top and about 1/4 inch from the edge. Check to see that the back panel edge and the side are flush. Drive the nail in part way.

4. Now check the bottom. Its outer corner may be sprung slightly. Press it into alignment with the back panel marks, hold, and drive the other bottom nail in part way. Check it over to see if the bottom is lined up. If so, place one more nail along the edge, 4 inches up from the bottom of the back panel, and drive in all the nails.

D

1. Turn the unit on its back. Lay out the front panel, weather side up—racing stripe dazzling your eyes—and start two nails 1/4 inch below the bottom line and 1 1/2 inches in from each edge. Be sure the points have just come through the other side.

2. Put the front in place, matching the lines marked at the bottom with the interior surface of the bottom panel. There should be about a 1/2-inch gap at the top of the right side when the roof is on.

3. Drive the nail into the bottom, nearest the enclosed side, until the nail holds. Then start a nail 2 inches down from the top of the front panel and 1/4 inch in from the edge. Make sure that the front panel edge and the side are flush. Drive the nail in part way. Spring the bottom corner into alignment, and drive the nail near the open edge part way into the bottom. Start another, 2 inches up from the bottom, and drive it in part way. If everything looks good, pound in all the nails.

E.

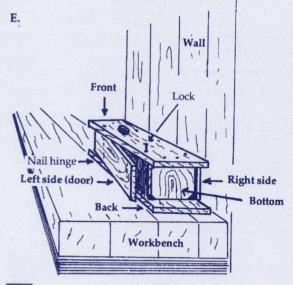

E

1. Fit the left-hand side panel into position. If it is tight, plane down the edge for a looser fit. You want this "door" to open easily even when the wood swells in wet weather, so you can inspect the nest and clean out the house at the season's end.

How to Build a Simple Birdhouse

2. Check for about a 1/2-inch gap at the top. Drive two nails—one into the bottom and one into the front, halfway up—part way in to hold temporarily. (They will be removed later.)

3. On the left edge of the front panel, make a mark 1 inch from the top. Using a square, draw a horizontal line across the left side panel on the mark. At one end of this line, drive a nail through the front panel into the edge of the left panel. At the other end of the line, drive a nail through the back panel into the edge of the left panel. These nail hinges will allow the "door" to be opened.

4. Put a mark on the front panel 2 inches up from the bottom and centered over the edge of the door. Drill a small hole, about 2 inches deep, at the mark. Use a right-angle screw hook twisted into place as a lock nail. It is not likely to fall out of the hole, as a nail might, when the box is tipped forward. Remove the temporary nails and test the door.

F

1. On the roof, start two nails, each 1/4 inch in from the back or top edge of the roof, and about 2 inches in from the left and right sides. Remember that the roof slants, and you want the nail angled so it goes straight into the edge of the back panel. Stand the box upright with a block under the front. Run a strip of caulking compound along the top edge of the back panel. Place the top on, with the wood grain running down the slant, not across it.

2. Adjust the roof for equal overhang on each side. It should be flush with the back. Drive the nail in part way.

3. Sight along the front and drive two more nails—gingerly—into the top edge of the front panel until they hold. If it looks right, hammer them in.

G

1. Now for hanging the birdhouse. If there are predators in your area, resist the temptation to hang your house on a tree or fencepost. If your area is predator-free (and not many areas are in North America), trees or fenceposts may be acceptable. To be safe, I suggest baffling all of your bird houses.

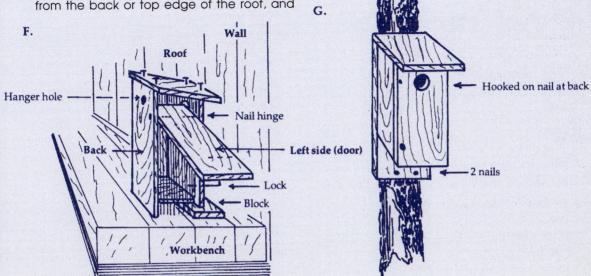

F.
Wall
Roof
Hanger hole
Nail hinge
Back
Left side (door)
Lock
Block
Workbench

G.
Hooked on nail at back
2 nails

161

Bird-Friendly Plants for Your Yard

TREES

Common Name	Latin Name	Good For/Other Notes
Apples	*Malus* spp.	Fruit, insects, cavities
Ashes	*Fraxinus* spp.	Seeds, insects, cover
Aspens	*Populus* spp.	Seeds, insects, cover, cavities
Birches	*Betula* spp.	Seeds, insects, cover
Cedars	*Juniperus* spp.	Fruit, year-round cover
Cherries	*Prunus* spp.	Fruit
Chokecherry, common	*Prunus virginiana*	Fruit
Cottonwoods	*Populus* spp.	Cavities, shelter
Crabapples	*Malus* spp.	Fruit, insects
Dogwoods	*Cornus* spp.	Fruit
Firs	*Abies* spp.	Year-round cover
Hackberries	*Celtis* spp.	Fruit, cover
Hawthorns	*Crataegus* spp.	Fruit, cover, nesting
Hemlocks	*Tsuga* spp.	Seeds, insects, shelter
Hollies	*Ilex* spp.	Fruit, year-round cover
Junipers	*Juniperus* spp.	Year-round cover
Larches	*Larix* spp.	Seeds
Madrones	*Arbutus* spp.	Fruit
Maples	*Acer* spp.	Seeds, cover
Mesquites	*Prosopis* spp.	Shelter
Mountain ashes	*Sorbus* spp.	Fruit
Mulberry, red	*Morus rubra*	Fruit
Oaks	*Quercus* spp.	Acorns, cover, insects
Pines	*Pinus* spp.	Year-round cover, insects
Poplars	*Populus* spp.	Cavities, shelter
Sassafras	*Sassafras albidum*	Fruit, cover, cavities
Shadbush, or serviceberry	*Amelanchier laevis*	Fruit, flowers
Spruces	*Picea* spp.	Year-round cover
Sycamores	*Platanus* spp.	Cavities, shelter, insects
Willows	*Salix* spp.	Cavities, shelter, insects

Bird-Friendly Plants for Your Yard

SHRUBS

Common Name	Latin Name	Good For/Other Notes
Arrowwood viburnum/ Viburnums	*Viburnum dentatum/ Viburnum* spp.	Fall fruit. Tolerates shade
Bayberry, northern	*Myrica pensylvanica*	Fruit. Male & female plants needed for fruit
Blackberry, American	*Rubus alleghaniensis*	Fruit, dense cover, nesting
Blueberry, highbush	*Vaccinium corymbosum*	Fruit, flowers, cover. Needs acid soil
Chokeberry, red	*Aronia arbutifolia*	Fruit. Moist soil preferred
Cranberry, highbush	*Viburnum trilobum*	Fruit. Shade tolerant
Dogwoods	*Cornus* spp.	Fall fruit, dense cover
Elderberry, American	*Sambucus canadensis*	Fruit, dense cover
Hercules' club	*Aralia spinosa*	Fruit
Hobblebush	*Viburnum alnifolium*	Fruit. Shade tolerant
Hollies, deciduous	*Ilex decidua, Ilex* spp.	Winter fruit. Male & female plants needed for fruit
Huckleberry, black	*Gaylussacia baccata*	Fruit. Sandy soil preferred
Inkberry	*Ilex glabra*	Fruit. Thicket-forming. Needs acid soil
Mahonia	*Mahonia aquifolium*	Fruit, year-round cover
Manzanitas	*Arctostaphylos* spp.	Early fruit, thick cover
Nannyberry	*Viburnum lentago*	Fruit. Shade-tolerant
Pokeweed	*Phytolacca americana*	Fall fruit.
Roses	*Rosa* spp.	Winter fruit. Summer flowers
Shadbushes	*Amelanchier* spp.	Early fruit
Spicebush	*Lindera benzoin*	Fruit. Needs moist soil
Sumacs	*Rhus* spp.	Fruit available all winter
Winterberry, common	*Ilex verticillata*	Fruit. Male & female plants needed for fruit
Yews	*Taxus* spp.	Year-round cover. Some fruit

VINES

Common Name	Latin Name	Good For/Other Notes
Ampelopsis, heartleaf	*Ampelopsis cordata*	Fruit. Resembles a grape vine
Bittersweet, American	*Celastrus scandens*	Fruit. Avoid Asian species.
Grapes, wild	*Vitis* spp.	Fruit attracts 100 species, cover

Bird-Friendly Plants for Your Yard

VINES

Common Name	Latin Name	Good For/Other Notes
Greenbriars	*Smilax* spp.	Fruit, thick cover
Trumpet honeysuckle	*Lonicera sempervirens*	Nectar, fruit, cover. Avoid Asian species
Trumpet vine	*Campsis radicans*	Nectar, summer cover
Virginia creeper	*Parthenocissus quinquefolia*	Fruit attracts 40 species

FLOWERS

Common Name	Latin Name	Good For/Other Notes
Asters	*Aster* spp.	Flowers attract butterlies, seed
Bachelor's button	*Centaurea cyanus*	Seed
Black-eyed Susan	*Rudbeckia serotina*	Seed
Blazing star	*Liatris* spp.	Seed, flowers attract butterflies
California poppy	*Eschscholzia californica*	Seed
Coneflower, purple	*Echinacea purpurea*	Seed, flowers attract butterflies
Coreopsis	*Coreopsis* spp.	Seed, flowers attract butterflies
Cornflower	*Centaurea cyanus*	Seed
Cosmos	*Cosmos* spp.	Seed
Daisy, gloriosa	*Rudbeckia* cv.	Seed
Goldenrods	*Solidago* spp.	Flowers for butterflies, winter cover
Joe-Pye weeds	*Eupaorium* spp.	Flowers for butterflies, winter cover
Marigolds	*Tagetes* spp.	Seed
Penstemons	*Penstemon* spp.	Nectar, seed
Poppies	*Papaver* spp.	Flowers attract butterflies, seed
Primroses	*Oenothera* spp.	Seed
Sedums	*Sedum* spp.	Flowers attract butterflies, seed
Sunflowers	*Helianthus* spp.	Seed
Thistles, globe	*Echinops* spp.	Flowers, seed, nesting material
Zinnias	*Zinnnia elegans*	Seed, flowers attract butterflies

Bibliography

American Bird Conservancy. 2003. *Guide to the 500 Most Important Bird Areas in the United States*. New York: Random House.

American Ornithologists' Union. 1998. *Check-List of North American Birds*. 7th edition. Washington, DC: American Ornithologists' Union.

Choate, E. A. 1985. *The Dictionary of American Bird Names, Revised Edition*. Boston: Harvard Common Press.

Ehrlich, P. R.; Dobkin, D. S.; and Wheye, D. 1988. *The Birder's Handbook*. New York: Fireside Books.

Kaufman, K. 1996. *Lives of North American Birds*. Boston: Houghton Mifflin Co.

Kaufman, K. 2000. *Birds of North America, A Kaufman Focus Guide*. Boston: Houghton Mifflin Co.

National Geographic Society. 1999. *Field Guide to the Birds of North America*. 3rd edition. Washington, D.C.: National Geographic Society.

Peterson, R. T. 1996. *A Field Guide to the Birds* (Eastern). Boston: Houghton Mifflin Co.

Poole, A., and Gill, F., eds. 1992–2002. *The Birds of North America*. Philadelphia, PA: American Ornithologists' Union/Birds of North American, Inc.,

Sibley, D. A. 2000. *The Sibley Guide to the Birds*. New York: Alfred A. Knopf, Inc.

Stokes, D., and Stokes, L. 1996. *Stokes Field Guide to Birds: Eastern Region*. Boston: Little, Brown and Co.

Terres, J. K. 1995. *The Audubon Encyclopedia of North American Birds*. New York: Wings Books.

Thompson III, B. 1995. *An Identification Guide to Common Backyard Birds*. Marietta, OH: Bird Watcher's Digest Press.

Thompson III, B. 1997. *Bird Watching For Dummies*. New York: John Wiley & Sons.

Thompson III, B. 2003. *The Backyard Bird Watcher's Answer Guide*. Marietta, OH: Bird Watcher's Digest Press.

Zickefoose, J. 1995. *Enjoying Bird Feeding More*. Marietta, OH: Bird Watcher's Digest Press.

Zickefoose, J. 2001. *Natural Gardening for Birds*. Emmaus, PA: Rodale Organic Living Books.

National Organizations for Bird Watchers

National Organizations

American Bird Conservancy
P.O. Box 249
The Plains, VA 20198
(540) 253-5780
www.abcbirds.org

American Birding Association
P.O. Box 6599
Colorado Springs, CO 80934-6599
800-850-2473
www.americanbirding.org

Cornell Laboratory of Ornithology
Attn: Communications
159 Sapsucker Woods Road
Ithaca, NY 14850
800-843-2473
www.birds.cornell.edu

National Audubon Society
700 Broadway
New York, NY 10003
(212) 979-3000
www.audubon.org

National Wildlife Federation
11100 Wildlife Center Drive
Reston, VA 20190-5362
800-822-9919
www.nwf.org

The Nature Conservancy
4245 North Fairfax Drive, Suite 100
Arlington, VA 22203-1606
800-628-6860
www.tnc.org

Field Guides to Birds

Griggs, J. L. 1997. *All the Birds of North America*. New York: Harper Collins.

Kaufman, K. 2001. *Birds of North America (Kaufman Focus Guides)*. Boston: Houghton Mifflin Co.

National Geographic Society. 1999. *National Geographic Field Guide to the Birds of North America, 3rd edition*. Washington, D.C.: National Geographic Society.

Peterson, R. T. 2002. *A Field Guide to the Birds of Eastern and Central North America (Peterson Series). 5th ed*. Boston: Houghton Mifflin Co.

Robbins, C. S., et al. 1983. *Birds of North America: A Guide to Field Identification (Golden Field Guide Series)*. Revised edition. New York: Golden Press.

Sibley, D. A. 2000. *The Sibley Guide to the Birds. New York:* Alfred A. Knopf, Inc.

Stokes, D., and Stokes, L. 1996. *Field Guide to the Birds of North America*. Boston: Little, Brown and Co.

Audio Guides to Birds

Elliott, L. 2004. *Know Your Bird Sounds, volumes 1 and 2.* Mechanicsburg, PA: Stackpole Books.

Elliott, L.; Stokes, D.; and Stokes, L. 1997. *Stokes Field Guide to Bird Songs: Eastern Region (Stokes Field Guide to Bird Songs).* New York: Time Warner Audio Books.

Peterson, R. T. 2002. *A Field Guide to Bird Songs of Eastern and Central North America. Revised edition.* Boston: Houghton Mifflin Co.

Walton, R. K., and Lawson, R. W. 1989. *Birding By Ear, Eastern and Central North America (Peterson Field Guide Series).* Boston: Houghton Mifflin Co.

Walton, R. K., and Lawson, R. W. 1994. *More Birding By Ear (Peterson Field Guide Series).* Boston, MA: Houghton Mifflin Co.

Periodicals for Bird Watchers

The Backyard Bird Newsletter
P. O. Box 110
Marietta, OH 45750
800-879-2473
www.birdwatchersdigest.com

Bird Watcher's Digest
P. O. Box 110
Marietta, OH 45750
800-879-2473
www.birdwatchersdigest.com

Living Bird
Cornell Laboratory of Ornithology
159 Sapsucker Woods Road
Ithaca, NY 14850
800-843-2473
www.birds.cornell.edu

Photography Credits

Arthur Morris/Birds as Art: Pages 35, 46, 47, 48, 49, 50, 51, 52, 53, 54, 55, 58, 59, 61, 62, 63, 64, 65, 66, 67, 68, 69, 70, 71, 72, 73, 74, 75, 76, 78, 79, 81, 84, 86, 87, 88, 89, 93, 95, 96, 97, 98, 99, 100, 101, 102, 103, 104, 106, 108, 110, 112, 113, 115, 116, 117, 118, 119, 122, 125, 127, 130, 132, 134, 135, 136, 137, 138, 139, 140, 141, 142, 143, 144, 145

Bird Watcher's Digest: Pages 34, 37, 38 (both photos), 39 (both photos), 40, 41

Tom Vezo: Pages 56, 57, 60, 80, 90, 91, 109, 121, 133

Barth Schorre: Pages 120, 123, 126, 128, 129

Maslowski Photography: Pages 77, 83, 85, 107

Brian Henry: Pages 94, 111, 124

Ron Austing: Page 82

Bill Beatty: Page 92

Cliff Beittel: Page 105

Bill Bevington: Page 131

Randall Ennis: Page 33

Robert McCaw: Page 114

Charles Melton: Page 42

Julie Zickefoose: Page 43

Index

Acadian flycatcher, 91, 92
albatross, 103
alder flycatcher, 92
American
    coot, 68
    crow, 100
    goldfinch, 144
    kestrel, 65
    redstart, 123
    robin, 93, 111, 112
anhinga, 47
Audubon's warbler, 122
August teal, 53

Bald eagle, 63
Baltimore oriole, 35, 142
bank swallow, 102
barn swallow, 39, 42, 102, 103
barred owl, 61, 78
beebird, 95
belted kingfisher, 84
Bicknell's thrush, 114
bittern, least, 49
black
    duck, 52
    vulture, 59
black-billed cuckoo, 76
black-capped chickadee, 105
blackbird, 138, 139, 140, 141
    red-winged, 139, 140
blue
    heron, great, 48, 77
    jay, 99, 100
bluebird, 39, 108, 111, 118, 145
    eastern, 111
blue-gray gnatcatcher, 110
blue-winged teal, 53
bobwhite, 66
bobwhite, northern, 66
Bohemian waxwing, 119
broad-winged hawk, 61
brown thrasher, 117
brown-headed
    cowbird, 113, 119, 124, 139, 144
    nuthatch, 106
bufflehead, 56

bunting, 131
    indigo, 36, 131
butcherbird, 96
butterbutt, 122

Canada goose, 50
Canadian goose, 50
canary, wild, 144
cardinal, 42, 104, 128, 130
    northern, 38, 110, 130
Carolina
    chickadee, 105
    wren, 39, 42, 104, 107, 108
catbird, 115
    gray, 115
cedar waxwing, 119
chat, yellow-breasted, 127
chewink, 132
chickadee, 36, 39, 89, 104, 105, 109, 120
    black-capped, 105
    Carolina, 105
chimney swift, 82
chipping sparrow, 133, 134, 139
chuck-will's widow, 80
clay-colored robin, 112
common
    grackle, 141
    merganser, 57
    moorhen, 68
    nighthawk, 80, 81
    pond heron, 49
    yellowthroat, 125
Cooper's hawk, 60, 65
coot, 68
    American, 68
cormorant, 47
    double-crested, 47
    neotropic, 47
cowbird, 97, 125, 139
    brown-headed, 113, 119, 124, 139, 144
crane, 48
crow, 100
    American, 100

cuckoo, 76
    black-billed, 76
    yellow-billed, 76

Dark-eyed junco, 137
double-crested cormorant, 47
dove, 74
    mourning, 42, 74
downy woodpecker, 87, 88
duck, 51, 52, 53, 54, 55, 56, 57, 68, 89
    black, 52
    ring-necked, 54
    ruddy, 56
    wood, 51, 54, 57, 78

Eagle, bald, 63
eared grebe, 46
eastern
    wood-pewee, 91
    bluebird, 111
    kingbird, 95
    meadowlark, 138
    phoebe, 91, 92, 93
    screech owl, 79
    towhee, 132
egret, 48
European starling, 39, 85, 86, 89, 101, 118, 139

Falcon, 65
    merlin, 65
    peregrine, 65
field sparrow, 133
finch, 43
    house, 42, 143
    purple, 143
fish hawk, 64
flicker, 60, 89, 90
    northern, 89
    red-shafted, 89
    yellow-shafted, 89
flycatcher, 39, 91, 92, 93, 94, 126
    Acadian, 91, 92
    great crested, 92, 94
    silky, 119
fox sparrow, 117

Gallinule, 68
   purple, 68
gnatcatcher, 110
   blue-gray, 110
golden-crowned kinglet, 109
goldfinch, 144
   American, 144
goose, 47
   Canada, 50
   Canadian, 50
goshawk, northern, 60
grackle, 139, 141
   common, 141
gray catbird, 115
gray-cheeked thrush, 114
great
   blue heron, 48, 77
   crested flycatcher, 92, 94
   horned owl, 77
   white heron, 48
greater
   scaup, 54, 55
   yellowlegs, 70
grebe, 46
   eared, 46
   horned, 46
   pied-billed, 46
green heron, 49
green-backed heron, 49
green-winged teal, 56
gull, 72, 73
   herring, 72, 73
   ring-billed, 72, 73

Hairy woodpecker, 87, 88
hawk, 60, 77, 81, 96
   broad-winged, 61
   Cooper's, 60, 65
   fish, 64
   red-shouldered, 61, 99
   red-tailed, 61, 62, 99
   sharp-shinned, 60, 65
hermit thrush, 112, 114
heron, 47, 48, 49, 77
   common pond, 49
   great
      blue, 48, 77

      white, 48
   green, 49
   little, 49
   squat, 49
herring gull, 72, 73
high-hole, 89
Hollywood
   linnet, 143
   robin, 132
hooded
   merganser, 57
   warbler, 126
horned
   grebe, 46
   owl, great, 77
house
   finch, 42, 143
   sparrow, 101, 111, 145
   wren, 108
hummingbird, 109, 110
   ruby-throated, 83

Indigo bunting, 36, 131

Japanese waxwing, 119
jay, blue, 99, 100
junco, 137
   dark-eyed, 137

Kestrel, 65
   American, 65
killdeer, 69
kingbird, 95
   eastern, 95
kingfisher, 36, 84
   belted, 84
kinglet, 104, 109
   golden-crowned, 109
   ruby-crowned, 109

Least
   bittern, 49
   flycatcher, 92
lesser
   scaup, 54, 55
   yellowlegs, 70
linnet, Hollywood, 143

little heron, 49
loggerhead shrike, 96
loon, 47

"**M**aggie", 121
magnolia warbler, 121
mallard, 52, 54
martin, 101
   purple, 39, 101, 118, 145
meadowlark, 138
   eastern, 138
merganser, 57
   common, 57
   hooded, 57
   red-breasted, 57
mockingbird, 96, 115, 116, 117
   northern, 116
moorhen, common, 68
mourning dove, 42, 74
myrtle warbler, 122

Neotropic cormorant, 47
nighthawk, 81
   common, 80, 81
northern
   flicker, 89
   bobwhite, 66
   cardinal, 38, 110, 130
   goshawk, 60
   mockingbird, 116
   rough-winged swallow, 102
nuthatch, 39, 106
   brown-headed, 106
   red-breasted, 106
   white-breasted, 106

Olive-backed thrush, 114
orchard oriole, 142
oriole, 142
   Baltimore, 35, 142
   orchard, 142
osprey, 63, 64
ovenbird, 124
owl, 77, 78, 79
   barred, 61, 78
   eastern screech, 79
   great horned, 77

screech, 79
spotted, 78

Pelican, 47
phoebe, 39, 42, 93
    eastern, 91, 92, 93
pied-billed grebe, 46
pigeon, 60, 74, 75
    rock, 75
pileated woodpecker, 90
plover, 69
    semipalmated, 69
purple
    finch, 143
    gallinule, 68
    martin, 39, 101, 118, 145

Quail, 66

Rail, 68
raincrow, 76
red-bellied woodpecker, 54, 85,
    86, 110
redbird, 128, 130
    summer, 128
red-breasted
    merganser, 57
    nuthatch, 106
red-eyed
    vireo, 97, 139
    warbler, 98
red-headed woodpecker, 85, 86
red-shafted flicker, 89
red-shouldered hawk, 61, 99
redstart, 123
    American, 123
red-tailed hawk, 61, 62, 99
red-winged blackbird, 139, 140
ring-billed gull, 72, 73
ring-necked duck, 54
robin, 39, 60, 71, 112, 113,
    128, 129
    American, 93, 111, 112
    clay-colored, 112
    Hollywood, 132
rock pigeon, 75
ruby-crowned kinglet, 109

ruby-throated hummingbird, 83
ruddy duck, 56
rufous-sided towhee, 132

Sandpiper, 71
    spotted, 71
scarlet tanager, 42, 128, 129
scaup, 54, 55
    greater, 54, 55
    lesser, 54, 55
screech owl, 79
    eastern, 79
seagull, 73
semipalmated plover, 69
sharp-shinned hawk, 60, 65
shrike, 96
    loggerhead, 96
silky flycatcher, 119
snowbird, 137
song sparrow, 136, 139
sparrow, 42, 43, 104, 132, 133,
    134, 137
    chipping, 133, 134, 139
    field, 133
    fox, 117
    house, 101, 111, 145
    song, 136, 139
    tree, 133
    white-throated, 135
spotted
    owl, 78
    sandpiper, 71
squat heron, 49
starling, 101, 111, 118
    European, 39, 85, 86, 89,
        101, 118
stork, 48
summer
    redbird, 128
    tanager, 128, 129
    teal, 53
Swainson's thrush, 114
swallow, 36, 39, 101, 102, 103, 145
    bank, 102
    barn, 39, 42, 102, 103
    northern rough-winged, 102
    tree, 39, 108

swift, 82
    chimney, 82

Tanager
    scarlet, 42, 128, 129
    summer, 128, 129
teal, 53
    August, 53
    blue-winged, 53
    green-winged, 56
    summer, 53
Tennessee warbler, 120
tern, 73
thrasher, 117
    brown, 117
thrush, 111, 112, 114, 117,
    123, 124
    hermit, 112, 114
    olive-backed, 114
    Swainson's, 114
    wood, 71, 113
titmouse, 39, 104, 109
    tufted, 104, 110
towhee, 43, 132
    eastern, 132
    rufous-sided, 132
tree
    sparrow, 133
    swallow, 39, 108
tufted titmouse, 104, 110
turkey, 67
    wild, 63, 67
turkey vulture, 58, 59

Vireo, 97, 98, 126
    red-eyed, 97, 139
    warbling, 98
    white-eyed, 98
vulture, 58
    black, 59
    turkey, 58, 59

Warbler, 97, 109, 120, 121,
    122, 123, 124, 125,
    127, 142
    Audubon's, 122
    hooded, 126

magnolia, 121
myrtle, 122
red-eyed, 98
Tennessee, 120
wood, 123, 126
yellow, 139
yellow-rumped, 122
yellow-throated, 98
warbling vireo, 98
waterthrush, 124
waxwing, 119
    Bohemian, 119
    cedar, 119
    Japanese, 119
whip-poor-will, 36, 80
white-breasted
    nuthatch, 106
white-eyed vireo, 98
white heron, great, 48
white-throated sparrow, 135

wild
    canary, 144
    turkey, 63, 67
willow flycatcher, 92
wood
    duck, 51, 54, 57, 78
    thrush, 71, 113
    warbler, 123, 126
wood-pewee, 91, 92
    eastern, 91
woodpecker, 36, 39, 86, 87, 88, 89, 90, 94, 104, 105
    downy, 87, 88
    hairy, 87, 88
    pileated, 90
    red-bellied, 54, 85, 86, 110
    red-headed, 85, 86
wren, 39
    Carolina, 39, 42, 104, 107, 108
    house, 108

Yawkerbird, 89
yellow warbler, 139
yellow-billed cuckoo, 76
yellow-breasted chat, 127
yellowhammer, 89
yellow-rumped warbler, 122
yellow-shafted flicker, 89
yellow-throated warbler, 98
yellowlegs
    greater, 70
    lesser, 70
yellowstart, 123
yellowthroat, 125
    common, 125

Sighting Notes

Date	Species/Description	Location

Sighting Notes

Date	Species/Description	Location

Sighting Notes

Date	Species/Description	Location

Meet Bill Thompson, III

Bill Thompson, III is the Editor of Bird Watcher's Digest, *the popular bimonthly magazine devoted to birds and bird watching. From an early age, Bill knew his life would be intertwined with birds and bird watching. One of his first words was "junco" and one of his early memories is of seeing a male cardinal in a tree. In 1978, his parents, Bill and Elsa Thompson, founded* Bird Watcher's Digest *in their living room, fulfilling their dream. It has been published continuously since its inception.*

In addition to this book for Cool Springs Press, Bill Thompson is the author of the best-selling book, *Bird Watching for Dummies*. He is also the author of many booklets published by *Bird Watcher's Digest*. His articles on bird watching have appeared in numerous books and magazines, including *National Gardening*. Bill is a frequent guest lecturer and speaker for many events. In addition, he is a longtime member of The American Birding Association and is a Director of the Ohio Ornithological Society.

Bill, his wife Julie Zickefoose (an acclaimed artist and nature writer), and their two children enjoy life on an 80-acre farm in Whipple, Ohio. One of their life dreams became a reality when they added a 50-foot-tall bird-watching observation tower to their home. To date, they have recorded sightings of more than 180 bird species. When he's not serving as an editor, traveling, lecturing, or writing books, Bill enjoys playing guitar in his band, *The Swinging Orangutangs*, with his wife and brother, Andy.